Svend Reuse

Corporate Evaluation in the German Banking Sector

WIRTSCHAFTSWISSENSCHAFT

Svend Reuse

Corporate Evaluation in the German Banking Sector

With a foreword by Prof. Dr. Eric Frère
and Prof. Dr. Burghard Hermeier

Deutscher Universitäts-Verlag

Bibliografische Information Der Deutschen Nationalbibliothek
Die Deutsche Nationalbibliothek verzeichnet diese Publikation in der
Deutschen Nationalbibliografie; detaillierte bibliografische Daten sind im Internet über
<http://dnb.d-nb.de> abrufbar.

1. Auflage März 2007

Alle Rechte vorbehalten
© Deutscher Universitäts-Verlag | GWV Fachverlage GmbH, Wiesbaden 2007

Lektorat: Brigitte Siegel / Anita Wilke

Der Deutsche Universitäts-Verlag ist ein Unternehmen von Springer Science+Business Media.
www.duv.de

Umschlaggestaltung: Regine Zimmer, Dipl.-Designerin, Frankfurt/Main
Gedruckt auf säurefreiem und chlorfrei gebleichtem Papier
Printed in Germany

ISBN 978-3-8350-0699-7

Foreword

Corporate Evaluation in the German Banking sector is becoming more and more important. In times of hostile takeovers, missing success in the retail market and an unpleasant cost income ratio, especially small cooperative banks and savings banks are facing a changed situation they have never expected. The changing speed has increased dramatically in the German banking sector. While selling of a savings bank was not possible even 5 years ago, this hard frontier is broken up now. Banks have to manage this changed situation – in order to prevent to be taken over or to increase the own value and the own independency accordingly. In both cases, the quantification of the own value is an essential aspect.

The presented Master Dissertation of Svend Reuse solves theoretical and practical problems according to this topic. It combines actual value oriented management tools with the classical methods of corporate evaluation and the results of the actual status quo in the German banking sector. The essentials can be summed up as follows:

First, the theoretical status quo of corporate evaluation in the German banking sector was defined. The result is that only the earnings value method, equity approach and multiplier method are useful for banks. All entity models must be rejected, as they do not consider the fact that a bank generates value with the liability side. Discussing several bank-individual evaluation models led to open questions. The discounting rate, the implementation of value corrections and the value of treasury are subject to discussion. Further, it was clearly investigated, why maturity transformation does not generate value, why the CAPM can only be used in some models and in which models the value corrections for lost loans have to be deducted. The theory-based demands on a new model are simplicity and the usage of secure cash flows in order to use other discounting rates than the CAPM.

An additional interesting aspect in this work is the connection to actual banking practice. Svend Reuse presents a representative empirical study. In total, 51 out of 750 banks took part in the study. The responses nearly always show a high quality. The main results can be summarized as follows: Shareholder value is not implemented in practice by many banks. Periodic variables are favoured to manage a bank. Intangible values as human resources or the own brand are not considered in the whole sector. The author developed a scoring model which proved this assumption to be correct. The second part of the survey analyzed the practical status quo of corporate evaluation. Almost 50% of the banks analyze their own value in order to do value based management. Nevertheless, the interlink between the bank's value and the related controlling numbers/tools is missing. Banks judge their value, but an integrated management process cannot be found. A practice-based impulse for a new model is that some existing controlling methods, especially those derived from the risk covering mass processes should be used.

The model developed by Svend Reuse took all these aspects into consideration. By an integrated usage of the market interest rate method and the usage of secure cash flows, the CAPM approach could be avoided. The model sets the value of treasury as zero and quantifies a more realistic bank value accordingly. Even though the single parts of the model are not new, the integration of them led to new, interpretable aspects. Really new for the German banking sector is that the model is verified in practice. A number of 19 of the 51 banks of the survey wanted a detailed corporate evaluation based upon the data of the survey. On average, the treasury approach leads to lower results than the equity and earnings value method, even though a risk-free rate is used. The further empirical analysis was able to generate internal based multiples to evaluate the value of classical banks in a very simple manner.

To the opinion of Svend Reuse it has to be criticized that banks do not interlink the evaluation of the own value with a value-oriented management process. In the last section of his work, he offers a solution to this problem. Further he recommends the integration of intangible assets. The value of the brand, customer satisfaction and the employees will be responsible for the bank's value in the future.

The presented Master Dissertation combines existing literature in a new way and extends it in some parts. Considering the aspect that Svend Reuse has written this dissertation beneath his work in a few months, the results are very impressing. Some aspects can be used directly in practice to manage a bank in a rather present value oriented way. We hope that this dissertation will become well-known in Germany.

With his work, Svend Reuse has proved that attaining an excellent academic level is not exclusively possible under the conditions of a full-time degree programme. Nevertheless, part-time-concepts as the FOM's MBA programme make high demands on the participants. Consistent discipline and the ability to self-motivation are the key skills to cope with the challenges of graduating alongside a career –attributes characterizing people with long-term success.

Prof. Dr. **Eric Frère**
Head of International Studies

Prof. Dr. **Burghard Hermeier**
Dean of FOM
University of Applied Sciences

Preface

Very early during the MBA course of studies, I found the topic of the Master Dissertation. One the one hand, nearly all my scientific work and publications handled with bank controlling and similar topics. On the other hand, the methods of corporate evaluation fascinated me. So I connected both aspects into the presented dissertation in order to develop some real new aspects. Combining the theoretical aspects with the practical status quo led to interesting results for the German banking sector.

Such a project can only be successful with the help and support of many persons closely connected with me. They all helped me – with good advice or psychological support in times of trouble. I want to give special thanks to some persons and organisations.

My first thanks go to my employer, Sparkasse Mülheim an der Ruhr. Sponsoring and supporting me during the MBA course of studies in a time of huge work helped me to complete the MBA and to write this book.

Certainly, my thanks go to the banks that answered the query. Only with investing time and manpower into answering the questions, the presented status quo became possible.

Further, I want to say thanks to Herbert Peters, Marc Quattelbaum and Jochen Rulhoff for finding the mistakes in the English formulations. Reading 200 pages of complex English under time pressure is not very easy, I know.

Next, I want to thank Birgit Rieforth. She has always been a good discussion partner, even at night if necessary. She was often the only one who understood my complex problems and helped me with good advice. Further, she checked the formalia – sometimes a very boring job as well.

Surely, my special thanks go to Prof. Dr. Eric Frère. Since the first semester, his courses inspired me to choose this Master dissertation topic and to specialize myself on the banking sector. He guided me to the good results in this dissertation during a time of pressure in the job and in the MBA. Further, it was him again who gave me the possibility to publish my work as a book. It is an honour for me that he wrote a foreword together with Prof. Dr. Burgard Hermeier for this book.

Further, the personal contacts have to be mentioned. I want to say thanks to my friends, especially Andreas Horn, as I had nearly no time for them during the time of writing the Master dissertation. Thank you for understanding me during this time.

Certainly, I want to thank my parents, Helke and Rüdiger Reuse. Thank you for supporting me in everything I did and helping me in times of trouble. Without your aid at the right time, some of my success would not have been possible.

Finally, my thanks go to my girl friend Anita. We got closer in a time I had a lot of stress. Thank you for having patience with me, thank you for packing 750 letters into the envelopes during the whole night and thank you for standing behind me in these hard times.

Even though the presented work is written in English, I hope that some German banks become aware of the results. I would feel pleased, if these banks get some additional value-added because of the presented content.

Svend Reuse

Table of Contents

List of Figures

List of Tables

List of Equations

List of Abbreviations

σ	=	Volatility
€	=	Euro
A	=	Annual surplus
AG	=	Aktiengesellschaft
APT	=	Arbitrage pricing theory
APV	=	Adjusted Present Value
AuM	=	Assets under Management
av.	=	Average
b	=	Parameter > 0
BaFin	=	Bundesanstalt für Finanzdienstleistungen
BFH	=	Bundesfinanzhof
BMW	=	Bayerische Motorenwerke
BS	=	Balance Sheet
CAPM	=	Capital Asset Pricing Model
CCA	=	Comparable Company Analysis
Cf.	=	Confer
CIR	=	Cost Income Ratio
CM	=	Contribution Margin
CV	=	Corporate Value / Company Value
DAX	=	Deutscher Aktienindex
DCF	=	Discounted Cash Flow
DDM	=	Dividend Discount Model
DiBa	=	Direktanlagebank *(Name of a company)*
DSGV	=	Deutscher Sparkassen- und Giroverband
E	=	Earnings
EBIT	=	Earnings Before Interest and Taxes
EBITDA	=	Earnings Before Interest, Tax, Depreciation and Amortization
EBT	=	Earnings Before Taxes
ed.	=	Editors
EQ	=	Book value of equity
etc.	=	et cetera
EV	=	Earnings Value
EVA	=	Economic Value Added
FCF	=	Free Cash Flow
FOM	=	Fachhochschule für Oekonomie und Management
FTE	=	Flow To Equity
Geno	=	Genossenschaftsbanken / cooperative bank

HGB	=	Handelsgesetzbuch
HVB	=	Hypovereinsbank
i	=	Interest rate
IAS	=	International Accounting Standard(s)
ID	=	Identification
IDW	=	Institut der Wirtschaftsprüfer
ifb	=	Institut für Bankmanagement
IFRS	=	International Financial Reporting System(s)
IS	=	Income Statement
IT	=	Information Technology
ITM	=	Integral Total Management
KWG	=	Kreditwesengesetz
m	=	Market
MaRisk	=	Mindestanforderungen an das Risikomanagement
max.	=	Maximum
MBA	=	Master of Business Administration
min.	=	Minimum
Mio.	=	Million
mult.	=	Multiplier
n	=	Number
n.a.	=	no answer
n.Y.	=	no year
No.	=	Number
NOPAT	=	Net Operating Profit After Taxes
OLG	=	Oberlandesgericht
p.	=	page
PDF	=	Adobe Portable Document Format
PF	=	Performance Factor
pp.	=	pages
r^2	=	Coefficient of determination
RAROC	=	Risk Adjusted Return On Risk Adjusted Capital
rf	=	risk free
RI	=	Residual Income
RIM	=	Residual Income Method
ROCE	=	Return On Capital Employed
ROE	=	Return On Equity
RORAC	=	Return On Risk Adjusted Capital
RSGV	=	Rheinischer Sparkassen- und Giroverband
SEV	=	Separate Evaluation Value

ß	=	Beta
t	=	Time period
TCF	=	Total Cash Flow
tr	=	Tax ratio
ts	=	Tax shield of debt
USA	=	Unites States of America
US-GAAP	=	Unites States Generally Accepted Accounting Principle
V	=	Value
VaR	=	Value at Risk
VBM	=	Value Based Management
vs.	=	versus
WACC	=	Weighted Average Costs of Capital
Y	=	Year
zdf	=	zerobond discounting factor
zeb	=	Zentrum für ertragsorientiertes Bankmanagement

1 Introduction

1.1 Problem Definition

Corporate Evaluation is often discussed in literature. In theory, the aspects and assumptions of several methods are clear. Practical application, however, in a certain sector or company type leads to various technical problems. Further, the quality and availability of data is not optimal[1].

With respect to the banking sector, literature offers rather theoretical methods to quantify the value of a bank[2]. However, nearly no practical solutions are available. Further, not all aspects of typical banking operations are integrated into the published models. A current and reliable model proven by empirical data is not known to exist.

Nowadays a shareholder value[3]-oriented management with the evaluation and improvement of the own value is more important for German banks than ever before[4]. Mergers between some banks and profitability problems of the whole sector lead to pressure and to the danger of hostile takeovers[5]. This is proven by table 1:

Kind of bank type	1990	2005	Percentage
Private Bank	338	302[6]	-10.65%
Clearing House	12	12	0.00%
Savings Banks	769	463	-39.79%
Geno / cooperative banks[7]	3,380	1,293	-61.75%
Sum	4,499	2,070	-53.99%

Table 1:   Development of the number of German banks[8]

---

[1]   Cf. *Drukarczyk* (1996), pp. 218.

[2]   Cf. *Sonntag* (2001), p. 5. Discussed in detail in section 2.3. The IDW offers a guideline for the evaluation of the needed data. Cf. *IDW* (2003).

[3]   Shareholder value is defined as a strategy to increase the value of the shareholders. Cf. *Stützer* (1976), columns 4404. Value based management is nearly the same, but the focus is laid on the management process. Cf. *Csoport/Linner* (2002), p. 2. Shareholder value and shareholder wealth are often used synonymicly in literature. Cf. for example *Volkart* (n.Y.), p. 18.
       As a consequence, all three definitions are used similarly in this dissertation. Further explanations can be found in section 3.3.2.

[4]   For a detailed discussion of shareholder value cf. *Stewart* (1991); *Rappaport* (1995) and *Copeland/Koller/Murrin* (1994). For the development from shareholder value to stakeholder value cf. *Krämer/Schäfer* (2005), p. 19. This differentiation will not be discussed in this dissertation as well.

[5]   Cf. *Die Welt* (2003).

[6]   Excluding 55 Investment Banks, which were added to this group in 2002. Cf. *Bankenverband* (2006).

[7]   Abbreviation for Genossenschaftsbank or cooperative bank. In some sources, cooperative bank and savings bank are used similar. Because of that, the abbreviation Geno will be used further on.

[8]   Author's own table referring to *Bankenverband* (2006). Partly including subsidiaries of foreign banks.

The total number of banks decreased by 54% from 4,499 in 1990 to 2,070 in 2006[9]. Analyzing the three pillars of the German banking sector (Private banks, Genos and savings banks)[10] leads to the result that especially the number of the rather small Genos and savings banks shrink strongly. Mergers and fusions in between these pillars led to this effect. The differentiation into these three banking groups is under discussion now[11]. While the private banks want to cancel it[12], the Genos and the savings banks[13] intend to keep it. Breaking up with that three-pillared system would lead to a wave of mergers with the central question about the value of the banks.

Further, the CIR[14] of German banks is about 67.7%[15]. This is too high compared to international competition[16]. The same effect can be stated according to the ROCE[17]. While German banks show a rate of 0.20%[18], the European average rate is about 0.72%[19].

A shareholder value-oriented management must be based on the corporate value of the bank. This value is the central strategic target. Regarding the German banking sector this dissertation answers the following questions:

- Do the existing approaches of corporate evaluation lead to the right values?
- How far is theory in quantifying the value of banks?
- What is the practical status quo of corporate evaluation in the German banking sector?
- What is the value of a typical German bank?
- Do banks manage their business in a shareholder value-oriented way?

---

[9]   Cf. *Bankenverband* (2006).

[10] For further explanation cf. *Süchting/Paul* (1998), p. 32 and *Voigtländer* (2004), pp. 3.

[11] For the current discussion cf. *Jennen* (2006). A structured analysis is given in *Simmert/Benölken* (2006), pp. 238.

[12] Cf. *WiWo* (2006).

[13] Cf. for example *Hoppenstedt* (2005), p. 3.

[14] Abbreviation for Cost Income Ratio.

[15] Cf. *Krabichler/Krauß* (2003), p. 18, data of 2002. The actual development is not even better in Germany. Cf. *Franke* (2004) and *Täubert* (2005).

[16] The average in Europe is about 64.7% in 2002. Cf. *Krabichler/Krauß* (2003), p. 21. The number one bank Citibank has a CIR of 52.5%. Cf. *Franke* (2004).

[17] Abbreviation for Return On Capital Employed. In the banking sector defined as annual surplus divided by average balance sheet sum.

[18] Cf. *Krabichler/Krauß* (2003), p. 19.

[19] Cf. *Krabichler/Krauß* (2003), p. 21.

1.2 Reasoning and Motivation

Current literature offers only some basic ideas to evaluate the corporate value of banks[20]. Theoretical or even empirical evaluations with respect to the German banking sector do not exist[21]. It is the aim of this dissertation to solve the open questions of theory[22] and practice[23], to develop a new evaluation model[24] and to apply it on the German banking sector[25].

In this dissertation, there are actually six aspects which can be stated as new:

1. A representative survey in the German banking sector according to the status quo of corporate evaluation was done recently.
2. A scoring model was defined to quantify the shareholder value-orientation of the bank.
3. The banks had the possibility to be valued by using several existing methods of corporate evaluation and a model developed by the author. Therefore, the internal data given in the survey were used. A total of 19 banks agreed to this option.
4. A new evaluation model was developed by integrating existing aspects of bank controlling with existing approaches of corporate evaluation.
5. This model was verified by applying it to the 19 banks.
6. Some reliable multiples were defined which facilitate the evaluation of the value of a bank in a brief and pragmatic way. They are based on the internal approaches.

Hence, general conclusions are given according to corporate evaluation in the banking sector. These findings are empirically proven. Finally, the results lead to the motivation of building up some general statements regarding the relation between bank's strategy, controlling process and corporate value.

1.3 Research Methods

The underlying research methods for this dissertation have to be structured. During the dissertation, secondary research data[26] was often used. On the one hand, section 2 and a part of section 4 consist of the analysis of current literature. On the other hand, in sections 3 and 5, primary research[27] was done. Sections 4 and 5 offer some additional new arguments in the

---

[20] Cf. section 2.3.
[21] Cf. section 3.4.1.
[22] Cf. section 2.3.
[23] Cf. section 3.
[24] Cf. section 4.
[25] Cf. section 5.
[26] Defined as data collected for another purpose. Cf. *Kotler/Armstrong* (2004), p. 149.
[27] Defined as data collected for a specific purpose. Cf. *Kotler/Armstrong* (2004), p. 149.

evaluation and verification process of the own model. This structure and visualized with the help of figure 1:

Section of the Dissertation	Secondary Research		Primary Research		
	Literature	Other Surveys	Own Survey	Own Model	Own Arguments
Section 1: Introduction					X
Section 2: Theoretical status quo	X				
Section 3: Practical status quo – Survey		X	X		
Section 4: New Model	X			X	X
Section 5: Valuing German Banks	X		X	X	X
Section 6: Final Conclusion					X

Figure 1:   Research methods and methodology[28]

These methods are transferred into a dissertation structure as follows: After a brief introduction in section 1, the classical theory and the application to the German banking sector is done in section 2. In this section, the theoretical status quo of the bank evaluation is presented. After that, a representative survey in the German banking sector is described and structured in section 3. The quality of shareholder value management is analyzed. Further, the status quo regarding the use and acceptance of corporate evaluation is analyzed. Section 4 develops a new model of corporate evaluation. Its usage is discussed when valuing German banks in section 5 – according to data resulting from the survey in section 3. Section 6 summarizes the main results, draws conclusions and offers general hints for the German banking sector.

---

[28]   Author's own figure. Certainly, literature as secondary research is used in every section. This figure visualizes the mainly used sources.

2 Theoretical Status Quo of Corporate Evaluation

2.1 Motivations for a Corporate Evaluation

2.1.1 Reasons for a Corporate Evaluation

Corporate Evaluation has its origin in different reasons. Shareholder value management[29] has become more and more popular[30] and the number of corporate transactions has increased during the last years[31]. The problem is that most of the transactions have been too expensive[32]. Hence, the evaluation of the right corporate value with the right approach for the right purpose[33] has become very important recently.

The motivations for a corporate evaluation can be classified in different ways. Life cycle of a company, obligation to do a corporate evaluation (duty by law, duty by contract or voluntarily) and can be mentioned[34].

A first famous way to distinguish the reasons in literature is the change of property. Reasons for corporate evaluation are divided into those which lead to different property circumstances in the end and into those that do not lead to different property conditions[35].

A second way is to differentiate reasons with respect to the dependency of the decision makers. This is nearly similar to the obligation criteria mentioned above. Some reasons can be determined by the valuator, some not – the company has the obligation to quantify its own value.[36].

Combining these two aspects leads to table 2:

---

[29]   For corporate management based on the shareholder value concept cf. *Lass* (2004), pp. 15.
[30]   Cf. *Rappaport* (1986); *Drukarczyk* (1996), p. 1; *Copeland/Koller/Murrin* (2002), p. 28 and *Kuhner/Maltry* (2006), p. 8.
[31]   Cf. *Drukarczyk* (1996), p. 1.
[32]   Cf. *Porter* (1987), pp. 43 – 89.
[33]   Cf. *Ballwieser* (2004), p. 1.
[34]   Cf. *Peemöller* (2005), p. 17.
[35]   Cf. *Sieben* (1993), column 4320 and *Mandl/Rabel* (1997), pp. 12.
[36]   This does not fit to Drukarczyks definition of domination – this is only a sub-category of the main category changing property. Cf. *Drukarczyk* (1996), p. 89.

	Change of property	**No change of property**
Depending on a decision	• Purchase or sale of companies or share of a company, business units, product groups, trademarks • Voluntary mergers, divestitures of companies • A new partner is joining an existing company • Going public • One partner leaves the company • Compensation payment quantification for several property changes • Rehabilitation/redevelopment • Capital participation of employees	• A company that has to be sold has to evaluate its own value • Shareholder value based management • Turnarounds • Risk/return controlling
Not depending on a decision	• All evaluations during the insolvency proceedings • Retirement of a partner by cancellation • Disqualification of a "annoying" partner • Calculation of compensatory payments • Expropriation • Squeeze out *With restrictions* • Divorce • Inheritance problem	• Goodwill-Impairment-Test according to $IAS^{37}/IFRS^{38}$ and US-GAAP • Calculation of the tax basis • Credit assessments and ratings • Balance Sheet aspects • Turnarounds

Table 2:   **Motivation for a corporate evaluation**[39]

In addition to that, Born mentions some reasons especially for the evaluation of the own company or a business unit. The evaluation could be used for the comparison of different strategic concepts with the current one and for the calculation of synergy effects in the own company when buying another. Further, the intended foundation of a joint venture or the performance assessment of the management has to be mentioned.[40]

2.1.2 The Difference between Price and Value

The objective of a corporate evaluation is to find the value of a company. It has always to be distinguished carefully between price and value of a company[41]. The value of an object always depends on the occasion and context of evaluation[42], while the price is an amount which has to be paid for this object[43]. Usually, the value of an object, which is also called "inner

---

[37]   Abbreviation for International Accounting Standard(s).

[38]   Abbreviation for International Financial Reporting System(s).

[39]   Author's own table referring to *Bellinger/Vahl* (1992), p. 31; *Drukarczyk* (1996), p. 89; *Born* (2003), pp. 1 and *Kuhner/Maltry* (2006), pp. 8.

[40]   Cf. *Born* (2003), pp. 2.

[41]   Cf. *Korth* (1992), p. 2 and *Picot/Jansen* (1999), p. K 3.

[42]   Cf. *Richter* (1942), p. 106 and *Winckelmann* (1953), p. 181.

[43]   Cf. *Tichy* (1992), p. 334.

value"[44], could be calculated in an analytical way from the object's potential of performance or output. In comparison to that a price will always be determined in the market by the law of supply and demand[45]. On both sides, there are different expectations influencing the price. On the one hand, a seller wants to maximise his assets, he will try to get the highest possible price for the object for example by evaluating the potential of synergies as very high. On the other hand, the buyer is keen on paying a possibly low price for the object. His arguments will be that the value of synergies is not that high, and he will additionally ask for a risk discount on the price.[46] In this context a differentiation of objective and subjective company values has to be made[47].

The **objective value** is the value of the company as defined by analysing the current situation of the company. This leads to the value the company is worth for the **owner**. Such a value depends on the structure of the industry, the strategic and operative abilities of the management.[48]

A **subjective value** depends on the benefit, which may result from a change in conception of the company[49]. Such a benefit may be determined by the **buyer's** strategy of acquisition, because he may have other intentions with the company's development, or he may have calculated other synergies. Therefore he attaches another value to the company than the current owner.[50]

This contradiction is summed up elegantly in the sentence of Warren Buffet "Price is what you pay. Value is what you get[51]". Price and even value differ from the purpose of evaluation, as mentioned above.

2.1.3 Functions of Corporate Evaluation

Literature goes one step further. The more practical based approach to structure reasons for corporate evaluation is renewed by the model of the functions of corporate evaluations[52]. This model integrates the subjective and objective value and solves the contradictions[53]. This de-

---

[44] Cf. *Tichy* (1992), p. 333.
[45] Cf. *Korth* (1992), p. 4 and *Funk* (1995), p. 492.
[46] Cf. *Picot/Jansen* (1999), p. K 3.
[47] Cf. *Viel/Bredt/Renard* (1970), pp. 21; *Göppl* (1980), p. 238 and *Gerling* (1985), p. 16.
[48] Cf. *Coenenberg/Sautter* (1988), p. 693 and *Korth* (1992), p. 2.
[49] Cf. *Korth* (1992), p. 2.
[50] Cf. *Göppl* (1980), p. 238.
[51] *Buffet* (n.Y.).
[52] Cf. *Gerling* (1985), p. 16 and *Ballwieser* (2004), p. 1. A short introduction is shown in *Bartke* (1978), pp. 238 – 250.
[53] Cf. *Gerling* (1985), p. 16.

pendency between corporate value and function is accepted in literature nowadays[54]. The main aspects are discussed in the current section.

Correct company values depend on the purposes and functions. Without fulfilling a function the company has no value at all[55]. Literature offers five functions for corporate evaluation[56] divided into main and sub functions[57]:

Function		Description
Main functions[58]	**1. Consulting function**	• Development of a decision price. • For buyer and seller. • Internal personal value for both parties. • At this price, a buyer would buy and a seller would sell.
	2. Argumentation function	• Supporting arguments of some stakeholders. • Not a "fair" or intrinsic" value. • Rather a tactical value that differs from the consulting function value – the buyer has a lower and the seller has a higher argumentation function price.
	3. Mediation function	• Price to solve conflicts. • Example: compensation payments.
Sub functions	**4. Tax calculation function**	• Evaluation of basic value for tax calculation. • Often only for parts of the company.
	5. Balance Sheet function	• Based on balancing rules, book values have to be established. • Value of equity is the resulting difference between assets and liabilities.

Table 3:   Functions for corporate evaluations[59]

These rather classical functions are extended and changed by Coenenberg/Schultze[60]. They define 5 functions as well but these functions differ from those in table 3. While an equivalent for function 1 and 2 exist, the function 3 (balance sheet) is extended to a value-oriented controlling function. Further a capital market evaluation function and a fair value reporting function are added[61]. This follows the current trend that a value-oriented controlling or a shareholder value or wealth oriented management needs the corporate value as a core variable to manage the company.

---

[54] Cf. *Coenenberg/Schultze* (2002), p. 599.
[55] Cf. *Ballwieser* (2004), p. 1.
[56] Cf. *Gerling* (1985), pp. 17 and *Ballwieser* (2004), pp. 3.
[57] Cf. *Sieben* (1977), pp. 28 – 30; *Moxter* (1983), pp. 9 – 22 and *Mandl/Rabel* (1997), pp. 15 – 17 and *IDW* (2002), pp. 10.
[58] Cf. *Kuhner/Maltry* (2006), p. 57.
[59] Author's own table referring to *Gerling* (1985), pp. 17; *Künnemann* (1985), pp. 32 and *Ballwieser* (2004), p. 1.
[60] Cf. *Coenenberg/Schultze* (2002), p. 599 and *Schultze* (2003a), p. 10.
[61] Cf. *Coenenberg/Schultze* (2002), p. 600.

By defining several functions of corporate evaluation, the argumentation according to a unique corporate value differs. As every function has several motivations, the company value must differ in order to fulfil the right function. A company can have more than one "right" value. It depends on the function vice-versa.

2.2 Methods of General Corporate Evaluation

Several approaches to define the value of a company can be found in literature. They differ regarding the time they were evaluated as well as regarding the assumptions they make. The higher the number of the approaches is, the higher is the number of special cases and the possibilities to structure the methods of corporate evaluation.

Drukarczyk offers one chapter of corporate evaluation[62] in which he differs the earnings value method from discounted cash flow methods and structures those into entity, equity and APV[63] approach[64]. Reproduction or liquidation methods, multiplier methods or real option approach are not presented[65].

Ballwieser offers a holistic structure of corporate evaluation methods. Separate evaluation methods, global evaluation methods, mixtures of both and multiplier approaches are mentioned[66]. The DCF[67] are structured into APV, FCF[68], TCF[69] and FTE[70] in the table of content. Chapter 5 on the other side offers a more structured overview according to the DCF methods[71].

Kuhner/Maltry do not structure all approaches consequently in the content table[72], but they give a main structure in section 2 similar to Ballwieser[73]. Nevertheless, they differ in some aspects. Their structure of the DCF approaches leads to a difference compared with Drukarczyk and Ballwieser – the APV is a sub-section of the entity approach[74]. Further, TCF and FCF approaches exist beneath the APV approach. All three build the entity approaches that exist beneath the equity approach.

---

[62]   Cf. *Drukarczyk* (1996), chapter 5, pp. 87 – 267.
[63]   Abbreviation for Adjusted Present Value.
[64]   Cf. *Drukarczyk* (1996), p. 143.
[65]   Cf. *Drukarczyk* (1996), chapter 5, pp. 87 – 267.
[66]   Definition follows. Cf. section 2.2.3 and 2.2.4.
[67]   Abbreviation for Discounted Cash Flow.
[68]   Abbreviation for Free Cash Flow.
[69]   Abbreviation for Total Cash Flow.
[70]   Abbreviation for Flow To Equity.
[71]   Cf. *Ballwieser* (2004), p. 111.
[72]   They structure the topic into 2 sections. Cf. *Kuhner/Maltry* (2006), p. VIII – X.
[73]   Cf. *Kuhner/Maltry* (2006), p. 52.
[74]   Cf. *Kuhner/Maltry* (2006), p. 200.

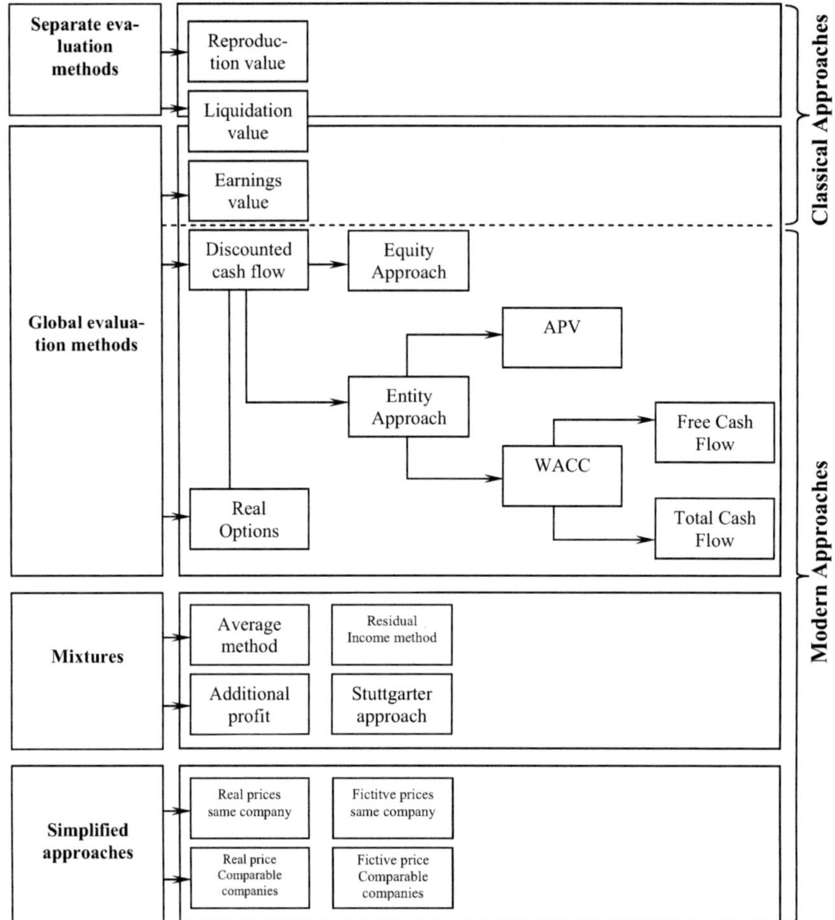

Figure 2:   **Main structure of corporate evaluation approaches**[75]

As the main structure of Ballwieser is common content in literature[76], figure 2 is based on his main assumptions and implements aspects of Drukarczyk and Kuhner/Maltry. However, some extensions are done. Due to the fact that some authors do not discuss classical and modern approaches together in one chapter[77], this is chosen to be an additional criterion to distinguish the approaches. Further, the market value based on the share price analysis and the real option

---

[75] Author's own figure referring to the sources mentioned above, but especially referring to *Ballwieser* (2004), p. 8, p. 111, p. 184, p. 190 and *Schierenbeck* (1998), p. 388.

[76] Cf. *Mandl/Rabel* (1997), p. 30; *Drukarczyk* (2003), p. 131 and *Ballwieser* (2004), p. 11.

[77] Schierenbeck for example chooses this procedure. Cf. *Schierenbeck* (1998), p. 388.

approach are inserted into the figure. In contrast to **Schierenbeck**, the mixture methods are treated as modern approaches[78]. As they combine modern and classical aspects with focus on the modern aspects, they are rather modern than classical.

Separate evaluation methods quantify the value of the company by adding the value of the company's parts[79] while global evaluation methods seek to evaluate the company as a whole[80] by considering future's income[81] and efforts[82]. Mixtures combine these two basic criteria. Simplified approaches seek to get a price for the company by comparing it to the market or to other companies[83].

Figure 2 is more detailed than the illustrations in existing literature. As a consequence, the real option approach is inserted into the DCF-sector, the simplified approaches are distinguished into four aspects and the DCF entity/equity structuring approach combines Ballwieser[84] and Kuhner/Maltry[85].

Even though this structure represents the status quo of modern literature, some aspects are still under discussion. Personal taxes are not always considered in literature[86] and the substantial value[87] is often set similar to the liquidation value[88]. This is wrong as the main assumption of the liquidation approach is the winding up of the company[89]. A typical example for another structure is given by **Schultze**. He defines several other global evaluation models. He offers a structure with the main sectors DDM[90], DCF, earnings value and RIM[91]. Differing between dividends to discount and earnings to discount[92] shows no real difference – defining the dividends as earnings solves this classification problem[93]. The RIM is based on the book value of the equity and compares expected earnings with the equity yield.[94] It can be defined as a mixture approach, a specialisation of an additional profit approach[95]. It is not an origin global evaluation model[96].

---

[78] Cf. *Schierenbeck* (1998), p. 388.
[79] Cf. *Kuhner/Maltry* (2006), p. 52.
[80] Cf. *Moxter* (1977), p. 254.
[81] Cash flows or earnings.
[82] Cf. *Ballwieser* (2004), p. 8.
[83] Cf. *Ballwieser* (2004), p. 8 and *Kuhner/Maltry* (2006), p. 52.
[84] Cf. *Ballwieser* (2004), p. 8.
[85] Cf. *Kuhner/Maltry* (2006), p. XI.
[86] Cf. *Ballwieser* (2004), p. 8.
[87] Another definition for reproduction value.
[88] Cf. *OLG Düsseldorf* (2003), p. 691 and *OLG Düsseldorf* (2004), p. 327.
[89] Cf. *Kuhner/Maltry* (2006), p. 42.
[90] Abbreviation for Dividend Discount Model.
[91] Abbreviation for Residual Income Method.
[92] Cf. *Schultze* (2003a), pp. 75.
[93] Cf. *Ballwieser* (2004), p. 11.
[94] Cf. *Schultze* (2003a), pp. 111.
[95] Argued in *Ewert/Wagenhofer* (2000), pp. 10.
[96] Cf. *Ballwieser* (2004), p. 11.

In the following sections, all presented approaches as outlined and structured in figure 2 will be dealt with in more depth. The structure of section 2.2 follows the structure of the figure accordingly.

2.2.1 Separate Evaluation Methods

The separate evaluation principle is regulated by German law[97]. By summarizing each part of a company's net assets stated in the balance sheet and by deducting all debts, the substance value or net asset value of a company could be calculated[98]. In general, reproduction and liquidation approach can be distinguished.[99] These two approaches differ from each other.

2.2.1.1 Reproduction Value Method

The reproduction value method assumes the asset-identical reproduction of the company[100]. Therefore the expenditure at replacement asset values should determine the value of a company's substance. Thus it is a synthetic value as only a fictitious selling and new building up is assumed[101]. Depending on the assumptions especially according to immaterial assets several different sub approaches can be defined[102]. They are not discussed here in detail. The reproduction approach has the advantage that the asset's value does not depend on intransparent assumptions[103]. Therefore it is often used for the purpose of tax evaluation, credit security and donations[104]. The tax function and the balance sheet function can be fulfilled by this approach. For decisions, however, it does not offer the right information for the management.

2.2.1.2 Liquidation Value Method

Contrariwise to this, the liquidation value method does not assume the principle of going concern, but a sale of company's assets[105] in case of liquidation[106]. According to this method, the asset value in the case of selling each single part will be evaluated. This gross value will be reduced by the debts of the company and maybe reduced by the costs for liquidation[107]. Prob-

---

[97] Cf. § 252 (1) No. 3 *HGB* ("Einzelbewertungsverfahren"). HGB stands for Handelsgesetzbuch.
[98] Cf. *Ballwieser* (2004), p. 10.
[99] Cf. *Kuhner/Maltry* (2006), p. 43.
[100] Cf. *Kuhner/Maltry* (2006), p. 43.
[101] Cf. *Kuhner/Maltry* (2006), p. 43.
[102] Cf. *Sieben/Maltry* (2002), p. 379.
[103] Cf. *IDW* (2002), A 401.
[104] Cf. *Sieben* (1992) and *Kuhner/Maltry* (2006), p. 43.
[105] Cf. *Mandl/Rabel* (2002), pp. 80.
[106] Cf. *Ballwieser* (2004), p. 10.
[107] Cf. *Jung* (1983), p. 209 and *Moxter* (1983), p. 41.

lems will occur, if parts of the company cannot be sold, because a market does not exist. An optimal liquidation period and the liquidation intensity, defined as the granularity of objects to sell, is very important[108]. This approach will only become interesting, if other approaches lead to a lower value than the liquidation approach. Normally, it is a kind of value floor for all other approaches, as the owner can decide to not to discontinue the company[109].

Nevertheless, the value calculated by liquidation or reproduction method does not correspond to the "real" value of the company[110]. The intangible assets[111] like human capital, customer relationships or organizational excellence could not be found in the balance sheet and, therefore, are not considered in the calculation. Further, all future expected earnings and growth possibilities are not considered as well. Especially in the case of a strong growing and knowledge intensive company these methods would lead to an undervaluation of the company.[112] However, a seller could understand the calculated values as minimum price for his company, if instead of a sale only a liquidation is possible, while the buyer could see it as risk limit, if an acquisition did not seem to be successful.

2.2.2 Global Evaluation Methods

As mentioned before a company could be more or less worth than the sum of its parts or its assets[113]. Therefore the value of the company should not be measured by the single assets. The whole company's potential in future is more important[114]. The central idea is to consider a company as an investment[115], so that present value approaches can be used. Before presenting the approaches some basic definitions are needed.

In all kinds of present value approaches, the discounting rate is crucial. A differentiation into equity yield and debt yield is useful[116], as the risk differs between a shareholder and a bank[117]. Risk can be implemented in two ways: decreasing the returns[118] or increasing the discounting factor[119]. In this section, only the adjustments of the risk premium but not the evaluation of

---

[108] Cf. *Bellinger/Vahl* (1992), p. 25; *Moxter* (1976), pp. 50 and *Kuhner/Maltry* (2006), p. 42.
[109] Cf. *Sieben/Maltry* (2002), p. 397.
[110] Assuming that at least one real value exists.
[111] For a short introduction into this topic cf. *Hopfenbeck* (1989), pp. 207.
[112] Cf. *Picot/Jansen* (1999), p. K 3.
[113] Cf. *Ballwieser* (2004), p. 9.
[114] Cf. *Picot/Jansen* (1999), p. K 3.
[115] Cf. *Ballwieser* (2004), p. 8.
[116] Cf. *Copeland/Koller/Murrin* (2002), p. 17.
[117] Cf. *Copeland/Koller/Murrin* (2002), p. 250.
[118] Cf. *Gerling* (1985), pp. 248; *Drukarczyk* (1996), pp. 96; *Ballwieser* (2004), p. 66, p. 89 and *IDW* (2005), p. 1312.
[119] Cf. *IDW* (2005), p. 1320 and *Kuhner/Maltry* (2006), p. 49.

risk adjusted cash flows is analyzed. For the banking sector, special models that reduce the earnings will be used, so that the methods to adjust earnings will be discussed later on[120].

Taking this into consideration, the discounting yield has to follow several equivalency principles[121] and can be distinguished into several parts[122]. These criteria are combined in the following table. Further, hints are given how these parts can be filled.

	Equity yield	**Debt yield**
Currency	Normally €	Normally €, depending on the debt structure.
Maturity	10 years or even longer, as equity has no maturity at all.	Depending on the individual liability structure of the bank loans and emissions.
Risk	Equity risk can be defined by the CAPM[123] or other approaches[124], as the spread[125] or individual models[126], which partly extend the CAPM.	Inherent in the offered rate. It covers bank's credit risk in form of expected and (partly) unexpected losses[127].

Table 4:   Parts of the discounting rate[128]

The currency should be the same as the opportunity the investor has[129]. A German investor would prefer a German yield curve. Problems will only occur, if complex situations exist. For example, if an American subsidiary of a German company buys a Mexican company. A calculation in Peso, Euro or Dollar is possible[130].

The maturity aspect is more difficult to handle. Discussing the debt yield leads to easy results: the offered rate by the bank has to be used[131]. Only if these rates are not available, for example when discounting pension reserves, a maturity conform market yield has to be used[132]. But analyzing the equity yield leads to other results. As the earnings or returns of the company are estimated for eternity, an eternal yield has to be chosen[133]. However, an eternal yield does not

---

[120]   Cf. section 2.3 and section 4.
[121]   Cf. *Moxter* (1983), pp. 155 – 202.
[122]   Cf. *Copeland/Koller/Murrin* (2002), p. 266.
[123]   Abbreviation for Capital Asset Pricing Model.
[124]   The model itself will be explained later on.
[125]   For a distinguishing of the spread to other risks cf. *Wiedemann/Hager* (2002), pp. 3. A short definition can be found in *Harter/Franke/Hogrefe/Seger* (2002), p. 143.
[126]   A stochastic analysis is done in *Schwetzler* (2000), pp. 478.
[127]   For these definitions cf. *Rolfes* (1999), pp. 332.
[128]   Author's own table referring to *Ballwieser* (2004), p. 82 and *Kuhner/Maltry* (2006), pp. 84.
[129]   Cf. *Ballwieser* (2004), pp. 82.
[130]   Cf. *Kengelbach* (2000), pp. 175 – 179.
[131]   Cf. *Copeland/Koller/Murrin* (2002), pp. 259 and *IDW* (2005), p. 1316.
[132]   Cf. *IDW* (2005), p. 1316.
[133]   Cf. *Drukarczyk* (1996), pp. 242.

exist. So the longest available yield, normally a 10-15 year yield, is used[134]. This is common usage in literature.

But the question, if the yield of the evaluation date[135], a sustainable average[136] or a future expected yield[137] has to be chosen is not finally solved[138]. The author follows the suggestion of Drukarczyk and the IDW[139] to choose a maturity equivalent[140]. But in contrast to the IDW, just following Drukarczyk, spot rates transformed into zero bond yields[141] shall be used. This might be argued as follows: if a corporate evaluation takes place, the value at a certain moment shall be evaluated. Therefore the spot rates have to be used. Analyzing the argumentation of the IDW leads to the following results. On the one hand, the IDW agrees that a corporate evaluation is a fixture of a moment, as the returns are moment-dependant[142]. On the other hand it states that the long-lasting average shall be used[143]. This is a contradiction in itself, so that Drukarczyk's argumentation is the more consistent one.

Despite these argumentations, the sustainable average of a yield was preferred in practice[144]. Nevertheless, legal acceptation demands other results again[145]. Sometimes a fix yield is used, nearly without connection to the capital market. Further some authors want to implement an inflation discount in order to define real instead of nominal discount rates. But in this case even the returns have to be calculated on a real instead of a nominal basis[146]. As a consequence, both approaches lead to the same result[147]. Summing up these facts leads to the following result: Even though the best way is to use actual spot rates, other methods are used in practice and the approaches accepted by law often differ from both. The author follows Drukarczyk's argumentation.

As the last factor to discuss, the risk premium offers various possibilities. With respect to the debt yield, the answer is clear. The conditions offered by banks or the yields of the emissions

---

[134] Cf. *Ballwieser* (2004), pp. 83.
[135] Cf. *Matschke* (1979), pp. 215.
[136] Cf. *Widmann/Schieszl/Jeromin* (2003), p. 800, p. 803 and *IDW* (2005), p. 1315.
[137] Cf. *Hetzel* (1988), pp. 725 and *Piltz* (1994), p. 173.
[138] Cf. *Drukarczyk* (1996), pp. 242.
[139] Abbreviation for Institut der Wirtschaftsprüfer.
[140] With respect to the maturity cf. *IDW* (2005), p. 1315.
[141] Cf. *Drukarczyk* (1996), pp. 242.
[142] Cf. *IDW* (2005), p. 1306.
[143] Cf. *IDW* (2005), p. 1315.
[144] For the history of jurisdiction cf. *Moxter* (1983), p. 146; *Hackmann* (1987), pp. 105 and *IDW* (1992), p. 94. Actual jurisdiction can be found in *Ballwieser* (2004), p. 87, pp. 105 – 107.
[145] Cf. *Drukarczyk* (1996), pp. 244 and *Ballwieser* (2004), pp. 104.
[146] Cf. *Kuhner/Maltry* (2006), p. 90.
[147] Cf. *Schildbach* (1977); *Moxter* (1983), p. 192; *Ballwieser* (1988), pp. 800 – 802 and *Ballwieser* (2004), p. 88.

have an inherent risk-equivalent spread. The better the solvency of a creditor is, the lower the expected default rate is[148]. The spread, defined as the risk premium, becomes lower as well.[149]

Discussing the equity yield leads to more differences in the evaluation of the discounting rate. The most common and accepted approach is the CAPM[150] or Tax-CAPM[151]. This model was developed by Sharpe[152], Lintner[153], Mossin[154] and Traynor[155], based on Markowitz[156] portfolio theory[157]. Only a short introduction into this model is given in this dissertation[158]. The CAPM states on the one hand that every investor has the same expectations of risk and return. On the other hand, it assumes the existence of a risk free rate of return.[159] In an efficient market, the expected risk premium varies proportionally to the accepted risk, because an unsystematic risk could be avoided by diversification[160], and a systematic risk usually is connected with movements of the whole market portfolio. Consequently, the following figure can be set up:

---

[148]   Cf. *Standard & Poor's* (2006).
[149]   Empirically proven in *Reuse* (2003.12), p. 17.
[150]   Cf.*Brealey/Myers* (1996), pp. 180;*Copeland/Koller/Murrin* (2002), pp. 264 and *IDW* (2005), pp. 1320.
[151]   Cf. *Jonas/Löffler/Wiese* (2004), pp. 898.
[152]   Cf. *Sharpe* (1964), pp. 425 – 442.
[153]   Cf. *Lintner* (1965), pp. 13 – 37.
[154]   Cf. *Mossin* (1996), pp. 768 – 783.
[155]   Traynor's article has not been published. Cf. *Brealey/Myers* (1996), pp. 180.
[156]   Cf. *Markowitz* (1952).
[157]   Cf. *Brealey/Myers* (1996), pp. 180.
[158]   Following the structure of several other approaches. Cf. *Drukarczyk* (1996), p. 179; *Copeland/Koller/Murrin* (2002), p. 265 and *IDW* (2005), p. 1320.
[159]   Cf. *Wöhe* (1996), p. 911.
[160]   Cf. *Copeland/Koller/Murrin* (2002), pp. 265.

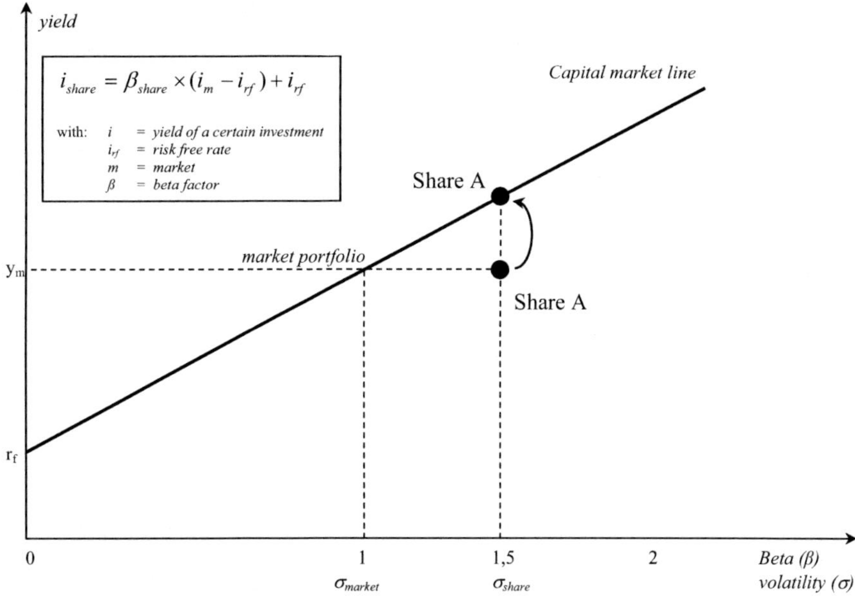

Figure 3:   **Graphical visualization of the CAPM**[161]

Regarding this figure and the equation, the expected risk premium on a stock corresponds to the expected risk premium of the market[162] multiplied with the beta factor[163]. This factor measures the sensitivity between the movement of a share and the movement of the whole market[164]. The beta factor for the whole market is 1, as the risk premium is the same on both sides[165]. If the beta factor is higher than 1, the expected risk premium for the share is higher than the market average[166]. This corresponds to a higher volatility as well[167]. The beta factor can be evaluated by historical correlation analysis of the volatility[168] of a certain industrial sector compared with the index volatility of land[169] or by serious estimations[170].

---

[161]   Author's own figure referring to *Brealey/Myers* (1996), p. 180; *Copeland/Koller/Murrin* (2002), p. 265 and *IDW* (2005), p. 1321. Assumption: linear efficiency line.

[162]   Defined as $(i_m - i_{rf})$.

[163]   Cf. *Schierenbeck* (1998), p. 382 and *Copeland/Koller/Murrin* (2002), pp. 265.

[164]   Cf. *Brealey/Myers* (1996), pp. 180.

[165]   Cf. *Copeland/Koller/Murrin* (2002), pp. 265.

[166]   Cf. *Drukarczyk* (1996), p. 182.

[167]   For the definitions of volatility and standard deviation cf. *Brealey/Myers* (1996), pp. 650; *Perriod/Steiner* (1997), pp. 326 and *Harter/Franke/Hogrefe/Seger* (2002), p. 155.

[168]   If a diagram is setup that shows the volatilities of the market on the x-axis and the volatility of the market on the y-axis, the beta is the ascent factor of the regression line of market risk and individual portfolio risk. Cf. *Sharpe* (1970), p. 91 and *Schmidt/Terberger* (1997), p. 357.

[169]   Cf. *Kuhner/Maltry* (2006), p. 167. This index represents the market yield. Cf. *Brealey/Myers* (1996), pp. 181.

[170]   Cf. *Kuhner/Maltry* (2006), p. 166.

In the example explained above, the share is an inefficient market position, as other positions exist that offer a better return at the same risk. All these efficient portfolios lay one the capital market line. So the expectations of the investor will be that the share reduces its risk or increases its expected return. In a corporate evaluation scenario, the risk is given, so the expectations according to the yield will increase. This has a direct influence on the resulting risk premium.

Despite its availability, the CAPM is not necessarily the best model[171], as it is eyed critically.[172] Even though the model is quite simple[173], empirical analysis has shown that betas can be instable[174] and that the model leads to contradictory results[175]. Nevertheless, the usage of this model is the only option a valuator has. The author will use this model as well – but it has to be emphasized that some extensions and the new bank-individual evaluation model will prevent the usage of CAPM in several situations[176].

Adding the risk premium to the risk free ratio leads to the equity yield to discount the returns with. The exact definition of the return and the related usage of the discounting factor led to the global evaluation methods structured above[177]. The following sections discuss these approaches.

2.2.2.1 Earnings Value Method

The earnings value method[178] calculates the company's value by capitalizing selected earnings and expenditures[179] with the formula of an eternal annuity[180].

$$CV = \sum_{1}^{n} \frac{\text{net return}_n}{(1+i)^n}$$

with:

i	=	interest rate
CV	=	Corporate value
n	=	number of periods

Equation 1:   The earnings value approach[181]

---

[171] Cf. *Copeland/Koller/Murrin* (2002), pp. 264.
[172] Cf. for example *Ossadnik* (1984), pp. 217 and *Kruschwitz/Löffler* (1997).
[173] Cf. *Drukarczyk* (1996), p. 179.
[174] Cf. *Kuhner/Maltry* (2006), p. 167.
[175] Cf. *Black/Jensen/Scholes* (1972); *Fama/MacBeth* (1973); *Banz* (1981); *Lakonishok/Shapiro* (1986); *Bhandari* (1988); *Fama/French* (1992) and *Black* (1993).
[176] Cf. sections 4 and 5.
[177] Cf. figure 2.
[178] Popular in Germany, but not in the USA, cf. *Drukarczyk* (1996), p. 209.
[179] Cf. *Mellerowicz* (1952), p. 17.
[180] Cf. *Jung* (1983), p. 207 and *Korth* (1992), p. 4.
[181] Cf. *Kuhner/Maltry* (2005), p. 48.

The capitalization is necessary, as earnings will be worth less, if they are generated in the far future[182]. Usually, these earnings could be either determined by extrapolating the past[183] and current earnings and by correcting them for extraordinary effects[184], or by taking them for example from a ten years budget.[185] The returns that have to be discounted are net returns[186] as personal taxes of the owner and capital inserts have to be deducted[187].

The calculation of the earnings value leads to some difficulties[188]. Kuhner/Maltry state three problems[189] as shown in the following table:

Problem	Description
Prognosis problem	Company's earnings expectations are influenced by general economical risks, the dependence on business cycles, the competition in the market, but also by specific company risks. Usually, such risks could only be determined in a subjective way[190]. However, by discounting them they will be partly equalized.[191]
Strategy problem[192]	Strategy determines the returns of the future. A simple interpolation of past returns does not lead to the right results. Transforming strategy into returns is difficult.
Capitalization problem	The main problem is the quantification of risk and transferring it into a suitable risk premium for the discounting rate[193]. For the discounting a cost of capital rate is used, which corresponds to the individual yield expectation of the investor. Such a rate will be determined by the yield expectations of alternative investments like long term bonds. Consequently a comparison of the expected earnings of the company with those from alternative investments has to be done. Additionally company's risk has to be considered, as it is not included in the basic capital rate. Therefore it has to be settled by a risk premium as well as probably an inflation premium[194].

Table 5:   **Problems of the earnings value method**[195]

The resulting present value should be higher than the liquidation or reproduction value[196]. It is closer to the corporate value expectations of a seller or buyer. Hence, the consulting function[197] is fulfilled. Further, mediation and argumentation function fit to the earnings value

---

[182] Cf. *Ballwieser* (2004), p. 9.
[183] Cf. *Drukarczyk* (1996), p. 218.
[184] Cf. *Bellinger/Vahl* (1992), pp. 145.
[185] Cf. *Fischer* (1989), p. 93 and *Beisel/Klumpp* (1991), p. 33.
[186] Cf. *Mandl/Rabel* (1997), p. 113.
[187] Cf. *Ballwieser* (2004), p. 13 and *IDW* (2005), p. 1306.
[188] Cf. *Drukarczyk* (1996), pp. 210.
[189] Cf. *Kuhner/Maltry* (2006), p. 49.
[190] For a detailed analysis of this problem cf. *Bretzke* (1975).
[191] Cf. *Göppl* (1980), p. 238; *Jung* (1983), p. 495 and *Korth* (1992), p. 14.
[192] Ballwieser combines the first two aspects. Cf. *Ballwieser* (2004), p. 14.
[193] Cf. *Coenenberg/Sautter* (1988), p. 703.
[194] Cf. *Jung* (1983), p. 207; *Moxter* (1983), p. 193 and *Korth* (1992), p. 11. The inflation problem has been discussed above.
[195] Author's own table referring to *Kuhner/Maltry* (2006), p. 49.
[196] Cf. *Kuhner/Maltry* (2006), p. 48.
[197] Cf. section 2.1.3.

method as well[198]. The earnings value and the DCF approach are the only global evaluation methods the IDW accepts as an official approach in Germany[199].

The equity yield evaluated by CAPM can be used to discount the earnings[200], but the explicit usage of the CAPM is not mentioned at all[201]. CAPM normally belongs to DCF approaches[202]. So how shall the risk premium for the earnings value method be evaluated? Literature does not offer a consistent solution. As mentioned in the table above, security discounts[203] derived from the personal usage function[204] are often used[205]. They generate the present value by adjusting the risk free rate in relation to this usage function. Reducing the returns respectively the expected values[206] must lead to the same result[207]. This is why these returns can be transferred into a risk premium and vice-versa. Further several ex-ante approaches to calculate the equity yield exist [208]. Their usage has to be eyed critically[209].

The earnings value approach has several inherent problems. First, the quantification of the earnings that can be paid out to the owner is very difficult to justify[210]. Further the discounting yield is not discussed consistently in literature. This leads to problems concerning the assumptions and the resulting corporate value.

2.2.2.2 Discounted Cash Flow Methods

The discounted cash flow methods were developed in order to solve the conception problems of the earnings value method. One of the major weaknesses of the earnings value approach is the question which earnings can be paid out to the shareholders. Even though the exact evaluation of payable returns in an earnings value method is possible, it is very difficult in practice[211].

---

[198] Cf. *Kuhner/Maltry* (2006), p. 57.
[199] Cf. *Ballwieser* (2004), p. 110; *IDW* (2005), p. 1313 and *Eisenmann/Höfele* (n.Y.), p. 4.
[200] Cf. *IDW* (2005), p. 1315.
[201] Cf. *Ballwieser* (2004), p. 111. Further, Ballwieser explains the CAPM under the structure of earnings value approaches. Cf. *Ballwieser* (2004), p. 92.
[202] Cf. *Drukarczyk* (1996), p. 179; *Schierenbeck* (1998), p. 390; *Ballwieser* (2004), p. 111 and *Kuhner/Maltry* (2006), pp. 127 – 176, p. 197;
[203] Cf. *Kuhner/Maltry* (2006), p. 135.
[204] Cf. *Neumann/Morgenstern* (1944).
[205] Cf. *Drukarczyk* (1996), p. 230.
[206] Cf. *Kuhner/Maltry* (2006), p. 130.
[207] Cf. *Ballwieser* (2004), p. 97.
[208] Cf. *Claus/Thomas* (2001); *Gebhardt/Lee/Swaminathan* (2001); *Gode/Mohanram* (2002) and *Daske/ Gebhardt/Klein* (2004).
[209] Cf. *Ballwieser* (2004), p. 100.
[210] Cf. *Drukarczyk* (1996), pp. 103 – 123.
[211] Cf. *Drukarczyk* (1996), p. 263.

This is solved elegantly by using the cash flow approach[212]. The corporate value is also calculated as a present value. The calculation however is not based on the future profits, but on the cash flows[213] generated in future[214]. These cash flows are discounted by a risk adjusted interest rate.[215] The bounds between DCF and earnings value method may be fluent, as both are based on discounted returns[216]. Therefore the DCF method could be seen as a special and more future oriented version of the earnings value method[217].

As earnings value approach, entity and equity approaches show different assumptions related to the discounting rate, the cash flow differs, too. A cash flow is defined as the internal financing power of a company[218]. It contains all earnings and expenditures that leads to a cash transfer as well. The classical way to develop this is as follows: adjust the annual surplus[219] with earnings that are no cash inflow and expenditures that are no cash outflow[220]. Its evaluation for the purpose of balance sheet analysis leads to three different cash flow definitions[221]. For the purpose of corporate evaluation, however, a different method has to be chosen. The cash flow that has to be derived has to be adjusted by several aspects[222]. It has to be kept in mind that every DCF approach requires its own cash flow[223]. The following table visualizes which cash flow has to be used for which approach. Further a differentiation into the operative and non operative return is given[224].

---

[212] Cf. *Drukarczyk* (1996), p. 263.
[213] Defined as free cash flows.
[214] Cf. *Ballwieser* (1998), p. 81.
[215] Cf. *Copeland/Koller/Murrin* (2002), pp. 251.
[216] Cf. *Funk* (1995), p. 495.
[217] Cf. *Börsig* (1993), p. 84 and *Steinöcker* (1993), p. 87.
[218] Cf. *Schierenbeck* (1998), p. 610.
[219] Cf. *Ballwieser* (2004), p. 39.
[220] Structured in *Buchner* (1981), pp. 78 and *Richard/Mühlmeyer/Bergmann* (1996), p. 382.
[221] Cf. *Schierenbeck* (1998), p. 610.
[222] Cf. *Schierenbeck* (1998), p. 390.
[223] Cf. *Kuhner/Maltry* (2006), p. 196.
[224] Useful for the earnings value approach, cf. section 2.2.2.1.

Component		Used for
Annual surplus − Earnings from shares − Extraordinary income + Non earning-relevant taxes	+ Cash inflow of normal operating − Cash outflow of normal operating incl. taxes	
= **Operative/sustainable earning after taxes**		**Earnings value approach**
+ Depreciation[225] + Interest payments + Earning relevant taxes		
= **EBITDA[226]**		
− Taxes at fictitious self financing + Changing of accruals		
= **gross cash flow / operating cash flow**		
− Extension investments + Disinvestments −/+ Changing of working capital		
= **Free cash flow (FCF)**		**WACC FCF & APV**
+ Tax shield		
= **Total cash flow (TCF)**		**WACC TCF**
− Interest payments[227] − Redemption payments + New loans − Other claims		
= **Flow to equity (FTE)**		**Equity Approach**

Table 6:   **Differentiation of cash flows[228]**

These cash flows are used in several models. As the cash flow differs, the discounting rate differs as well[229]. But in total, however, the results of the usage of all three approaches have to be the same[230] – if consistent assumptions are used[231]. The exact definition of the cash flow and the discounting rate are based on several assumptions. They will be presented in the following section.

2.2.2.2.1 Equity Approach

As mentioned above, the DCF methods could be divided into an equity approach and entity approaches[232]. The equity approach calculates the corporate value by using the expected cash

---

[225] Not including value corrections for financial assets. Cf. *Copeland/Koller/Murrin* (2002), p. 18.

[226] Abbreviation for Earnings Before Interest, Taxes, Depreciation and Amortization.

[227] Defined as flow to debt. Cf. *Casey* (2003), p. 14.

[228] Author's own table referring to *Fischer* (1999), p. 29; *Copeland/Koller/Murrin* (2002), p. 18; *Casey* (2003), p. 14; *Ballwieser* (2004), p. 112; *IDW* (2005), p. 1316 and *Kuhner/Maltry* (2006), p. 196.

[229] Cf. *Ballwieser* (2004), p. 112.

[230] Cf. *Breuer* (2001), pp. 1511. He compares equity, entity and APV approaches.

[231] Cf. *Drukarczyk* (1996), p. 142 and *Eisenmann/Höfele* (n.Y.), p. 6.

[232] Given in *Schierenbeck* (1998), p. 390 and *Ballwieser* (2004), p. 111.

flows as given by the FTE and discounting them by the cost of equity capital, as defined above[233]. The formula can be set up as follows:

$$CV = \sum_{1}^{n} \frac{FTE_n}{(1+i)^n}$$

with:

i	=	interest rate, equity yield per CAPM
FTE	=	Cash flows as per flow to equity
n	=	number of periods
CV	=	corporate value

Equation 2:　The equity approach[234]

The value of debt must not be discounted – this is inherently done by implementing interest payments[235].

On the one hand several authors state that earnings value approach and equity approach will lead to the same results, if the same assumptions and related yields are used[236]. On the other hand the usage of the CAPM is only demanded in a clear way when discussing the equity approach[237]. Even Drukarczyk offers inconsistent argumentations: At first he states that earnings value approach and equity approach differ according to the risk equivalent rate[238], secondly he states the identity of both approaches[239]. The result is that these approaches are identical in theory only – in practice, they will differ.

All DCF methods have the same disadvantages as the earnings value approach. The definition of the terminal value is the most sensible value driver[240]. Not all the problems concerning constant growing earnings[241] or full payout situations[242] can be solved in theory or practice.

Even though the equity approach seems to be simple, it is only rarely used in practice[243]. On the one hand compared with the other DCF approaches, no advantages can be stated by Dru-

---

[233]　Cf. *Drukarczyk* (1996), p. 176 and *Ballwieser* (1998), p. 82.

[234]　Cf. *Kuhner/Maltry* (2006), p. 197.

[235]　Cf. *Ballwieser* (2004), p. 111.

[236]　For the equivalence of DCF and earnings value approaches cf. *Schmidt* (1995), pp. 1087; *Sieben* (1995), pp. 714; *Drukarczyk* (1996), p. 263; *Jakubowicz* (2000), pp. 191; *Ballwieser* (2004), p. 111, p. 169 and *Ballwieser* (2005), pp. 365.

[237]　Cf. *Drukarczyk* (1996), p. 17; *Schierenbeck* (1998), p. 390; *Ballwieser* (2004), p. 111 and *Kuhner/Maltry* (2006), pp. 127 – 176, p. 197.

[238]　Cf. *Drukarczyk* (1996), p. 178.

[239]　Cf. *Drukarczyk* (1996), p. 263.

[240]　Cf. *Copeland/Koller/Murrin* (2002), p. 325 and *Ballwieser* (2004), p. 65.

[241]　Cf. *Aders/Schröder* (2004).

[242]　Cf. *Laitenberger/Tschöpel* (2003).

[243]　Cf. *Kuhner/Maltry* (2006), p. 197.

karczyk[244]. The reason is the fictitious complete self-financing of the company. Only one re-financing situation can be analyzed, the influence of the leverage effect is not discussable[245]. On the other hand, according to Ballwieser, the equity approach is more suitable, as it does not touch the question of financing, so that in a diversified company group, the cash flows could be forecasted independently from the assumptions regarding a financing with debt or equity capital.[246]

In the context of bank evaluation approaches the equity method will become more important[247]. Even though authors of classical corporate evaluation consider this approach as not optimal, it will be the only DCF approach that can be used for evaluating the value of a bank[248].

2.2.2.2.2 Entity Approach – WACC

The corporate evaluation following the entity approaches consist of two stages[249]. At first the present value of the cash flows available for the shareholders and debt financiers is calculated[250]. In a second step the value of the debt capital will be deducted from the value of the whole capital[251]. The difference should be the value of equity capital respectively the shareholder value[252]. Because of this procedure the entity method is also called gross method in German literature[253]. The idea is to separate the operating section from the (re)financing section[254].

From this it can be concluded that the forecasted earnings should serve the equity and debt financiers. Only FCF and TCF fulfil these conditions[255]. Therefore the cost of capital should also consider this mixture[256]. According to theory a weighted average cost of capital, the so-called WACC, should be used for discounting[257]. Usually, a constant rate of debt financing based on market conditions is assumed, which is determined by a defined target capital structure[258]. The yield expectation of debt financiers is usually known, as the effective costs have

---

[244] Cf. *Drukarczyk* (1996), p. 177.
[245] Cf. *Kuhner/Maltry* (2006), pp. 197 – 198.
[246] Cf. *Ballwieser* (1998), p. 85.
[247] Cf. *Sonntag* (2001), p. 6.
[248] Cf. *Sonntag* (2001), p. 6.
[249] Cf. *Ballwieser* (1998), p. 84.
[250] Cf. *Copeland/Koller/Murrin* (2002), p. 172.
[251] Cf. *Kuhner/Maltry* (2006), pp. 198.
[252] Cf. *Drukarczyk* (1996), p. 143; *Ballwieser* (1998), p. 84 and *Steiner/Bruns* (2000), p. 226.
[253] Cf. for example *Schierenbeck* (1998), p. 390.
[254] Cf. *Kuhner/Maltry* (2006), pp. 198.
[255] Cf. *Ballwieser* (2004), p. 112.
[256] Cf. *IDW* (2005), p. 1313.
[257] Cf. *Drukarczyk* (1996), p. 144.
[258] Cf. *Ballwieser* (1998), pp. 84.

been negotiated. So only costs of equity capital have to be determined, which usually are estimated by using the CAPM[259].

According to the cash flow to use, two classical WACC approaches[260] exist[261]: The FCF and the TCF approach[262]. The FCF is based on the wrong tax payments, as the possibility of deducting interest payments in form of a so-called tax shield is not considered[263]. The cash flows base on the assumption of a 100% self-financed company[264]. This "mistake" in the assumptions is corrected by implementing the tax rate into the denominator[265]. The TCF eliminates this mistake by using the right and adjusted taxes in the numerator[266]. The WACC does not have to be adjusted; only interest payments before taxes are implemented[267]. These two approaches are explained in the following table:

	FCF approach	**TCF approach**
Definition of cash flow	FCF, cash flow before interest payments and not including tax shield.	TCF cash flow before interest payments but including tax shield.
Tax shield	Denominator	Numerator
Definition of discounting rate and formula[268]	$$CV = \frac{FCF}{i_{equity} \cdot \frac{V_{equity}}{V_{gross}} + i_{debt} \cdot (1-tr) \cdot \frac{V_{debt}}{V_{gross}}} - V_{debt}$$ *with:* CV = Corporate Value; i = interest rate; tr = tax rate; V = value	$$CV = \frac{TCF}{i_{equity} \cdot \frac{V_{equity}}{V_{gross}} + i_{debt} \cdot \frac{V_{debt}}{V_{gross}}} - V_{debt}$$
Critical valuation	• Constant capital structure is not given in reality[269].	• Inconsistent argumentation: a fictitious 100% self-financed company is combined with a tax shield[270]. • Constant capital structure is not given in reality as well[271]. • Not established in practice[272].

Table 7:   **FCF vs[273]. TCF approach[274]**

---

[259] Cf. *IDW* (2005), p. 1316.

[260] Without the APV approach. It is an entity approach, but **not** a WACC approach. Cf. *Ballwieser* (2004), p. 111.

[261] Cf. *Ballwieser* (2004), p. 111.

[262] Drukarczyk does not make this differentiation. Cf. *Drukarczyk* (1996), p. 143.

[263] Cf. *Ballwieser* (2004), p. 112.

[264] Cf. *Ballwieser* (2004), p. 112.

[265] Cf. *Drukarczyk* (1996), p. 145. Implicitly, he uses the FCF approach.

[266] Cf. *Kuhner/Maltry* (2006), p. 192.

[267] Cf. *Ballwieser* (2004), p. 113.

[268] Cf. *Ballwieser* (2004), p. 140, p. 166 and *Kuhner/Maltry* (2006), p. 203. Assumption: eternal cash flows.

[269] Cf. *Drukarczyk* (1996), p. 155; *Steiner/Bruns* (2000), p. 226 and *Ballwieser* (2004), pp. 145 – 146.

[270] Cf. *Ballwieser* (2004), pp. 168 – 169 and *Kuhner/Maltry* (2006), p. 198 – 200.

[271] Cf. *Ballwieser* (2004), p. 169.

[272] Cf. *Ballwieser* (2004), p. 169 and *Kuhner/Maltry* (2006), p. 199.

[273] Abbreviation for versus.

[274] Author's own table referring to *Copeland/Koller/Murrin* (2002), p. 18; *Ballwieser* (2004), p. 140, p. 166 and *Kuhner/Maltry* (2006), pp. 198 – 203.

The WACC is discussed critically in literature[275]. On the one hand the structure of debt is considered in the model[276]. On the other hand this capital structure is fixed for eternity[277]. The APV approach presented in the following section is often considered as the best entity approach, as it solves the problem of a constant capital structure[278].

2.2.2.2.3 Entity Approach – APV

In the APV approach, the components of the corporate value are quantified separately[279]. The FCF is used as well[280]. This is shown in the following equation.

$$CV = CV_{no\,debts} + ts - V_{debt}$$

$$CV = \frac{FCF}{i_{equity}} + (1 - tr) \cdot V_{debt}$$

with:

CV	=	corporate value
i	=	interest rate
ts	=	tax shield of debt
tr	=	tax rate
V	=	value

Equation 3:   The APV approach[281]

At first, the market value of the whole capital is calculated, based on the assumption of a complete internal financing[282]. Hence, the forecasted free cash flows will be discounted with the cost of equity capital[283]. In addition, the net present value effect of debt financing would be considered. It is caused by the tax-deductible interests for debt capital, the so-called tax shield[284]. By deducting the net debts, the market value of equity capital could be determined[285].

---

[275] Cf. *Drukarczyk* (1996), pp. 144; *Ballwieser* (2004), pp. 145 – 146, pp. 175 – 176 and *Kuhner/Maltry* (2006), pp. 198 – 200.

[276] Cf. *Drukarczyk* (1996), pp. 145.

[277] Cf. *Steiner/Bruns* (2000), p. 226.

[278] Cf. *Drukarczyk* (1996), p. 265.

[279] Cf. *Kuhner/Maltry* (2006), p. 200.

[280] Cf. *Ballwieser* (2004), pp. 112.

[281] Cf. *Ballwieser* (2004), p. 114 and *Kuhner/Maltry* (2006), p. 201. Assuming an eternal value.

[282] Cf. *Drukarczyk* (1996), p. 157.

[283] Cf. *Kuhner/Maltry* (2006), p. 201.

[284] Cf. *Drukarczyk* (1996), pp. 156 and *Ballwieser* (1998), p. 82.

[285] Cf. *Kuhner/Maltry* (2005), p. 200.

The separation of the components that determine the corporate value is the advantage of the APV [286]. Varying capital structure can be modelled very easily[287] and the tax shield is more transparent[288]. If significant changes in the capital structure are probable, the APV method shall be used[289]. Changes in capital structure have only an effect on the tax shield but not on the discount rate. The complex calculation of a WACC does not have to be done any longer. Even in those cases, the classical WACC approaches fail, the APV will work[290]. Further, mistakes cannot be made as easy as in the WACC approach[291].

However, the APV model has some difficulties, in particular in the determination of the costs for equity capital as well as in the adjustment of the interest rates for equity capital[292]. Equity yields for a 100% self-financed company are not available[293]. They have to be reconstructed manually[294]. In literature, an adjustment of the beta factors is mentioned[295]. This is shown in the following equation:

$$\beta_{indebted} = \beta_{self\ financed} \cdot \left[1 + (1 + tr) \cdot \frac{debt}{equity_{indebted\ company}} \right]$$

with:

tr = tax ratio

Equation 4:   Beta transformation[296]

The beta of the indebted company can be evaluated by the market data, but therefore, the value of the indebted company is required. This is an inconsistency so that in practice the approach can be difficult[297].

Considering the main arguments, the APV is often viewed as the best entity approach[298], as it separates the components of corporate value and allows volatile capital structures[299].

---

[286] Cf. *Drukarczyk* (1996), pp. 156 and *Kuhner/Maltry* (2006), p. 201.
[287] Cf. *Kuhner/Maltry* (2006), p. 202.
[288] Cf. *Kuhner/Maltry* (2006), p. 202.
[289] Cf. *Copeland/Koller/Murrin* (2002), p. 171.
[290] Cf. *Luehrman* (1997), p. 145. The advantages are attackable, as APV and WACC assume different financing assumptions.
[291] Cf. *Ballwieser* (2004), pp. 113.
[292] Cf. *Ballwieser* (1998), p. 91.
[293] Cf. *Miles/Ezzel* (1980), p. 720.
[294] Cf. *Drukarczyk/Honold* (1999), p. 343.
[295] Cf. *Copeland/Koller/Murrin* (2002), p. 372.
[296] Cf. *Copeland/Koller/Murrin* (2002), p. 372 and *Ballwieser* (2004), pp. 129.
[297] Cf. *Ballwieser* (2004), pp. 129.
[298] Cf. *Drukarczyk* (1996,) pp. 265.
[299] Cf. *Copeland/Koller/Murrin* (2002), p. 171.

All approaches of discounting returns must lead to the same result in the end, consuming consistent assumptions.[300] At first, following Copeland/Koller/Murrin, the equity approach and entity approaches in general must lead to a similar value, as long as the cash flows are discounted with the related risk-adjusted yield[301]. Further the earnings value method and DCF approaches in general must lead to the same results, if the assumptions are set similarly[302]. Finally, the WACC and the APV approaches[303] must lead to the same results as well, if the dependency between debt ratio and equity yield is set as constant[304]. All approaches show equal results in theory accordingly[305]. But in reality this consistence is not given. Different assumptions lead to different corporate values[306].

2.2.2.2.4 Real Options Approach

The real option approach can be defined as an extension of existing DCF approaches[307]. The disadvantage of the DCF approaches is that they assume a rigid continuation of the current situation[308]. The implicit value of existing alternatives to act is not quantified at all. The presented approach is an alternative investment calculation method based on the shareholder value concept. With its help, real economic projects or even companies could be valuated[309]. Modelling the options leads to the solution that a real option is comparable to a stock option[310]. It is the right but not the duty to buy or sell a share within a determined time period at a certain price.[311]

Real options can be distinguished as follows[312]:

---

[300] Cf. *IDW* (2005), p. 1313.

[301] Cf. *Copeland/Koller/Murrin* (2002), p. 172.

[302] Cf. *IDW* (2005), p. 1313.

[303] Defined below in section 2.2.2.2.3.

[304] Cf. *Modigliani/Miller* (1958) and *Modigliani/Miller* (1963).

[305] Cf. *Hachmeister* (2000), pp. 101.

[306] Cf. *Kuhner/Maltry* (2006), p. 263.

[307] Cf. *Kuhner/Maltry* (2006), p. 289. Therefore, the real option approach is structured into this section.

[308] Cf. *Kuhner/Maltry* (2006), p. 275.

[309] Cf. *Ernst/Thümmel* (2000), pp. 667.

[310] Cf. *Rams* (1998), pp. 676; *Crasselt/Tomaszewski* (1999), p. 517 and *Ernst/Thümmel* (2000), p. 667. For the theory of real options cf. *Trigeorgis* (2000).

[311] Cf. *Grill/Perczynski* (1998), p. 293.

[312] A more detailed but not really consistent structure can be found in *Copeland/Koller/Murrin* (2002), pp. 472 – 474.

	Invest Option	**Flexibility Option**	**Production Option**	**Divest Option**
Definition	The company has the possibility to do a prolongation investment. Other companies do not have this option.	The company has the option to wait and learn before doing something.	The company has the chance to vary output and production methods.	The company has the chance of getting out of a certain market or of selling certain parts of its own.
Direction	Expansion.	Increasing efficiency by learning and doing.	Optimizing existing core competences.	Restrict the loss of a certain project, insurance.
Example[313]	Planning of an investment.	Rearrange a market entry.	Restructuring the production process.	Insolvency in case of a limited liability.

Table 8:   Structure of real options[314]

The stock option model is transferable to entrepreneurial decision making[315]. Real options represent possibilities or opportunities, which can be used in future by doing an investment – but there is no obligation to exercise them[316]. Normally, the value of an option is calculated by using the perfect equilibrium model of Black and Scholes[317].

The character of a real option can be made clear by giving an example. The investment into a production plant could enable the investor to produce some other products in future, maybe by expanding the original plant only. If the planned production turns out to be successful, the opportunity to expand the production will be very valuable. The initial investment is the foundation for following investments. Just by doing this investment, all further investments and therefore, additional cash flows become possible. According to financial options, the owner of an option will execute his right, when the present value of the cash flows will be higher than the expenses for the investment. In addition to that, he has the opportunity of waiting for risky or uncertain developments. An economical value arises from this flexibility, as flexible projects are worthier than fixed projects.[318]

---

[313] For the status of the real option and detailed practical examples cf. *Copeland/Koller/Murrin* (2002), pp. 488 and *Hommel/Scholich/Baecker* (2003).

[314] Author's own table referring to *Rams* (1998). Extended by information referring to *Brealey/Myers* (1996), p. 589.

[315] Cf. *Kuhner/Maltry* (2006), p. 276.

[316] Cf. *Herter* (1992), p. 321.

[317] Cf. *Black/Scholes* (1973), pp. 637 and *Herter* (1992), p. 332. The formula and the derivation are not described in this dissertation.

[318] Cf. *Crasselt/Tomaszewski* (1999), p. 518 and *Ernst/Thümmel* (2000), p. 668.

The real options method is not a new independent evaluation method in principle. The present value of an investment must be calculated by using a DCF method[319]. This method will not be replaced, but enlarged by adding the view on options. The value of a flexible investment depends on the net present value, calculated by the DCF method, plus the value of the real option:

$$CV_{total} = V_{DCF} + V_{options}$$

with:

CV   =   Corporate value
V   =   Value
DCF   =   Discounted cash flow

Value drivers:

	For a high call value	For a high put value
Volatility	High	High
Strike	Low	High
Maturity	High	High
Present value of investment	High	Low
Risk free rate	High	Low
Dividends	Low	High

Equation 5:   Corporate value by real option [320]

The latter value in this equation increases with a higher volatility and is always positive, because the chance for realisation will rise, if it is not executed[321]. However, several influencing aspects have to be taken into consideration. The real option may be exclusive, so that only one company could take the opportunity, maybe because of market entry barriers[322].

By taking into consideration flexibility and uncertainty, the scope of entrepreneurial decisions becomes quantifiable, so that the value of investments could be determined more exactly[323]. However, the calculation of options is difficult. The opportunities of the company have to be estimated or derived in a comprehensive manner[324]. On the one hand, Copeland/Koller/Murrin suppose that the real option approach will even replace the DCF methods[325]. In their opin-

---

[319] Cf. *Kuhner/Maltry* (2006), p. 289.
[320] Cf. *Brealey/Myers* (1996), p. 589; *Kuhner/Maltry* (2006), p. 282 and *Copeland/Koller/Murrin* (2002), p. 471, p. 487. The latter consider dividends as well, but they define them as correction cash flows for the case of not exercising the option. For general value drivers of options cf. *Rolfes* (1999), p. 89.
[321] Assuming that the company has bought the option. If it has been sold, a negative value might occur as well.
[322] One further typical example is the abandon option. Cf. *Kuhner/Maltry* (2006), p. 288.
[323] Cf. *Copeland/Koller/Murrin* (2002), pp. 466.
[324] Cf. *Amely/Suciu-Sibianu* (2001), p. 92.
[325] Cf. *Copeland/Koller/Murrin* (2002), p. 466.

ion the value of the company will be too low, if real options are not implemented[326]. On the other hand, this has to be seen critical. Kuhner/Maltry stated that only in case of exclusiveness the option has an inherent value[327]. Quantifying the value of this option would overestimate the company's value[328]. Further, the assumptions lying behind the model have to bee seen critically.[329] Getting reliable results requires data of high quantity and quality. The main assumption of tradability is not given in reality[330]. This is why the practical usage is not very high.[331]

At current, the real options method is used less often[332]. This model is only in use in industries with intensively growing projects and companies with high uncertainty, for example IT[333] or biotechnology.[334]. With the decreasing importance of the new markets, it has become less important. The results may only be treated as a qualitative hint, but not as a quantitative company value compared to classical DFC or earnings value approaches [335].

2.2.3 Mixture Methods

Mixture methods combine aspects of separate evaluation methods with parts of the global evaluation methods[336]. The general equation can be set up as follows:

$$CV = SEV + b \cdot (EV - SEV)$$

with:

CV	=	Company value
SEV	=	Separate evaluation value
EV	=	Earnings value[337]
b	=	parameter > 0

Equation 6:   Mixture methods[338]

---

[326]   Cf. *Copeland/Koller/Murrin* (2002), p. 500.
[327]   Cf. *Kuhner/Maltry* (2006), p. 288.
[328]   Cf. *Witt* (2003), pp. 134 – 140.
[329]   Cf. *Brealey/Myers* (1996), p. 609.
[330]   Cf. *Brealey/Myers* (1996), p. 609.
[331]   Cf. *Kuhner/Maltry* (2006), p. 290.
[332]   Cf. *Copeland/Koller/Murrin* (2002), p. 466.
[333]   Abbreviation for Information Technology.
[334]   Cf. *Kuhner/Maltry* (2006), p. 290.
[335]   Cf. *Kuhner/Maltry* (2006), p. 290.
[336]   Cf. *Ballwieser* (2004), pp. 184.
[337]   Including DCF approaches.
[338]   Cf. *Jacob* (1960), p. 134 and *Moxter* (1983), p. 58.

The higher b is, the more influence the earnings value or DCF approach has. The difference between EV and SEV is also defined as goodwill. Four approaches can be defined in practice. They are structured in the following table:

	Simple average approach	Simple additional profit	Stuttgarter Approach	Residual Income Method
Formula	$CV = SEV + b \cdot (EV - SEV)$ $b = 0.5$ $CV = \dfrac{(SEV + EV)}{2}$	$CV = SEV + b \cdot (EV - SEV)$ $b = i_{rf} \cdot n$ $CV = SEV + n \cdot add.profit$ $n =$ periods of additional profit $i_{rf} =$ risk free ratio	$CV = SEV + i \cdot n \cdot (EV - CV)$ $n = 5$ $i = 9\%$ $CV = SEV + 0.45 \cdot (EV - CV)$ $CV = 0.69 \cdot SEV + 0.31 \cdot EV$	$EV = \sum\limits_{t=1}^{T} \dfrac{E_t}{(1+i)^t}$ $\quad = \sum\limits_{t=1}^{T} \dfrac{RI_t}{(1+i)^t} + EQ$ $\quad = \sum\limits_{t=1}^{T} \dfrac{A - i \cdot EQ_{(t-1)}}{(1+i)^t} + EQ$ $E =$ Earnings $t =$ time period $i =$ interest rate $A =$ annual surplus $EQ =$ Book value of equity $RI =$ Residual income
Critical discussion	No additional information according to the two separate approaches[339].	As only a modification of the SEV occurs, no additional information is generated[340].	Modified additional profit approach that is often used for settlement procedures[341]. Even though they are accepted by law[342], the usage is not recommended[343].	Used for quantifying the depreciation for the goodwill in a consolidation[344]. It is defined as a mixture approach because the annual surplus is the basis[345]. Even though this approach is the best of the presented four models, it has the same disadvantages[346].

Table 9:   Mixture methods[347]

In practice, these models have nearly no relevance as they combine the disadvantages of the two basic approaches. However, they legally accepted in 1986[348]. For the banking approach evaluated by the author, these models will become more important – without the disadvantages mentioned in this section. But this is discussed below[349].

---

[339] Cf. *Helbing* (1998), pp. 131 and *Mandl/Rabel* (2005), p. 82.
[340] Explicitly proven in literature. Cf. *Moxter* (1983), pp. 41 – 55.
[341] Cf. *Kuhner/Maltry* (2005), p. 46. Critically discussed in *Göllert/Ringling* (1999).
[342] Cf. *BFH* (1991). BFH stands for Bundesfinanzhof.
[343] Cf. *Kuhner/Maltry* (2006), p. 46.
[344] Cf. *Coenenberg/Schultze* (2002), p. 616.
[345] Cf. *Coenenberg/Schultze* (2002), p. 606.
[346] Cf. *Ballwieser* (2004), pp. 189.
[347] Author's own table referring to *Ballwieser* (2004), pp. 184 – 187.
[348] Cf. *Piltz* (2005), p. 784.
[349] Cf. section 4.3.1.

2.2.4 Simplified Approaches

Simplified approaches are all defined as market-oriented approaches that assume fictitious or real prices[350]. These prices can be used for the company to evaluate or for fictitious companies. This is shown in the following figure:

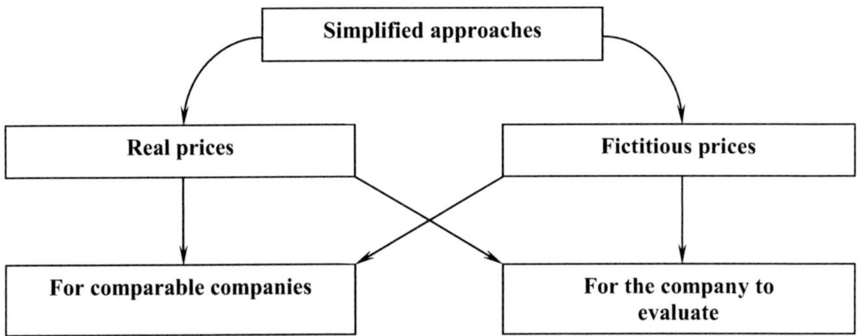

Figure 4: **Structure of simplified approaches** *351*

A central assumption of these methods is that the stock value quoted at the stock exchange, resulting from supply and demand of the market participants and depending on their information, corresponds to the value of the share as well as to the value of the company behind the share[352]. Comparable companies should have comparable values[353]. The approach is objectified, if enough transactions on the market are done – in form of share deals or complete company deals. In this case subjective or individual aspects cannot lead to wrong results[354]. However, the user has to keep in mind that only prices but not values are quantified[355]. As a result the methods are usable to validate the value coming out of a DCF or earnings value approach[356].

In principle, four kinds of calculation are possible. They are explained in the following sections.

---

[350] For further details cf. *Benninga/Sarig* (1997), pp. 305 – 311; *Mandl/Rabel* (1997), pp. 258 – 274; *Böcking/Nowak* (1999); *Achleitner/Dresig* (2002); *Ballwieser* (2003), pp. 17 – 26; *Moser/Auge-Dickhut* (2003a); *Moser/Auge-Dickhut* (2003b); *Nowak* (2003), pp. 159 – 185; *Seppelfricke* (2003), pp. 133 – 166 and *Freiburg/Timmreck* (2004).

[351] Author's own figure referring to *Olbrich* (2000), p. 457 and *Ballwieser* (2004), p. 190. Discussed contrary in *Kuhner/Maltry* (2006), p. 267.

[352] Cf. *Olbrich* (2000), p. 454.

[353] Cf. *Kuhner/Maltry* (2006), p. 266.

[354] Cf. *Kuhner/Maltry* (2006), p. 266.

[355] Cf. *Kuhner/Maltry* (2006), p. 266.

[356] Cf. *IDW* (2002), p. 134.

2.2.4.1 Real Prices of the Same Company

The easiest way for a stock-listed or merged company is to use historical market prices[357]. The disadvantage consists of the time lag between the old price and the current situation. Further, the number of shares held determines the price, too. 25% have a different value than $1/3^{rd}$ of 75%[358], as the value of voting rights may differ in practice.

2.2.4.2 Real Prices of a Comparable Company

The next step is to compare realized or published prices of similar companies with the company to value. The problem of section 2.2.4.1 can be transferred to this model as well. When can two companies be considered as equal or similar? The underlying assumptions lead to critical results. BMW[359] and Fiat work in the same sector – but using the price of the first for the price of the latter would lead to wrong results[360]. Solving this problem would also require the complete information that is necessary for a detailed DCF or earnings value approach. Therefore the only advantage of simplicity[361] would not exist any longer[362].

2.2.4.3 Fictitious Prices of the Same Company

If the company is listed current market prices can be used. The company's value would correspond to the value at the stock exchange, which is the market capitalization at the market or the shareholder value[363]. The calculation is done by multiplying the stock quotations by the number of shares. Usually a control premium[364] has to be taken into consideration. Both the claim for dividends and the possibility of getting influence on company's management decisions are connected with the purchase of all shares or at least of a large number of shares[365]. This add on, historically given with 40%[366] in the USA[367], has to be paid on top of the market capitalization. However, these 40% have to be eyed critically – their historical volatility is very high and values are not available for the German sector[368].

---

[357] Cf. *Ballwieser* (2004), p. 190.
[358] Cf. *Ballwieser* (2004), p. 190.
[359] Abbreviation for Bayerische Motorenwerke.
[360] Cf. *Ballwieser* (2004), p. 190.
[361] Cf. *Nestler/Kraus* (2003), p. 1.
[362] Cf. *Ballwieser* (1997), pp. 186 and *Ballwieser* (2001), p. 26.
[363] Cf. *Bausch* (2000), p. 450.
[364] Cf. *Ballwieser* (2004), p. 190.
[365] Cf. *Olbrich* (2000), p. 455.
[366] Cf. *Gaughan* (2002), p. 621.
[367] Abbreviation for United States of America.
[368] Cf. *Ballwieser* (2004), pp. 192 – 193.

2.2.4.4 Fictitious Prices of the Peer Group – Multiplier Approach

If the company is not listed at the stock exchange, the original multiplication method, the so-called CCA[369], has to be used. It is based on the assumption that comparable companies could be sold or purchased at a comparable price[370]. Therefore, the data of the company to be evaluated and the available data for other comparable reference companies in the same sector[371] are taken and put into relation. Therefore, the market capitalization of the comparables[372] is used. The resulting relations are used to define the value of the company as shown in the following set of equations:

$$CV = mult_{PF} \cdot PF_{company}$$

with:

CV   =   Company value
PF   =   Performance factor like EBIT[373], balance sheet sum or equity
mult   =   multiplier for a certain performance factor

Equation 7:   Multiplier approach[374]

The PF depend on the value to be quantified. Equity value, enterprise value or goodwill require different PF[375]. EBIT, sales and EBITDA are normally used for evaluating the enterprise value[376], because these basic variables are independent of the debt ratio[377]. EBT[378] and net profit are used to determine the value of the equity[379]. The multiple is evaluated by generating an average or a median[380]. However, in addition, the standard deviation of the multiple is considered as well[381]. Otherwise, the resulting value would lead to a false conclusion.

The empirical evaluation of the quality of possible multiples can be summarized as Liu/Nissim/Thomas did: "Second, we confirm that forward earnings contain considerably more value-relevant information than historical data, and they should be used as long as fore-

---

[369]   Abbreviation for Comparable Company Analysis.
[370]   Cf. *Weston/Chung/Siu* (1998), p. 176.
[371]   Cf. *Kuhner/Maltry* (2006), p. 268.
[372]   Cf. *Ballwieser* (2004), p. 193.
[373]   Abbreviation for Earnings Before Interest and Taxes.
[374]   Cf. *Nestler/Kraus* (2003), p. 1 and *Kuhner/Maltry* (2006), p. 267.
[375]   Visualized in *Ballwieser* (2004), p. 194.
[376]   Cf. *Liu/Nissim/Thomas* (2002), p. 137.
[377]   Cf. *Ballwieser* (2004), p. 193.
[378]   Abbreviation for Earnings Before Taxes.
[379]   Cf. *Löhnert/Böckmann* (2002), pp. 410 – 411 and *Nestler/Kraus* (2003), p. 3. The usual multiples are discussed here.
[380]   Cf. *Kuhner/Maltry* (2006), p. 266.
[381]   Cf. *Ballwieser* (2004), p. 195.

casted earnings are available. Third, contrary to general perception, different industries are not associated with different best multiples.[382]"

Advantages of the multiplier methods can be stated as follows: First, they are quite simple in their usage[383]. Soffer/Soffer stated concretely: "The main reason analysts use the multiples approach for evaluation is it is much quicker than discounted cash flow techniques[384]". The prognosis problem is solved elegantly – a prognosis of several data is not necessary at all[385], if the multiples are evaluated onto a historical basis. Further, it is stable according to the assumptions[386] and it is easy to communicate[387]. It can be even used for "faceless" companies[388] and it is a first, extendable quantification method. The results are a kind of self-fulfilling prophecy[389]. As all market partners know the method and rely on it, the offered (and very often paid) prices are similar to those in the model[390].

However, the quality of the evaluation method depends on the comparison with the reference companies[391]. They have to be carefully chosen by market share, market position, capitalization, company's structure, and much more[392]. Another critical factor is the data availability, which can be considered as given for listed companies. Nevertheless, for German companies, the data basis is much smaller than for companies in the USA due to the number of stock quotations[393]. However, the multiplier methods require an information efficiency of the capital market[394]. Additional problems will arise from the assumption that the price for a share depends on supply and demand. This is influenced by the usual anticipation of future developments and maybe less by the actual profit situation[395] and the effect that prognoses of analysts have a direct impact on forecasted earnings[396]. Additionally, it may be influenced by short term or speculative intentions. To keep comparability, it is usually necessary to make corrections like a control premium or a fungibility premium, which has to be discussed as well[397]. Last, multiples are often past-oriented. Actual aspects are not always considered accordingly[398].

---

[382] *Liu/Nissim/Thomas* (2002), p. 138.
[383] Cf. *Kuhner/Maltry* (2006), p. 269.
[384] *Soffer/Soffer* (2003), p. 389.
[385] Cf. *Kuhner/Maltry* (2006), p. 269 and *Ballwieser* (2004), p. 197.
[386] Cf. *Ballwieser* (2004), p. 197.
[387] Cf. *Liu/Nissim/Thomas* (2002), p. 136.
[388] Cf. *Ballwieser* (2004), p. 197.
[389] Cf. *Kuhner/Maltry* (2006), p. 270.
[390] Cf. *Kaplan/Ruback* (1995), p. 1067 for the empirical verification.
[391] Cf. *Nestler/Kraus* (2003), p. 2. For further argumentations according to the similarity discussion cf. *Achleitner/Dresig* (2002), column 2422.
[392] Cf. *Kuhner/Maltry* (2006), p. 270.
[393] Cf. *Bamberger* (1999), p. 667.
[394] Cf. *Kuhner/Maltry* (2006), p. 270.
[395] Cf. *Olbrich* (2000), pp. 458.
[396] Cf. *Ballwieser* (2004), p. 195.
[397] Cf. *Nestler/Kraus* (2003), p. 4
[398] Cf. *Kuhner/Maltry* (2006), p. 271.

The multiplication method is very helpful for the purpose of additional checks of a company's value, but its sole relevance for decisions has to be rejected.[399] A combination with a DCF approach, however, might be useful[400]. Its usage to get first orientation results is accepted in literature[401].

2.3 Bank Individual Approaches

2.3.1 Reasons for a Bank Individual Approach

All presented approaches of corporate evaluation show useful aspects. But all those theories imply that the value of a classical industrial company instead of a bank has to be defined[402]. The banking sector shows several special aspects. Whenever the value of a bank has to be determined, these special features have to be considered. Banks differ from classical industrial companies[403]. This is discussed in the following section.

2.3.1.1 Generating Value with the Liability Side

In contrast to other companies that take credits in order to receive money to invest, banks generate earnings with the liability side[404]. The market yield method is the basic idea for this[405]. On the asset side customers pay more than they would pay on the capital market[406]. On the contrary they receive less interest payments for savings or deposits, than they would receive at the market[407]. This is pointed out by the following figure. A bank's balance sheet may just consist of two transfers: a 10 year loan and a 10 year refinancing customer bond[408].

---

[399] Cf. *Kinast* (1991), pp. 37; *Bamberger* (1999), p. 667 and *Bausch* (2000), p. 459
[400] Cf. *Schmidtbauer* (2004), p. 151.
[401] Cf. *Hafner* (1993), pp. 88; *Hayn* (2003), p. 112; *Löhnert/Böckmann* (2002), pp. 406 – 408 and *Nestler/Kraus* (2003), p. 5.
[402] Cf. *Sonntag* (2001), p. 1.
[403] Cf. *Koch* (2004), p. 119.
[404] Cf. *Sonntag* (2001), p. 2 and *Adamus/Koch* (2006), p. 153.
[405] For a short overview cf. *Reuse* (2002.12), pp. 24. For further details cf. *Rolfes* (1999), pp. 12 – 18, pp. 270 and *Schierenbeck* (2001a), pp. 43, pp. 70. An example with realistic data is given in *Reuse* (2003.02), pp. 30 – 31.
[406] Cf. *Reuse* (2002.12), pp. 24.
[407] Cf. *Rolfes* (1999), p. 13.
[408] Maturity transformation is not discussed in this example.

Assets					**Liabilities**			
	amount in EUR	interest rate	market rate	interest margin		amount in EUR	interest rate	market rate	interest margin
Loan, 10Y	100,000	4.30%	3.31%	0.99%	Bond, 10Y	100,000	3.20%	3.31%	0.11%
	100,000	4.30%	3.31%	0.99%		100,000	3.20%	3.31%	0.11%

net interest revenue   **1.10%**
interest /contribution margin   **1.10%**

Figure 5:   **Contribution margin of a fictitious bank**[409]

As figure 5 shows, a bank generates its earnings by receiving the so-called interest margin[410]. This is defined as follows: If a bank grants a credit and issues a risk free bond as liability, the above mentioned earnings of 0.99% per year will be realized[411]. Emitting a customer bond leads to cheaper costs vice-versa[412]. If the bank invests this money in a risk free 10Y[413] interbank deposit by using this money, 0.11% of additional earnings would occur. In total, the net interest revenue consists of 1.10%.

Only due to the effect that the liability side shows lower interest rates than market rates, banks are able to generate value. This effect is not concerned correctly in the classical approaches described above. All entity methods require the market value for the liabilities[414]. However, this value is difficult to quantify as savings and deposits cannot be traded[415]. Using the nominal value would be the wrong way as well[416]. Therefore, the approaches that deal with a fictitious equity finance situation as WACC and APV would not lead to the "right" corporate evaluation[417]. Even small mistakes in the assumptions concerning the debt side would lead to a high variance of the corporate value[418].

2.3.1.2 Maturity Transformation

Further, in contrast to industrial companies, banks do maturity transformation[419]. This means that the assets have another maturity than the liabilities[420]. Short term liabilities are normally

---

[409] Author's own figure based on *Rolfes* (1999), p. 13. For market data cf. *Bundesbank* (2006a).
[410] Cf. *Rolfes* (1999), p. 271.
[411] Cf. *Rolfes* (1999), p. 271 and *Schierenbeck* (2001a), p. 73, p. 75.
[412] Cf. *Reuse* (2002.12), p. 25.
[413] Abbreviation for Year.
[414] Cf. Section 2.2.2.2.
[415] Cf. *Koch* 2000, p. 45 and *Adamus/Koch* (2006), p. 153.
[416] For further arguments cf. *Strutz* (1993), p. 87; *Behm* (1994), p. 59; *Vettiger* (1996), pp. 125 – 126 and *Copeland/Koller/Murrin* (1998), p. 488.
[417] For example discussed in *Adamus/Koch* (2006), p. 153.
[418] Cf. *Copeland/Koller/Murrin* (1994), p. 377.
[419] Cf. *Sonntag* (2001), p. 1 and *Koch* (2004), p. 119.
[420] Cf. *Schierenbeck* (2001a), p. 72.

transformed into long term assets[421]. In case of a normal yield structure[422], this leads to additional earnings, which depend on the current market interest rates[423]. Maturity transformation is a part of the market interest rate method. This method is able to divide the interest earnings of a bank into those generated by customer deals and those generated by maturity transformation[424]. The central question remaining is, whether and how this has to be implemented into the corporate value of a bank[425]. This will be discussed critically later on.[426]

2.3.1.3 Structure of the Balance Sheet

Further, the measurable assets of a bank are typically low, as the balance sheet nearly consists of credits and savings only[427]. As a consequence, the expenditures of the profit and loss account show a very high part of interest payments and depend on the current interest rates[428]. Market values do not exist for customer deals[429] and the nominal values would lead to wrong results[430].

2.3.1.4 Risk Transformation

Last, banks do risk transformation[431]. Liabilities in form of customer savings are transformed into loans. While the liability side does not have an inherent risk, the assets side does. This leads to the most important value and risk driver for banks: the provisions for lost loans which have been the largest problem in the recent past[432]. Traditional approaches of corporate evaluation do not consider the fact that the credits a bank grants may be lost because of customers' bankruptcy[433]. The expected losses of the credit portfolio have to be considered accordingly[434].

---

[421] Cf. *Reuse* (2003.03), p. 26.

[422] Short term interest rates are lower than long term interest rates. Cf. *Schierenbeck* (1998), p. 352 and *Schierenbeck* (2001a), p. 71. For a detailed analysis of yield curves cf. *Beer/Goj* (2002), pp. 156.

[423] Cf. *Rolfes* (1999), p. 271 and *Schierenbeck* (2001a), p. 73, p. 75. A simple example is given in *Reuse* (2003.03), p. 27.

[424] Cf. *Rolfes* (1999), pp. 12. For a detailed overview onto the calculation methods cf. *Reuse* (2002.12) and *Reuse* (2003.02). Done with real banks in 2006, cf. *Adamus/Koch* (2006), p. 148.

[425] Cf. *Sonntag* (2001), p. 3.

[426] Cf. section 2.3.3.1.

[427] Cf. *Kirsten* (2000), p. 134 and *Zessin* (1982), p. 28.

[428] Cf. *Sonntag* (2001), p. 2.

[429] Exception: Lost loans can be corrected in the balance sheet with §340f *HGB* reserves. Cf. *Koch* (2004), p. 120. Further, traded shares and bonds have to be balanced with the market value.

[430] Cf. *Adamus/Koch* (2006), p. 153.

[431] Cf. *Koch* (2004), p. 119.

[432] Cf. *Adamus/Koch* (2006), p. 143.

[433] Cf. *Sonntag* (2001), p. 2 and *Koch* (2004), p. 119.

[434] Done in *Sonntag* (2001), p. 202.

2.3.2 Structuring the Status Quo in Current Literature

	Zessin[435]	Adolf/Cramer/Ollmann[436]	Strutz[437]	Behm[438]	Kümmel[439]	Miller[440]	Vettiger[441]	Börner/Lowis[442]	Copeland/Koller/Murrin[443]	Höhmann[444]	Hörter[445]	Sonntag[446]	Koch, Adamus/Koch[447]
Year	1982	1989	1993	1994	1995	1995	1996	1997	1998	1998	1998	2001	2004
Kind of return[448]													
to shareholders	X	X	X	X	X	X	X	X	X	X	X	X	X
also to investors													
Used interest rates													
Equity interest rate[449]	X	X	X	X	X	X	X	X	X	X	X	X	X
WACC													
Valuation granularity													
Direct evaluation of the whole value.	X		X	X	X	X	X	X	X	X	X	X	X
Indirect evaluation: • Sum of strategic business units.		X	X						X				
Indirect evaluation: • Private customers • corporate customers • Treasury								X	X				
Indirect evaluation: • Asset side • Liability side • Treasury				X			X					X	
Using multiples to receive the bank value.													X

Figure 6:   **Status quo of existing bank-individual evaluation approaches[450]**

---

[435] Cf. *Zessin* (1982), p. 57, p. 61, pp. 161 – 165.
[436] Cf. *Adolf/Cramer/Ollmann* (1989a), pp. 485 – 492 and *Adolf/Cramer/Ollmann* (1989b), pp. 546 – 554.
[437] Cf. *Strutz* (1993), pp. 87 – 97.
[438] Cf. *Behm* (1994), p. 59, pp. 83 – 85.
[439] Cf. *Kümmel* (1995), p. 104, p. 107. First edition was placed in 1994.
[440] Cf. *Miller* (1995), pp. 196 – 199.
[441] Cf. *Vettiger* (1996), pp. 126 – 135.
[442] Cf. *Börner/Lowis* (1997), pp. 87 – 133.
[443] Cf. *Copeland/Koller/Murrin* (1998), p. 489, p. 493, pp. 514 – 524, *Copeland/Koller/Murrin* (2002), pp. 501 – 524.
[444] Cf. *Höhmann* (1998), pp. 37 – 39, pp. 168 – 171.
[445] Cf. *Hörter* (1998), pp. 56.
[446] Cf. *Sonntag* (2001).
[447] Cf. *Koch* (2004), pp. 119 – 136 and *Adamus/Koch* (2006), pp. 131 – 162. Even though Koch presented his first work in 2000, this year was chosen.
[448] No difference is made between cash flow and earning, as the definitions of the authors are not always consistent.
[449] A differentiation between the equity approach yield and earnings value approach yield is not done here.
[450] Author's own figure, following the basic idea of *Sonntag* (2001), p. 6, extended by the data of the other authors.

All these aspects led to the requirement for bank-individual approaches in the past. Literature offers several bank evaluation approaches[451]. This is shown in figure 6.

Zessin was the first one who discussed the evaluation of banks in his work. He worked out that banks do not produce real products, but deal with monetary assets[452]. He prefers an equity approach combined with an equity yield to discount the cash flows with. The result is the enterprise value. But a more detailed analysis, from which part of the bank the value results, was not done.[453]

Adolf/Cramer/Ollmann argue by using the earnings value approach. They add the value of strategic business units to the bank value[454]. They are the first ones who demand a differentiated quantification of return and risk, depending on the strategic business unit[455]. A direct prognosis of the bank's expected returns is not useful, as the value drivers (nominal value and net interest margin of the customer deals) can only be estimated in the subunits[456]. Adolf/Cramer/Ollmann discuss the CAPM approach as well[457]. The final conclusion according to its practicability is very critical. The equity yield defined by CAPM does not represent the threshold value an investor would pay for a bank[458]. Adolf/Cramer/Ollmann demand an external and an internal yield evaluation. The yield of an opportunity investment the investor has should be quantified in an external evaluation. This yield is based on the risk free ratio and a risk premium[459]. In an internal evaluation, Adolf/Cramer/Ollmann demand the yield of banking obligations that are traded at the stock exchange[460].

Strutz, on the other hand keeps the classical CAPM approach[461]. But he follows Adolf/Cramer/Ollmann in the differentiated quantification of the single values of the strategic business units[462].

Behm defines so called value centers[463] asset side, liability side and treasury for the purpose of a value based management or shareholder value management[464]. Adding the market value of these centers leads to the bank value. He is the first one who structures a bank like this[465].

---

[451] A first structure was given in *Sonntag* (2001), p. 6.
[452] Cf. *Zessin* (1982), p. 28.
[453] Cf. *Zessin* (1982), p. 57, p. 61, pp. 161 – 165.
[454] Cf. *Adolf/Cramer/Ollmann* (1989b), p. 546.
[455] Cf. *Adolf/Cramer/Ollmann* (1989a), p. 486.
[456] Cf. *Adolf/Cramer/Ollmann* (1989a), p. 486.
[457] Cf. *Adolf/Cramer/Ollmann* (1989b), pp. 550.
[458] Cf. *Adolf/Cramer/Ollmann* (1989b), pp. 550.
[459] Cf. *Adolf/Cramer/Ollmann* (1989b), p. 552.
[460] Cf. *Adolf/Cramer/Ollmann* (1989b), p. 552.
[461] Cf. *Strutz* (1993), pp. 90.
[462] Cf. *Strutz* (1993), pp. 87 – 97.
[463] Cf. *Behm* (1994), p. 73, p. 83.
[464] Cf. *Behm* (1994), p. 74.
[465] Cf. figure 6.

The free cash flows of all three value centers are discounted at the end[466]. The main advantage of this procedure is that the above explained market yield method can be used by Behm[467]. With respect to the equity yield, Behm did an empirical analysis. He estimated the equity yields in July 1993 for the following years[468]. He uses three approaches including the CAPM to define the equity yield and compares them to each other[469]. The CAPM is used, but it is only one of several solutions.

Kümmel evaluates the bank's value by using an equity approach and discounting the cash flows with an equity yield[470]. He criticises the CAPM as well. To his opinion, beta factors are instable and their historical values are not representative[471]. Further, the main assumption of the CAPM is the tradability. If a CAPM should be used, the equity should be differentiated according to a fictitious or real maturity[472].

Miller offers no new results. He uses the equity approach combined with an equity yield as well[473].

Vettiger follows Behm in the definition of the value centers and the usage of the market yield method[474]. He is the second one who uses the market yield method. Value based management or shareholder value is the main purpose for corporate evaluations. [475]

Börner/Lowis follow the main arguments of the equity approach[476] and the resulting equity discounting yield[477]. Further, they offer a detailed cash flow evaluation approach[478] and implement a three-phase model for the evaluation of the cash flows[479]. The cash flows are structured into those coming out of operating activities, investments and business structure – for example maturity transformation[480]. The usage of the market yield method was mentioned,

---

[466] Cf. *Sonntag* (2001), p. 11.
[467] Cf. *Sonntag* (2001), p. 9.
[468] Cf. *Behm* (1994), p. 118.
[469] Cf. *Behm* (1994), chapter 4. German banks show a ratio between 8.32% and 9.86%. Visualized in *Kirsten* (2000), p. 159.
[470] Cf. *Kümmel* (1995), p. 104, p. 107.
[471] Cf. *Kümmel* (1993), p. 34.
[472] Cf. *Kümmel* (1993), p. 35.
[473] Cf. *Miller* (1995), pp. 196 – 199.
[474] Cf. *Vettiger* (1996), pp. 133.
[475] Cf. *Vettiger* (1996), pp. 125.
[476] Cf. *Börner/Lowis* (1997), p. 112, p. 116.
[477] Cf. *Börner/Lowis* (1997), pp. 116.
[478] Cf. *Börner/Lowis* (1997), p. 106.
[479] Cf. *Börner/Lowis* (1997), pp. 100, extending the approach of *Adolf/Cramer/Ollmann* (1989a), p. 488.
[480] Cf. *Börner/Lowis* (1997), p. 104.

too[481]. They discuss the CAPM critically[482] and offer the more general APT[483] model as an alternative approach[484].

Copeland/Koller/Murrin follow Behm when doing a corporate evaluation[485]. In contrast to Behm they define private and corporate customers as the parts to evaluate[486]. As well as in Behm's work, the value of treasury is isolated in the end. Its value varies in the case of market yield change. The strategic business units, private and corporate clients, remain constant in this case[487]. Copeland/Koller/Murrin demand transfer prices for the cash flows between the three units. The disadvantage is that they do not use the market yield method. An exact interest rate risk free situation does not exist[488], even though they offer a consistent example, in which both approaches lead to the same result[489]. Copeland/Koller/Murrin follow the mainstream to use the equity approach for a bank evaluation, even though they recommend an entity approach for all other corporate evaluations[490].

Höhmann and **Hörter** offer no new ideas[491]. Höhmann's model of external evaluation[492] and Hörter's argumentations[493] come to the same conclusion as the authors before: equity approach with equity costs as a discounting factor.

Sonntag defines the three value centers as well and adds them to the value of the bank[494]. He uses the market yield method[495] and distinguishes the customer deals into existing deals and possible new deals[496]. This differentiation and the analysis of the treasury value[497] are the main new add ons, Sonntag presents. According to his argumentation the value of treasury is zero[498]. Sonntag's work is the most detailed and structured one up to this moment.

---

[481] Cf. *Börner/Lowis* (1997), p. 103.
[482] Cf. *Börner/Lowis* (1997), pp. 118.
[483] Abbreviation for Arbitrage Pricing Theory.
[484] Fur more detailed information cf. *Brealey/Myers* (1996), pp. 190. The APT is a more general approach than the CAPM. Cf. *Börner/Lowis* (1997), pp. 118.
[485] Cf. *Copeland/Koller/Murrin* (1998), p. 514.
[486] Cf. *Copeland/Koller/Murrin* (1998), p. 487.
[487] Cf. *Copeland/Koller/Murrin* (1998), pp. 514 – 524.
[488] Argued in *Sonntag* (2001), p. 9.
[489] Cf. *Copeland/Koller/Murrin* (2002), p. 506.
[490] Cf. *Copeland/Koller/Murrin* (2002), p. 503.
[491] Cf. *Sonntag* (2001), p. 6.
[492] Cf. *Höhmann* (1998), pp. 37 – 39, pp. 168 – 171.
[493] Cf. *Hörter* (1998), pp. 56.
[494] Cf. *Sonntag* (2001), p. 241.
[495] Cf. *Sonntag* (2001), pp. 91.
[496] Cf. *Sonntag* (2001), pp. 113 – 135, pp. 136 – 163.
[497] Cf. *Sonntag* (2001), pp. 15 – 90.
[498] Cf. *Sonntag* (2001), pp. 82. Argued in detail in section 2.3.3.1.

Last, **Koch** and **Adamus/Koch** offered some new ideas. They use the equity approach with equity costs as well[499]. Further, the market interest rate method is discussed but not used[500]. The reason is that external investors do not know the part of the net interest revenues that belong to maturity transformation[501]. Further, they offer a detailed approach to evaluate the cash flow statement of a bank[502]. Even though a detailed cash flows analysis would be better[503], an evaluation by using the income statement is the most practical way[504] because the investor does not have the necessary detailed information[505]. According to the equity yield, some further arguments are added. They accept the CAPM as a possible approach and prove that the equity yield is independent from the leverage[506]. Choosing the right comparables for evaluating the beta is more important. Adamus/Koch offer a last new point. They are the first who recommend a multiplier approach, at least as a plausibility check[507]. The preferred multiples are Market/Book, Price/Earnings and Price/AuM[508]. A balance sheet sum and a net interest revenue multiple are missing[509].

Even though all presented approaches differ in evaluating the cash flows, the central assumption of the equity approach is the same: all of them discount the net cash flows with the equity interest rate[510]. No one uses an entity approach. In combination with the argumentation above, the entity approaches seem to be not useful in the banking sector.

---

[499] Cf. *Koch* (2000), p. 44 and *Koch* (2004), p. 123, p. 126.
[500] Cf. *Koch* (2004), p. 122.
[501] Cf. *Adamus/Koch* (2006), p. 148.
[502] Cf. *Koch* (2004), p. 129 and *Adamus/Koch* (2006), p. 155.
[503] Cf. *Koch* (2004), p. 130.
[504] Cf. *Becker/Seeger* (2003), p. 23. As they do not offer a complete approach of bank evaluation, they are not presented in figure 6.
[505] Cf. *Koch* (2004), p. 130.
[506] Cf. *Adamus/Koch* (2006), p. 156. Contrary discussed in *Kirsten* (2000), pp. 163.
[507] Cf. *Adamus/Koch* (2006), p. 160.
[508] Abbreviation for Assets under Management.
[509] Done in section 5.
[510] Even argued in *Sonntag* (2001), p. 5.

2.3.3 Debatable Problems in Current Literature

2.3.3.1 The Value of Treasury

As mentioned above Sonntag pointed out that the value of treasury is zero. This can be proven as follows. Extending the above mentioned example[511] by implementing maturity transformation leads to figure 7. The bank decides not to refinance the loan with a 10Y bond, but with a 3M[512] deposit. As an assumption, the contribution margin of the liability side stays constant, but the maturity of the refinancing side changes. The whole contribution margin of 1.10% can be found again in this example accordingly:

Assets   **Liabilities**

	amount	customer yield	market yield	interest margin		amount	customer yield	market yield	interest margin
Loan, 10Y	100,000	4.30%	3.31%	0.99%	Deposits 3M	100,000	2.38%	2.49%	0.11%
	100,000	4.30%	3.31%	0.99%		100,000	2.38%	2.49%	0.11%

net interest revenue	**1.92%**
interest /contribution margin	**1.10%**
transformation margin	**0.82%**

Figure 7: **Additional earnings generated by maturity transformation**[513]

Compared to a situation without maturity transformation, the net interest earnings are much higher. According to the argumentation above, the net interest revenue of a bank can be divided into the contribution and the transformation margin[514]. The fictitious bank does maturity transformation and gets earnings coming out of the asset and the liability side. While the contribution margin is fixed, the transformation margin varies according to the yield structure[515]. In this case, the secure net interest rate margins could be summed up to 1.10% of the balance sheet sum. The additional transformation margin is about 0.82%. The longer the asset maturity is and the shorter the liability side is, the higher the earnings coming out of the ma-

---

[511] Cf. section 2.3.3.1, figure 5.
[512] Abbreviation for Month.
[513] Author's own figure referring to *Rolfes* (1999), p. 13. For market data cf. *Bundesbank* (2006a) and *Bundesbank* (2006b). Building up a fictitious balance sheet for a whole bank can be found in *Reuse* (2003.02), pp. 30 – 31.
[514] Cf. section 2.3.1.2.
[515] Cf. *Schierenbeck* (2001a), pp. 194.

turity transformation will be[516]. However, it has to be kept in mind that a risk exists[517]. If the market interest rates increase, the liabilities will become more expensive:

Assets   **Liabilities**

	amount	customer yield	market yield	interest margin		amount	customer yield	market yield	interest margin
Loan, 10Y	100,000	4.30%	3.31%	0.99%	Deposits 3M	100,000	3.38%	3.49%	0.11%
	100,000	4.30%	3.31%	0.99%		100,000	3.38%	3.49%	0.11%

net interest revenue	**0.92%**
interest /contribution margin	**1.10%**
transformation margin	**-0.18%**

Figure 8:   Additional earnings generated by maturity transformation, i +1%[518]

The fixed interest margins stay constant, but the transformation margin decreases by about 1% because of the more expensive deposit – the transformation margin becomes negative. Hence, the question, whether such a theory leads to additional earnings in the long run has to be answered. A backtesting of several maturity strategies answers this question[519]. This is presented in figure 9.

---

[516] For a detailed evaluation of yield curves cf. *Beer/Goj* (2002), pp. 156.
[517] Cf. *Sonntag* (2001), p. 43 for the status quo of the definitions of interest rate risk.
[518] Author's own figure. For data cf. *Bundesbank* (2006a) and *Bundesbank* (2006b).
[519] Discussed for example in *Wimmer* (2006), pp. 320. Empirical evidence is proven in *Sievi* (2000), chapter 8, 9; *Sievi* (2001), pp. 48 – 63 and *Hillmer* (2002), pp. 495 – 500. A short discussion of benchmarks can be found in *Goebel/Schumacher/Sievi* (1998b), pp. 340.

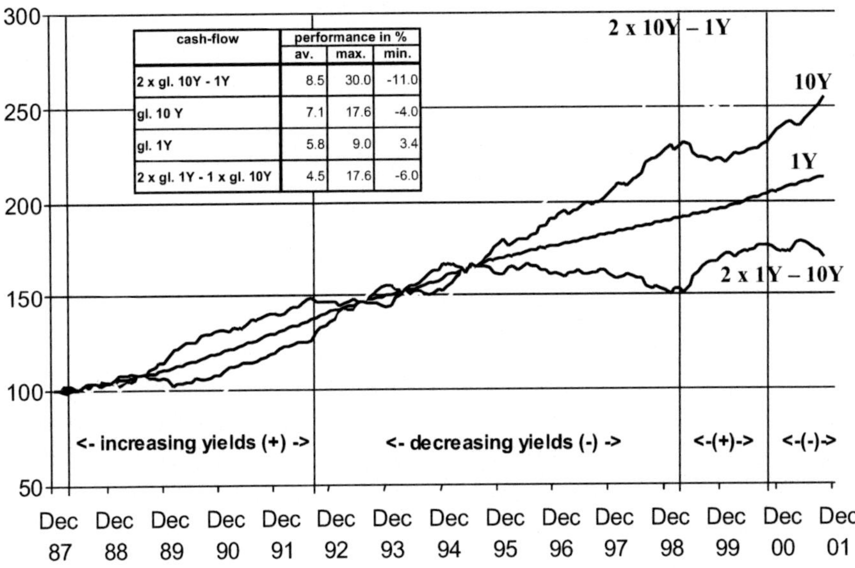

cash-flow	performance in %		
	av.	max.	min.
2 x gl. 10Y - 1Y	8.5	30.0	-11.0
gl. 10 Y	7.1	17.6	-4.0
gl. 1Y	5.8	9.0	3.4
2 x gl. 1Y - 1 x gl. 10Y	4.5	17.6	-6.0

Figure 9:   **Ex post performances of several treasury strategies 12/87 – 10/01**[520]

Four strategies are presented here. The first one is the gliding 1 year strategy[521]. The cash flows are distributed like the gliding 1 year. One cash flow becomes due after one month, the next after two months and the last after 12 months. The second presented approach is the gliding 10 year approach. The cash flows are distributed over 120 months. Every due cash flow is again invested in a ten year bond, so that this strategy consists of 120 bonds, which are invested in a 10 year maturity[522]. They are due between 1 and 120 months. The last two strategies use the leverage effect. The 2 x 10Y – 1Y strategy does not only invest the existing cash flow: the bank goes short in the 1 year maturity and invests this sum again in the gliding 10Y-strategy. The chances, but also the risks are duplicated by this. The last strategy 2 x 1Y – 10Y is the opposite: going short with a long maturity and going long with a short maturity. It is empirically proven that a 1Y liability side and a 10Y asset side lead to an optimal return. This strategy was the most efficient one in the past. Often, it is used as a benchmark in the German banking sector[523]. So the first conclusion is that such a strategy leads to additional earnings for a bank.

---

[520] Figure based on data of ifb AG. [av. = average, min. = minimum, max. = maximum].

[521] For the definition of gliding averages cf. *Sievi* (1999), pp. 31 – 39; *Böttrich/Drosdzol/Hager/ Schleicher* (2004), pp. 28 – 31 and *Reuse* (2006), p. 407. It is discussed in more detail in section 4.2.1.1.

[522] Explained in *Parchert/Markus* (2002), p. 26 and *Schierenbeck* (2001a), pp. 106.

[523] Cf. for example *Goebel/Schumacher/Sievi* (1998b), pp. 340; *Sievi* (2000), chapter 8, 9; *Sievi* (2001), pp. 48 – 63; *Hillmer* (2002), pp. 495 – 500 and *Wimmer* (2006), pp. 324.

But will an investor have to pay additional sums for the generation of maturity transformation, if he buys a bank? All authors before 2001 did not consider this aspect. But after 2001 this question was discussed in literature very often. On the one hand, Sonntag proved in 2001 that the value of treasury is zero, as everyone can duplicate a maturity transformation portfolio[524]. On the other hand, Bartetzky/Oesterhelweg argued in 2002 that a high maturity transformation leads to a higher corporate value[525]. Entrop/Scholz/Wilkens contradicted a few months later[526]. According to their argumentation treasury has a value of zero as well. The investor has two possibilities: Treating treasury as zero and discounting the value with a small yield or implementing the additional earnings, but discounting them with a higher yield, because transformation results are earnings under risk[527].

As to the author's opinion, Sonntag and Entrop/Scholz/Wilkens are right. No additional sums have to be paid for these strategies, as they could be duplicated with several derivatives as swaps[528] or caps[529]. The following example might clarify this. It is assumed that a private customer wants to speculate on the interest market. With a market partner, he draws a swap deal. He will receive a fix 10Y- interest rate payment and he has to transfer a variable 3M-interest payment to the contracting party. The reason why he makes such a deal is that he expects constant or decreasing interest rates. In this case, he will receive more funds than he has to pay. The contracting party expects the opposite: increasing interest rates. In this case, the contracting party would receive more variable interest payments than it has to pay fixed interest payments[530].

This can be transformed into a fictitious balance sheet as well, as figure 10 shows. It has to be kept in mind that a swap is only mentioned beneath the balance sheet.

---

[524] Cf. *Sonntag* (2001), p. 79.
[525] Cf. *Bartetzky/Oesterhelweg* (2002), pp. 508.
[526] Cf. *Entrop/Scholz/Wilkens* (2002), pp. 360.
[527] Cf. *Entrop/Scholz/Wilkens* (2002), p. 364.
[528] For the general structure of a swap cf. *Eller* (1996), pp. 401 and *Rolfes* (1999), pp. 74.
[529] Cf. *Bartetzky/Oesterhelweg* (2002), pp. 508.
[530] A practical implementation is discussed in *Bertsch* (2002), pp. 449 – 473 and *Heinzel* (2002), pp. 404 – 448.

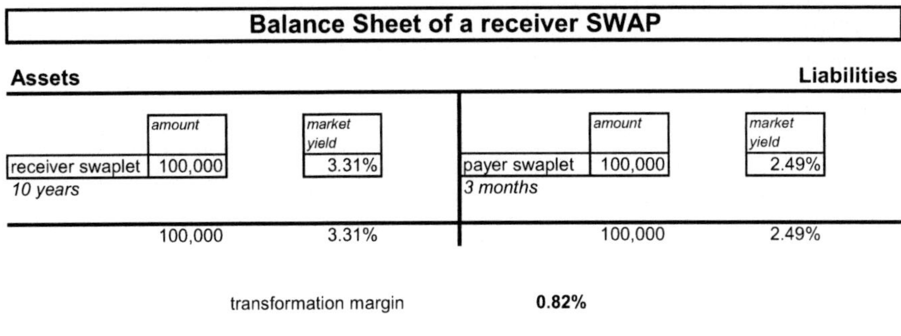

Figure 10:   **Fictitious balance sheet of a swap including interest rate risk**[531]

Compared with the above mentioned balance sheet of a bank, it becomes clear that the margin generated by the maturity difference (0.82% or -0.18%) and the risk is the same. As a conclusion, nearly everyone can duplicate a bank's strategy, when he has access to the capital market. Sonntag calls this a "homemade interest rate risk[532]". The only margin a normal customer cannot generate is the above described contribution margin. This is why treasury and maturity differences have no influence on a bank's value.

The only component that might lead to an additional value for the bank is the knowledge of the treasurers. As they might have an information advantage and more experience, they would probably build up more efficient structures than anybody else[533]. However, this has to be eyed very critically. In the long run, nearly no one can beat the market[534], so the strategies as men-

---

[531]   Author's own figure. For market data cf. *Bundesbank* (2006a) and *Bundesbank* (2006b).
[532]   *Sonntag* (2001), p. 41.
[533]   Cf. *Sonntag* (2001), p. 83.
[534]   Cf. *Stulz* (1996), p. 15.

tioned above (10Y refinanced by 1Y etc[535].) are the most efficient ones and are treated as benchmarks for the treasury department[536].

It is correct that the share prices of a bank include the value of an inherent interest rate risk. But an investor can hedge it, if he has an access to the capital market[537]. Hence, it is proven that in the case of a perfect market, the value of the treasury center is zero[538]. In case of an intransparent market, only the small bid/ask spread generates value for the bank[539] – but this value is almost zero as well.

Last, it has to be stated that realized profits of treasury will increase the value of a bank, if the treasury does not close a loan position and the yield curve is declining. The present value of this credit is higher than in the beginning accordingly[540]. So in sum, the realized present value of maturity transformation can be stated[541]. But no future expected returns have to be discounted.

2.3.3.2 The Value of Trading

This idea can be extended to the trading of banks. Can a bank beat the market in a sustainable way? The answer is no, according to Sonntag[542]. Further, the performance of the trading book normally is relatively low compared with the yield book, so that this aspect can be neglected.

2.3.3.3 Quantifying the Cash Flow for an Equity Approach

Even though existing literature is consistent according to the equity approach, the exact cash flow definition is not clear. While Copeland/Koller/Murrin[543], Koch[544], Kirsten[545] and Becker/Seeger[546] demand a complete full cash flow statement, the practical approaches are only based on the balance sheet data, as detailed information often is not available[547]. Another problem is the approach to use: equity or earnings value method. The cash flows will differ depending on the used approach.

---

[535] Abbreviation for et cetera.
[536] Cf. *Heinrich* (2002), pp. 575.
[537] Cf. *Sonntag* (2001), p. 41.
[538] Cf. *Sonntag* (2001), p. 82.
[539] Cf. *Sonntag* (2001), p. 90.
[540] Cf. *Reuse* (2003.03), p. 28.
[541] Cf. *Rolfes* (1999), p. 283.
[542] Cf. *Sonntag* (2001), p. 83.
[543] Cf. *Copeland/Koller/Murrin* (2002), p. 504.
[544] Cf. *Koch* (2004), p. 129.
[545] Cf. *Kirsten* (2000), p. 140.
[546] Cf. *Becker/Seeger* (2003), p. 23.
[547] Cf. *Becker/Seeger* (2003), p. 23.

For a good banking evaluation, an exact and consistent definition of the cash flow and the related discounting rate has to be done.

2.3.3.4 Discounting Factor – Equity Yield

The same problem can be stated when analyzing the equity yield. The more insecure cash flows are discounted, the higher the discounting yield has to be[548]. While Adolf/ Cramer/Ollmann partly recommend the yield of the bank obligation[549], the CAPM is preferred by most of the authors[550]. Nevertheless, the CAPM has to be eyed very critically. Several aspects are discussed in literature. While Koch found out that the leverage effect does not influence the equity yield[551], Zimmermann discusses a complex, transformation risk adjusted beta factor for the equity costs[552]. Further, Adamus/Koch state that the risk of the asset side is absorbed by the debt financiers, only 14% have to be carried by the shareholders[553]. This would mean that the equity ratio would consist of 86% bank obligation yield.

The complexity of the equity yield will increase dramatically, if these adjustments are made. The danger of mistakes occurs, too. According to the author, a simple definition of the equity costs, based on stable assumptions would lead to more reliable results than the high sophisticated ones.

2.3.4 Theoretical Impulses for a New Evaluation Model

A new, all embracing model should consider all aspects mentioned in section 2.3.3. A clear and consistent definition of cash flows and equity yield is the central quality driver. The more cash flows are inserted into the model, the more complex the equity yield will have to be defined. The following figure visualises, which combinations between complexity, scope of cash flow and yield exist:

---

[548] Cf. *Entrop/Scholz/Wilkens* (2002), p. 364.
[549] Cf. *Adolf/Cramer/Ollmann* (1989b), p. 552.
[550] Cf. section 2.3.2.
[551] Cf. *Adamus/Koch* (2006), p. 156.
[552] Cf. *Örtmann/Zimmermann* (1997), pp. 39 – 43 and *Zimmermann* (1995), pp. 4, cited and discussed in *Kirsten* (2000), pp. 163.
[553] Cf. *Adamus/Koch* (2006), p. 157.

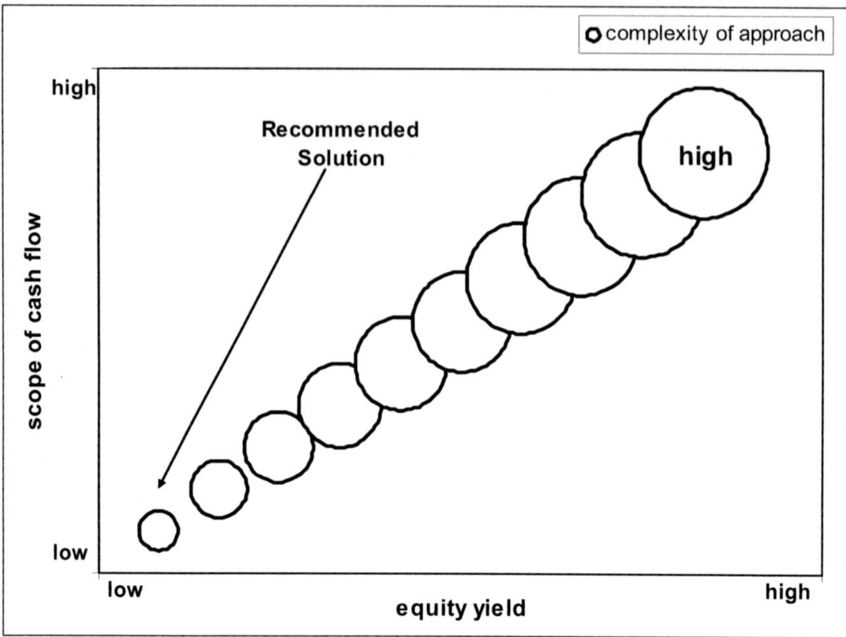

Figure 11:   **Dependence between cash flow, equity yield and complexity**[554]

A new model should be kept as simple as possible. If earnings or cash flows that have an inherent risk are not considered, the equity yield can be reduced on a bond yield, perhaps with a spread add on. Expanding this main idea, expected returns form maturity transformation must not be implemented either.

---

[554]   Author's own figure.

3 Practical Status Quo: An Empirical Study in the German Banking Sector

3.1 Modeling the Survey

3.1.1 Central Idea of the Survey

The theoretical requirements for a bank evaluation approach have been pointed out[555]. The next step is to verify this in practice. This is done by a survey in the German banking sector. As theory and practice might differ, the following central questions have to be answered:

- Do German banks know about the theoretical status quo?
- Do German banks evaluate their own value?
- Do German banks have a shareholder value-oriented management?
- Does the survey offer further impulses for a new evaluation approach?

The main aim is to come to further conclusions for a bank individual approach and to define the status quo with its strengths and weaknesses.

3.1.2 Theoretical Aspects for Modeling a Survey

As current data according to corporate evaluation in the German banking sector are not available, primary research has to be done[556]. For this dissertation, a survey is used to gather primary data. A survey can be defined as a method that stimulates the answerer in order to get the right results[557]. These stimulations can be verbal communication, pictures or presentations[558]. Surveys should be structured in order to receive high-quality information[559]. After a definition of the problem, the data have to be collected, interpreted and added with arguments of the researcher[560]. Surveys can be clustered according to different views: communication form, survey tactic, frequency, target group and scope[561]. For this dissertation, the following sample is used:

---

[555] Cf. section 2.
[556] For the definition and explanation of primary research cf. *Sudman* (1998), p. 87 and *Kotler/Armstrong* (2004), p. 154.
[557] Cf. *Lötters* (2000), p. 61.
[558] Cf. *Lötters* (2000), p. 61.
[559] Cf. *Schnell/Hill/Esser* (1999), p. 301.
[560] Cf. *Sudman* (1998), p. 84.
[561] Cf. *Kotler/Armstrong* (2004), pp. 151.

Aspect	Possibilities	Structuring the survey
Communication form	• Written form • Telephonic fom • Oral form • Computer assisted	A **written survey** is used. The reason is that banks would probably react more often than in an email survey. The probability that it reaches the right person is higher than by using an email. Further, the optic of a questionnaire can influence the reader, if it is printed out. Last, the reader recognizes that the sender has paid a lot of money to send the postal questionnaire. This is normally only done in case of a professional work.
Survey tactic	• Direct questions • Indirect questions	**Direct and indirect forms** of questions will be used – related to the problem. In some cases, it is useful to receive a "yes" or a "no" – but only in those situations, the author wants to have these two-dimensional answers.
Survey strategy	• Standardized interviews • Structured interviews • Free interviews	In order to receive standardized answers, a **standardized questionnaire** is used in order to cluster the answers before[562]. Only in some special cases, a free sentence can be inserted.
Frequency of survey	• One time • Repeated	The query is done only **once** for the master dissertation.
Target Group	• Organizations • Consumers • Experts • *Several others*	The target group consists of **organizations** – German banks. It has to be kept in mind that the survey's language must be target group conform – otherwise, no consistent results will be gathered[563].
Scope of survey	• One issue • More issues	The scope consists of **one direct** issue. The status quo of corporate evaluation combined with several aspects according to a shareholder wealth management will be analyzed.

Table 10:   Aspects for the questionnaire[564]

The advantages of surveys are that a structured questionnaire enables the researcher to control the interview without being present. It allows all participants to be asked the same questions in the same order. This makes the analysis of data easier. Furthermore, a structured questionnaire offers the possibility of interviewing the target group by mail or telephone. This is less expensive than interviews by researchers. Finally, using mail and telephone gives the possibility of doing many interviews with a broader cross section of the market.[565]

However, survey research involves also some disadvantages. Occasionally, participants are not able to answer the questions because they have never thought about what they do and why or because they cannot remember. Perhaps, participants try to answer even not understood

---

[562]   Cf. *Schnell/Hill/Esser* (1999), p. 301.
[563]   Cf. *Berekoven/Eckert/Ellenrieder* (2004), pp. 100.
[564]   Author's own table based referring to *Kotler/Armstrong* (2004), pp. 151.
[565]   Cf. *Sudman* (1998), pp. 84.

questions because they pretend to be smart. Participants may not reply because of believing survey themes are private.[566]

3.1.3 Structure of the Questionnaire

The questionnaire has to be answered within a short time in order to receive many responses. Only if answering does not take too much time, the answers will be complete and of a high quality[567]. Tests have shown that responding the survey should only take about ten minutes in order to be accepted by the user[568]. Further, the questionnaire should be structured and clear.

Using all theoretical aspects mentioned above the developed questionnaire shows five sections.

Section	Description	Questions
1. **General data of the answering banks**	It is important to know what type of bank answered the questionnaire. Legal form, age, size in form of balance sheet sum or number of employees, trading book character and stock listing help to verify the representativeness of the survey.	6
2. **Questions related to the used bank controlling**	Shareholder value management and evaluation of the bank's value belong together. Perhaps, some relations between the evaluation method and the level of bank controlling can be stated.	3
3. **Questions according to the methods of corporate evaluation**	This central part of the survey contains the most important questions according to the presented models and their usage or recognition in practice. Further, this section quantifies the number and form of used models.	8
4. **Data for an individual corporate evaluation**[569]	The survey consists of 2.5 pages asking for the individual bank data as balance sheet, income statement and internal controlling data. Based on this information, the banks' value will be quantified later on[570].	5
5. **Final questions**	The answerers had the possibility to give final comments. Further, the aspect of anonymity was asked. The question, whether the bank likes to be informed about the results constitutes the end of the questionnaire.	3
		25

Table 11:   Structure of the questionnaire[571]

---

[566] Cf. *Kotler/Armstrong* (2004), p. 154.
[567] Cf. *Perseus* (2004), p. 14.
[568] Cf. *Perseus* (2004), p. 14.
[569] Analyzed in detail in section 4.
[570] Cf. section 5.
[571] Author's own table, cf. appendix 3.

The questionnaire consists of 8 pages[572] – answering all questions within 10 minutes is not possible as the evaluation of the needed data in part 4 leads to research work for the answerer. But sections 1-3 and 5 can be answered within 11 minutes[573]. The questionnaire was accompanied by an introduction letter[574] and a confirmation letter of the FOM[575] in which the university asks the banks to answer the survey[576]. In total, 10 pages, printed on 5 pieces of paper were sent via post. The questionnaire contained several definitions and explanations of special aspects. Accordingly, it could be assured that the interviewees understand the questions similarly.[577]

3.1.4 Defining the Target Group

In the next step the target group has to be modelled. In general, all banks in Germany could be examined. The Bundesbank publishes a paper every year[578] in which all those banks are structured that do banking as per definition of § 1 KWG[579]. These banks belong to several groups[580]. In order to receive reliable results for classical all purpose banks, only those banks that are independent and have a classical customer liability side were addressed[581]. Hence, the addressable number of the target group decreases to 1,951 banks[582]. This number forms the whole target group. Not the whole target group was considered for the survey. 750 banks (38.44%) were set up manually in a database and addressed by mail.

---

[572] Cf. appendix 3.
[573] Betatests with banking colleagues.
[574] Cf. appendix 1.
[575] Abbreviation for Fachhochschule für Oekonomie und Management.
[576] Cf. appendix 2.
[577] Cf. appendix 3.
[578] Cf. *Bundesbank* (2005).
[579] Abbreviation for Kreditwesengesetz. Cf. § 1 *KWG*. This paragraph defines all possible activities that are defined as "banking".
[580] Cf. *Bundesbank* (2005), pp. 1.
[581] Cf. *Bundesbank* (2005), chapter II, section 1 without §53 *KWG* banks and subsections 1.4, 1.5, 1.6 and 1.8.
[582] Cf. *Bundesbank* (2005), own counting.

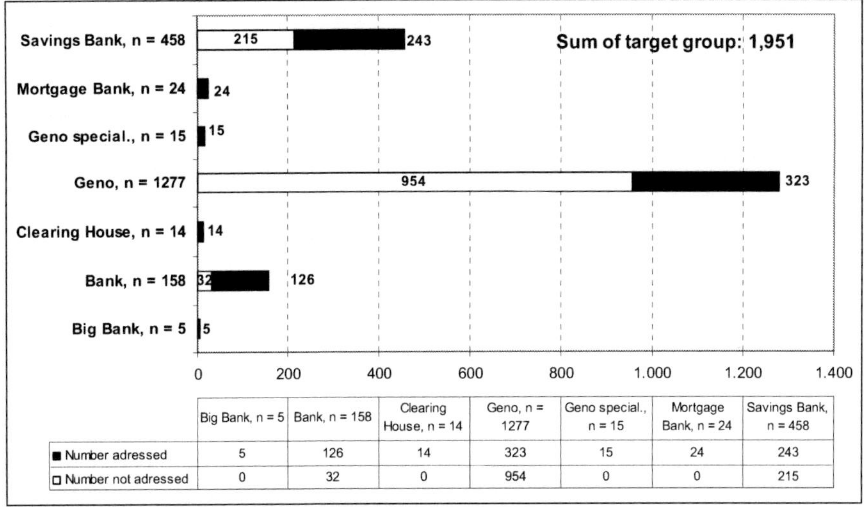

	Big Bank, n = 5	Bank, n = 158	Clearing House, n = 14	Geno, n = 1277	Geno special., n = 15	Mortgage Bank, n = 24	Savings Bank, n = 458
■ Number adressed	5	126	14	323	15	24	243
□ Number not adressed	0	32	0	954	0	0	215

Figure 12: **Target group and sample of the survey**[583]

Deducting the number of addressed banks had to be done proportionally in order to address a representative sample[584]. This was done accordingly, the whole target group and the sample is represented in figure 12. The small subgroups were addressed completely as the response probability decreases the bigger a company is. About half of the savings banks, 25% of the Genos and 80% of the private banks were addressed. The survey was sent out on Monday, May 15th, 2006 in order to be received by the banks at a Tuesday or Wednesday, as this is an optimal receiving day[585].

3.2 Quantification of the Answers

3.2.1 Return Ratio and Representativeness

Before discussing the results, the return rate and the representativeness of the survey have to be analyzed. Exactly 750 letters were sent out, 15 negative responses came in. In 17 cases[586], a 2nd attempt was done. This led to 3 more responses, including one big bank. All in all, 51

---

[583] Author's own figure referring to *Bundesbank* (2005), pp. 3. Changes: Deutsche Postbank AG was defined as big bank, DekaBank, clearing houses of the savings bank sector, DZ Bank and WGZ Bank were subsumed under the category clearing house. n = number in the whole target group.

[584] Cf. *Höpflinger* (2002).

[585] Cf. *Dillman* (1978), pp. 180.

[586] Including some personal contacts. Not all negative responses were contacted twice. But some banks that gave no answer were asked again.

banks answered the questionnaire[587]. This leads to a response rate of 6.80%, as the following table shows:

All banks		Adressed banks		Answering banks		
Kind of Bank	Number in Germany	Number adressed	Percentage contacted	Number answered	Percentage answered	Percentage of all banks
Big Bank	5	5	100.00%	2	40.00%	40.00%
Bank	158	126	79.75%	7	5.56%	4.43%
Clearing House	14	14	100.00%			
Geno	1,277	323	25.29%	21	6.50%	1.64%
Geno special.	15	15	100.00%	3	20.00%	20.00%
Mortgage Bank	24	24	100.00%	2	8.33%	8.33%
Savings Bank	458	243	53.06%	16	6.58%	3.49%
Sum	1,951	750	38.44%	51	6.80%	2.61%

Table 12:   **Response rate and representativeness, n = 51[588]**

Even though this rate seems to be low at a first glance, the quality of the return ratio has to be verified. Several arguments have to be mentioned: First, some German savings banks have the order of the local RSGV[589] not to answer any queries without the consent of the RSGV. Even good personal contacts of the author did not always lead to a result. Further, the survey asked for secret data a bank often does not want to publish. Last, the topics of the survey and even some questions are relatively complex. Even though all models were defined and explained in the questionnaire, the understanding of the presented models just based on a short introduction in the questionnaire is difficult, if the interviewee has never heard about these topics before. This is perhaps a first hint that German banks do not focus on corporate evaluation at the moment.

In addition, it has to be mentioned that similar professional surveys[590] that usually generate higher ratios show similar results, whenever banks are not obliged to answer[591]. For example, Ernst & Young did a survey according to shareholder value in the German banking sector in 1996. About 80% refused to answer the questionnaire[592]. Baetge/Heumann received 11.5%[593] and only Grimmer can offer a rate of 25%[594,595]

---

[587]   Cf. the answers of the survey.
[588]   Author's own table referring to the survey.
[589]   Abbreviation for Rheinischer Sparkassen- und Giroverband.
[590]   Discussed in detail in section 3.4.1.
[591]   An obligation often occurs in surveys of the BaFin, Bundesbank or even DSGV (Deutscher Sparkassen- und Giroverband).
[592]   Cf. *Ernst & Young* (1997), p. 2.
[593]   Cf. *Baetge/Heumann* (2006), p. 348.
[594]   Cf. *Grimmer* (2003), p. 200.
[595]   These surveys are discussed later on. Cf. section 3.4.1.

The consideration of those aspects leads to the conclusion that 6.80% can be treated as a relative good ratio – as 750 banks were addressed, the total number of 51 surveys leads to reliable results. Furthermore, it has to be mentioned that only a few answers were not filled in. The quality of the answers is very high.

With respect to the question as to whether the results were representative, it can be said that the results are positive. 2 of 5 big banks answered, 7 private banks, many Genos and many savings banks[596]. This represents almost the whole target group. As the return ratio is 6.80%, the ratio related to the target group is 2.61%. All banking groups show similar results – only big banks and specialized Genos show a higher rate, as they have a small basis number. There is only one exception that needs to be mentioned. No clearing house answered the questionnaire. However, for all other banks, the survey can be treated as representative. Only in cases very few banks answered, the results might be treated carefully when doing general conclusions according to the target group.

3.2.2 Date of Return

The addressed banks were asked to answer the questionnaire as soon as possible. Nevertheless, it took about 6 weeks, up to July 1st, until all questionnaires were returned to the author. This period is visualized in the following figure:

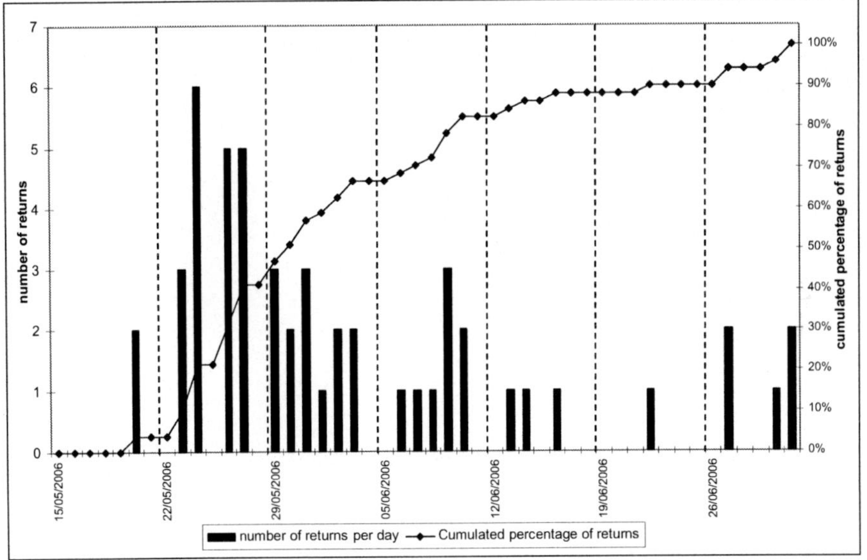

Figure 13:   **Distribution of returns of the survey, n = 51**[597]

---

[596]   Cf. table 12.
[597]   Author's own figure. The date of return was defined as the date of postal income at the author's home.

The reason was often that internal data had to be evaluated. The banks that only answered the sections 1, 3 and 5 responded earlier, on average on June 1st, 2006. Banks with the interest in a corporate evaluation answered on average 5 days later[598]. Within a month, 44 banks of the 51 answered the questionnaire. It was surprising that many banks took such a long time. This is again a hint for the fact that German banks are not familiar with corporate evaluation. Gathering the data is a difficult process. For this reason, 51 responses have to be treated as a good result.

3.3 Analyzing the Results

Analyzing surveys belongs to the deductive statistics, as the main objective of deductive statistics is to describe the data selected and to analyze them[599]. Several approaches will be used here. They can be clustered according to the number of variables used[600]. If only one variable is used, frequency allocation is the main analysis tool[601]. If two variables are combined, cross tables[602], correlation analysis[603] or regression analysis[604] can be done. Approaches using three or more variables have different methods to generate dependence or independence analysis[605]. Discriminates analysis, multiple analysis of variance, tree analysis, cluster analysis and factor analysis can be mentioned[606].

During this analysis, the frequency analysis will be the most important tool, but some of the approaches using two or more variables will be used as well. The questionnaire will be analyzed according to its five sections.

3.3.1 Section 1: General Data according to the Bank

The first section wanted to find out some general criteria of the answering banks. The first question asked for the number of employees. This was one of the questions the interviewee had to fill in a number. The clustering of the employees was done afterwards as the exact number has to be used later on[607]. The reason is that the same question should not be asked twice in a survey. The same was done with question 2, in which the balance sheet sum was

---

[598] Author's own calculations based on the return date.
[599] Cf. *Bleymüller/Gehlert/Gülicher* (1996), p. 1.
[600] Cf. *Berekoven/Eckert/Ellenrieder* (2004), p. 197, p. 211.
[601] Cf. *Bleymüller/Gehlert/Gülicher* (1996), p. 8 and *Berekoven/Eckert/Ellenrieder* (2004), p. 198.
[602] Cf. *Berekoven/Eckert/Ellenrieder* (2004), pp. 203.
[603] Using the correlation coefficient, cf. *Poddig/Dichtl/Petersmeier* (2000), pp. 144.
[604] Cf. *SPSS* (2003), p. 2 and *Berekoven/Eckert/Ellenrieder* (2004), p. 206.
[605] Cf. *Berekoven/Eckert/Ellenrieder* (2004), pp. 197, p. 211.
[606] Cf. *Berekoven/Eckert/Ellenrieder* (2004), pp. 197, p. 211.
[607] Cf. Section 5.

evaluated. The bank had to fill in the actual balance sheet sum. Visualizing both results leads to the following figure[608]:

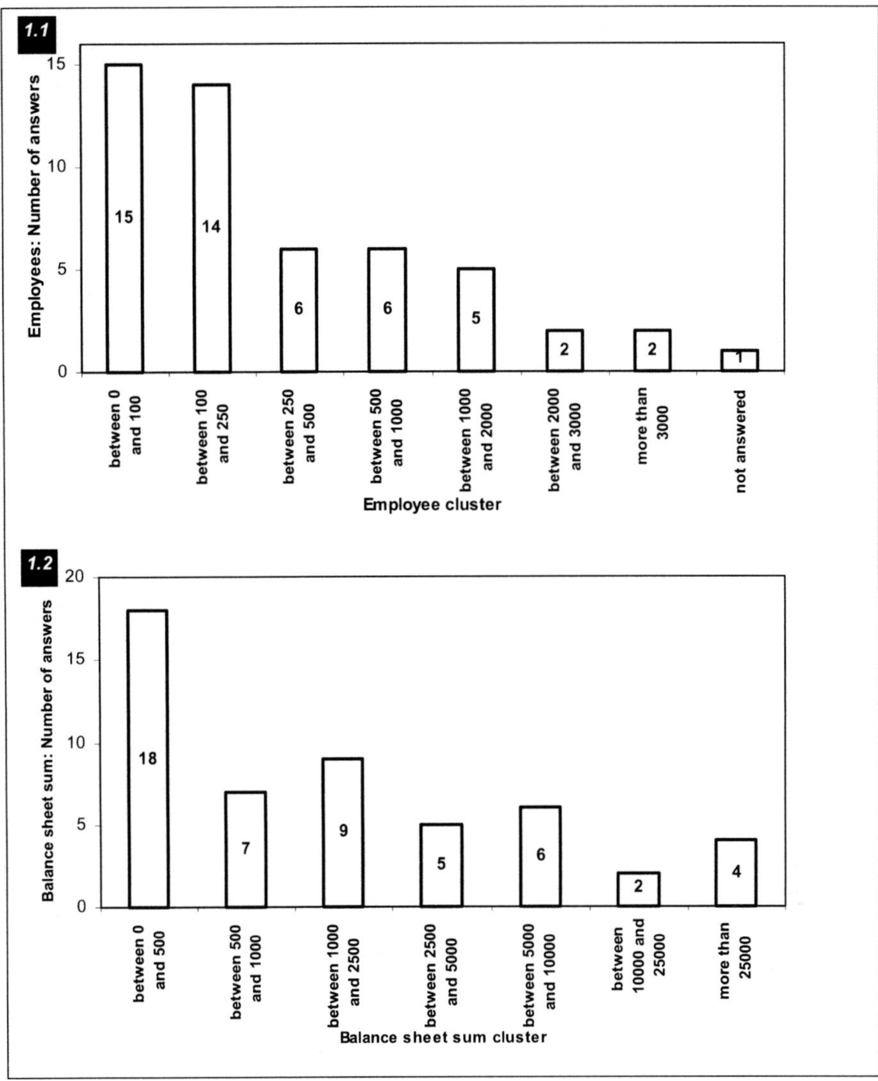

Figure 14:   **Clusters of employees and balance sheet sum, n = 51**[609]

---

[608]   All figures show the number of the related question in the upper left corner.
[609]   Author's own figure based on the results of the survey. Balance sheet sum in Mio. €.

The first conclusion coming out of this figure is that the answering banks are widespread in their size. The majority however comes from small banks with a low balance sheet sum and a small number of employees. Most German banks are small, so this confirms the statement that the study is representative.

Both results can be combined in order to find out what kind of banks answered the questionnaire. Classical all purpose banks must have a certain relation between employees and balance sheet sum. If the balance sheet of the bank consists of customer deals, many employees will be needed to serve the customers. So questions 1.1 and 1.2 are combined in the following table:

1.1 & 1.2		Balance Sheet sum in Mio. €							
		0 - 500	500 - 1000	1000 - 2500	2500 - 5000	5000 - 10000	10000 - 25000	> 25000	Sum
Employees	between 0 and 100	13	1					1	15
	between 100 and 250	4	6	3			1		14
	between 250 and 500			5	1				6
	between 500 and 1000			1	4	1			6
	between 1000 and 2000					4		1	5
	between 2000 and 3000					1	1		2
	more than 3000							2	2
	not answered	1							1
	Sum	18	7	9	5	6	2	4	

Table 13:   **Employees vs. balance sheet, n = 51**[610]

The table makes clear that most of the banks must be classical all purpose banks, as there is a dependency between the number of employees and the balance sheet sum. Only two banks do not fit into this scheme: both can be found in the upper right corner. The balance sheet sum is high while a relatively low number of clerks is employed. The analysis leads to the result that the two banks are exactly the two mortgage banks that answered the questionnaire[611]. But in general, the dependency between employees and balance sheet sum is significant. This is important for the analysis afterwards. First, the answers during the following sections are typical for general banks but not for specialized banks. Further, the corporate evaluation[612] can be based on similar assumptions, as the structure of the banks seems to be the same.

The age of the company was quantified in question 1.3. The reason for that is rather simple. The probability that young companies were created by a merger is relatively high. A corporate evaluation had to take place for this. Further, this question should prove the survey to be representative. The following figure visualizes the results:

---

[610] Author's own table referring to the analyzed data of the survey.
[611] Banks 173 and 185.
[612] Cf. section 5.

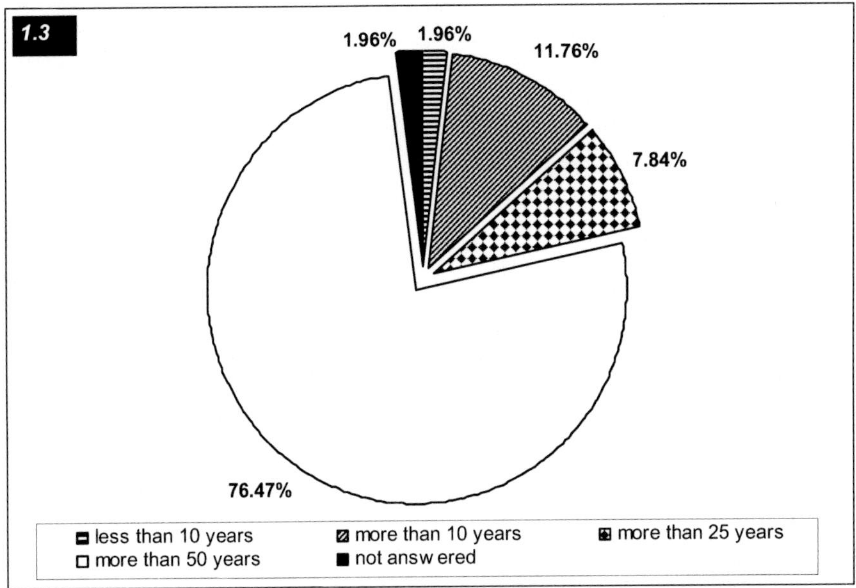

Figure 15:   Age of the company, n = 51[613]

In total, 39 banks have existed for more than 50 years. The German banking sector is relatively old. Even though many mergers took place[614], the banks that bought other companies continue to exist under the old name. Another interpretation can be that only a few banks did a merger in the past. A consolidation will perhaps take place, as many small banks exist.

Questions 1.1 – 1.3 lead to the result that the survey is at least representative in a qualitative way. The target group is represented in an adequate way. The first result coming out of these questions is that the German banking sector is again under pressure to merge or to buy other companies. A very old structure with a high number of small-sized banks forms attractive targets for institutional investors, for example big banks or even foreign banks.

Questions 1.4 and 1.5 deal with the trading book character[615] and the stock listing. From the 51 answering institutes, 16 are defined as a trading book bank and two are stock listed[616]. So all possible bank types answered the questionnaire; the representativeness is given.

---

[613] Author's own figure based on the results of the survey.
[614] Cf. section 1.1.
[615] For the definition of a trading book cf. *BaFin* (1999), discussed in detail in *Reuse* (2006), p. 380.
[616] Cf. questions 1.4 and 1.5 of the survey.

The last question of section 1 deals with the spread a bank has to pay for unsecured debt finance at the capital market. Not all banks answered this question, as the following table shows:

Type of Bank	Number of surveys answered	Number of responses	Spread in %
Big Bank	2	1	0.115%
Bank	7	3	0.193%
Clearing House			
Geno special.	3	2	0.325%
Geno	21	16	0.159%
Mortgage Bank	2	2	0.093%
Savings Bank	16	12	0.158%
Sum	**51**	**36**	**0.166%**

Table 14:   **Average spread of the banks, n = 36[617]**

The question aims at two purposes. First, the average risk premium a bank has to pay for its own risk shall be quantified, as it will be used later on[618]. Further, banks that have a high spread have a high risk as well – they and their answers have to be treated differently, as they could perhaps almost be bankrupt. The result is interesting, as the spread of all banking groups is almost the same. All spreads are below 0.35%, the average is about 0.17%. This is relatively low compared with other companies[619]. Therefore, the German banking sector has a good image at the capital market; banks have the market power to set low spreads[620]. Further, the analyzed banks are homogenous enough to be treated similarly when analyzing the corporate value[621].

3.3.2 Section 2: Bank Controlling and Value Based Management

Value based management or shareholder value and corporate evaluation determine each other[622]. The main target of shareholder value is to increase the value for the shareholders[623] – quantified by the (market) value of the company. Integrating these aspects into the management became famous in the eighties[624]. Hence, the form of bank controlling, the used ratios

---

[617] Author's own table based on the survey.
[618] Cf. section 5.2.2.3.
[619] Cf. for example *Reuse* (2003.12).
[620] Exceptions surely exist, as some interviewees offered a higher rate in the questionnaire.
[621] Cf. section 5.
[622] Cf. *Copeland/Koller/Murrin* (2002), p. 27.
[623] For the economic definition of value cf. *Bretzke* (1976), p. 153 and *Stützer* (1976), columns 4404.
[624] Cf. *Günther* (1995), p. 13.

and values to control a bank determine the importance of corporate evaluation in the German banking sector. If value-oriented numbers are not quantified, evaluating the company's value will not be useful for a bank. So section 2 of the survey wants to show, how good the conditions for corporate evaluation in the German banking sector are. Only if these conditions are good, a German bank will evaluate its own value voluntarily – and not only in case of a takeover.

Question 2.1 deals with the integrated bank controlling. This can be defined as an optimal risk/return allocation of economic equity[625]. Management has to set strategic goals, in which market or asset the economic equity has to be invested in. This is a typical behaviour of a value based management, so fulfilling this criterion would lead to the conclusion that a bank does shareholder value management. The banks answered the question as shown in figure 16.

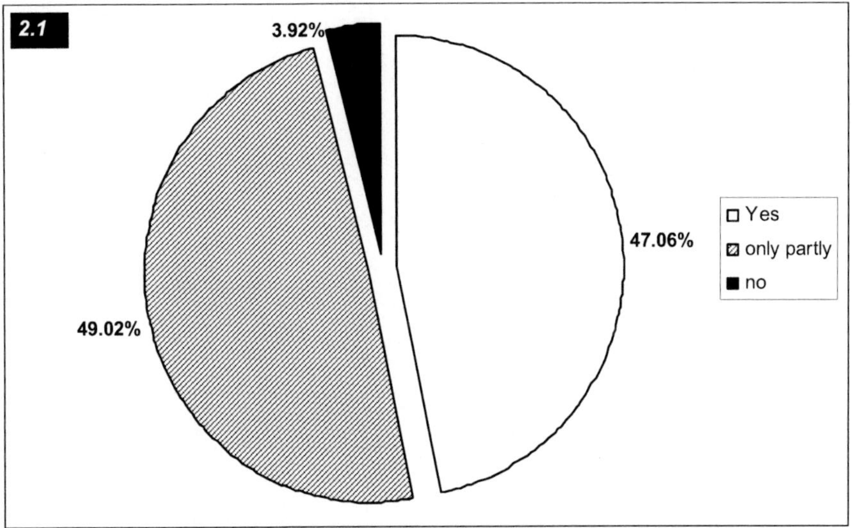

Figure 16:   **Integrated bank controlling, n = 51**[626]

At first glance, the result seems to be positive. About 49% or 25 banks offer an integrated bank controlling, 24 banks at least partly and only 2 banks answered "no" to this question. Having an integrated bank controlling would mean that the bank is able to define the present value of its own in order to define, which parts of this present value can be set "under fire" as

---

[625]   Cf. *Rolfes* (1999), p. 3; *Rolfes* (1999.04); *Schierenbeck* (2001a), pp. 22 and *Propach/Reuse* (2003), pp. 324.
[626]   Author's own figure based on the survey.

economic equity[627]. A present value-oriented risk capacity is the first step for an integrated bank controlling[628].

Question 2.2 asked for the priority of the banks in their controlling process. Optimizing the income statement was opposed to optimizing the value of the bank. It was the intention not to offer a solution in between, as most would have chosen this one, even if they do not manage the bank based on shareholder value. The result was interesting: 40 banks (78%) answered that optimizing the income statement has priority while 11 banks[629] prefer value based optimization[630]. This result seems to be more typical for German banks – the income statement and the balance sheet still remain the most important value drivers in practice.

In order to verify the quality of these responses, the result was combined with question 2.1. An integrated controlling should normally lead to an optimization of the present value. Otherwise, it is not installed correctly. The integration of the two questions is visualized in figure 17:

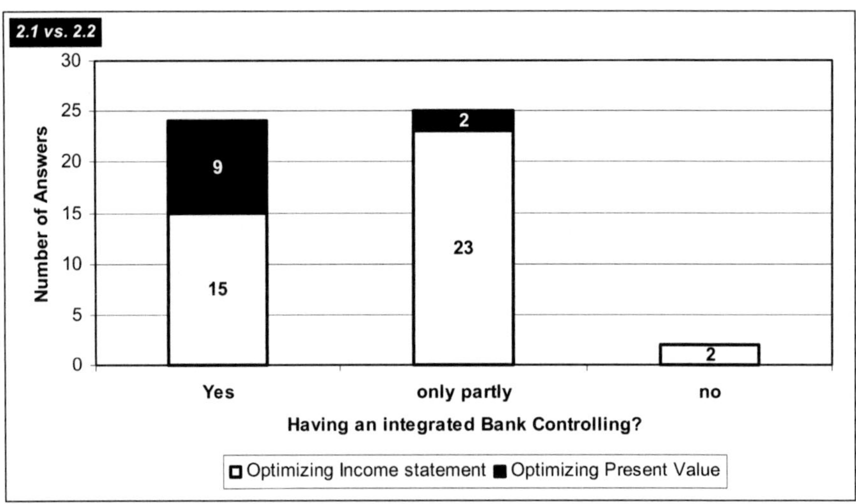

Figure 17:   Integrated bank controlling vs. priority of optimizing, n = 51[631]

---

[627] Cf. *Reuse* (2006), pp. 427 and *Rolfes* (1999), p. 5.

[628] Cf. *Rolfes* (1999), p. 4.

[629] Two banks marked both solutions, even though only one answer was requested. But they offered an additional text that proved that value-orientation seems to have a higher priority. So "optimizing the value" was chosen. Banks 657, 750.

[630] Cf. question 2.2.

[631] Author's own figure based on the survey.

This result qualifies the results of question 2.1. Only in 9 of 24 cases (38%), the optimization of the present value fits with the usage of an integrated bank controlling. 15 banks answering that they have an integrated bank controlling do not optimize the bank's value. These answers are inconsistent, so that 17.7%[632] are the only banks that do real value based management in Germany. The distribution is interesting: 3 savings banks, 3 Genos, one big bank, one private bank and one mortgage bank have chosen this combination[633].

Question 2.3 deals with several controlling ratios. Their usage[634] and their valuation[635] were tested in order to find out, whether value based controlling numbers are accepted or even used in practice. But therefore, a short introduction of these numbers shall be given[636]. This is done in the following table, in which all ratios are clustered. Ratios that consider more than one period and have a focus on the value of the bank are rather defined as shareholder value-oriented, one-periodic variables and income statement based methods belong to the periodic variables. These ratios almost do not have anything to do with optimizing the shareholder value or the corporate value.

Value / ratio	Short explanation	Rather periodic view or SV[637]
a) Present value of the bank	Defined as the value of all assets, especially the yield book[638]. This is the central controlling number for a shareholder value based management.	*SV*[639]
b) EBT	Classical part of the income statement[640]. In the query, a value before or after value corrections was used.	*Periodic*
c) Value at Risk	The Value at Risk defines the maximal loss that may occur in a certain time with a certain probability[641]. Normally used for a shareholder value management.	*SV*
d) RORAC[642]	Defined as net return of an asset divided through the corresponding Value at Risk[643]. Used to optimize the expected return on a present value basis.	*SV*
e) RAROC[644]	Defined as RORAC (Benchmark) minus RORAC (own Asset)[645] in order to measure if the own assets are better than the benchmark[646].	*SV*

---

[632] 9 of 51 banks.
[633] Cf. questions 2.1 and 2.2 of the survey.
[634] Yes or no.
[635] In a range of 1 (best) – 4 (worst).
[636] The questionnaire contained a short German explanation of all variables, cf. appendix 3.
[637] A similar structure can be found in *Weber* (2004), pp. 246.
[638] Cf. *Reuse* (2006), pp. 409, 428.
[639] Abbreviation for Shareholder Value.
[640] A typical structure can be found in *Schierenbeck* (2001a), p. 417.
[641] Cf. *Rolfes* (1999), p. 104; *Gramlich/Peylo* (2000), pp. 508; *Reuse* (2003.10), pp. 25 and *Reuse* (2006.07-08), pp. 366.
[642] Abbreviation for Return On Risk Adjusted Capital.
[643] Cf. *Rolfes* (1999), pp. 32 and *Schierenbeck* (2001b), p. 42, p. 544.
[644] Abbreviation for Risk Adjusted Return On Risk Adjusted Capital.
[645] Cf. *Rolfes* (1999), p. 32 and *Schierenbeck* (2001b), p. 46.
[646] Cf. *Rolfes* (1999.04), p. 18.

Value / ratio	Short explanation	Rather periodic view or SV[637]
f) EVA[647]	Defined as NOPAT[648] - (capital yield · invested capital)[649]. Describes the value that is generated after having paid out yield to shareholders and debt holders. The EVA is the central value based ratio[650], as the correlation between EVA and share price is very high[651].	*SV*
g) CIR[652]	The cost income ratio divides the costs through the earnings[653] and defines, how much one € of earnings cost on average. It is rather a periodic variable as only income statement aspects are considered.	*Periodic*
h) ROE[654]	Return in relation to the equity[655]. As the return from the income statement is used, this ratio is rather periodically oriented[656].	*Periodic*
i) Growth of BS growth[657]	Some banks define growth as a strategic goal. As this has only influence onto the balance sheet and not directly onto the shareholder value, it is rather a periodic variable.	*Periodic*
j) Market share	Market share cannot be found in the income statement, but it has an influence on expected earnings and is thus defined as rather shareholder value-oriented.	*SV*
k) Value of brand	The value of a brand as an intangible asset leads to expected add ons in the earnings as well. As the direct value cannot be seen in the income statement, it is rather a shareholder value-oriented number.	*SV*
l) Contribution margin	Defined as customer yield compared to market yield minus variable costs[658]. As only one period is considered, it can be treated as a periodic variable[659].	*Periodic*
m) Present value of CM[660]	Discounting the contribution margin considers all periods. The present value of all contribution margins has a direct impact onto the company's value. It is a shareholder value-oriented number.	*SV*
n) Balanced Scorecard	The balanced scorecard[661] is a multidimensional, all-embracing set of controlling numbers. Its target is to control the transformation of strategic goals into operative actions[662]. In case of a divergence, hints shall be given[663]. It consists of four perspectives[664] that are long-term oriented. Therefore, it is rather shareholder value-oriented.	*SV*

Table 15:   Structure of controlling variables/ratios[665]

---

[647]   Abbreviation for Economic Value Added.
[648]   Abbreviation for Net Operating Profit After Taxes.
[649]   Cf. *Stewart* (1991) and *Weber* (2004), p. 250.
[650]   Cf. *Kuhner/Maltry* (2006), pp. 75.
[651]   Cf. *Schultze* (2003b), p. 462 and *Ballwieser* (2004), p. 187.
[652]   Abbreviation for Cost Income Ratio.
[653]   Cf. *Schierenbeck* (2001a), p. 422, p. 437.
[654]   Abbreviation for Return On Equity.
[655]   Cf. *Schierenbeck* (1998), pp. 64 and *Schierenbeck* (2001a), p. 431.
[656]   Cf. *Weber* (2004), p. 246.
[657]   Abbreviation for Balance Sheet.
[658]   Cf. *Schierenbeck* (2001a), pp. 305.
[659]   A full cost approach is done in *Frère/Reuse* (2006), p. 488.
[660]   Abbreviation for Contribution Margin.
[661]   Cf. *Kaplan/Norton* (1992), pp. 71 and *Kaplan/Norton* (1997), pp. 23.
[662]   Cf. *Kaninke/Wiedemann* (n.Y.), p. 3.
[663]   Cf. *Propach/Reuse* (2005), p. 440.
[664]   Cf. *Kaplan/Norton* (1997), pp. 23.
[665]   Author's own table based on the survey.

The banks were asked to describe the usage and importance of these ratios. But the above mentioned categorization was not given in order not to influence the answers of the banks. At first, the usage of the ratios is analyzed, independently from the valuation:

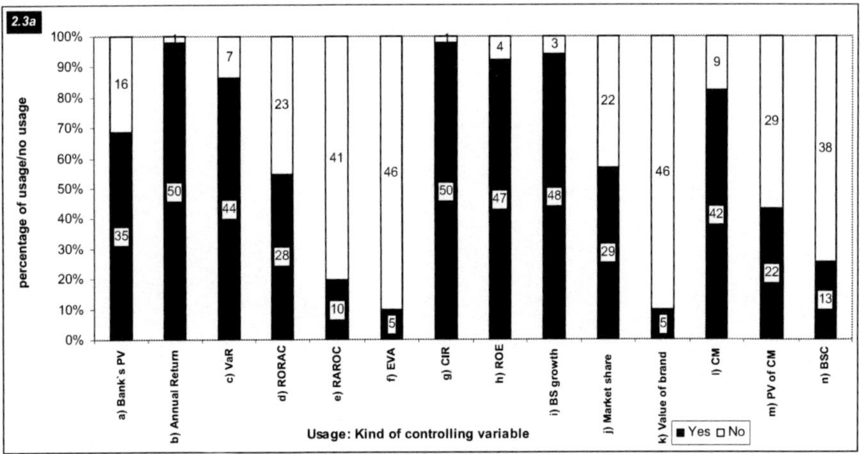

Figure 18:   **Usage of controlling variables, n = 51**[666]

The result is disappointing. The CIR, ROE, annual return and the growth of balance sheet are the top four used variables – all of them are rather periodically oriented and have not much to do with shareholder value. The only positive aspect is that the VaR is the 5th value mentioned. However, the combination of risk and return often is not done in the German banking sector, as EVA, RORAC and RAROC are not used very often. The impulse for the corporate evaluation aspect is that real shareholder value management is not done – and thus the necessity of an evaluation is not given.

This is supported by the average grade the banks gave to the variables:

---

[666] Author's own figure referring to the above mentioned sources and the survey.

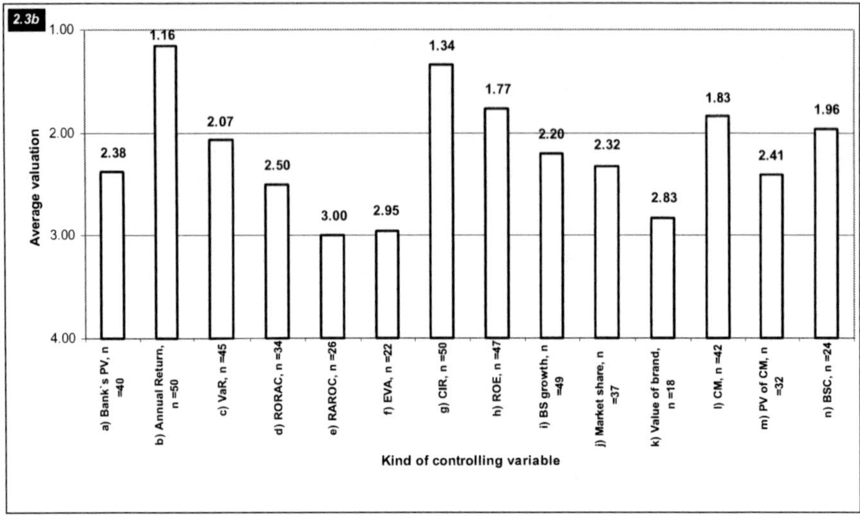

Figure 19:   Average grade of controlling variables, n = 51[667]

Annual return, CIR and ROE get the best marks. RAROC as the best approach in theory gets the worst mark with a 3.00. Further, the intangible aspects as for example the value of a brand get a very low importance. This shows that banks have not recognized that their brand may lead to real shareholder value.

Combining usage of the variables and the valuation is interesting again. The average usage of periodic and value-oriented numbers are aggregated. This leads to table 16:

Kind of Variable	Cumulated average usage		Average valuation
	Yes	No	
Periodic variables (5)	92.94%	7.06%	1.65
Shareholder Value (9)	41.61%	58.39%	2.44

Table 16:   Usage and valuation of controlling variables, n = 51[668]

On the one hand, German banks use the given periodic variables on average in 93% and give them an average degree of 1.65. On the other hand, only 42% of the shareholder value-

---

[667] Author's own figure based on the survey. The ratio n differs in relation to the valued variable as not all banks valued every ratio.

[668] Author's own table based on the survey. PV is an abbreviation for Present Value.

oriented numbers are in use in practice. The grade given is 2.44. This visualizes the inherently and not directly mentioned mentality. Many banks say that they do shareholder value management. Taking a closer look leads to the result that the real management does not consist of shareholder value management. This significant difference would not come up, if shareholder value was practiced in German banks. This can be complemented with a last cross check. Combining question 2.2 and 2.3a leads to the result that 25 of 40 banks that optimize their income statement use the present value of the bank[669]. So, both controlling mentalities are represented in the German banking sector – but none is transferred into practice consequently.

Summarizing the main results of section 2 of the questionnaire leads to the following aspects: Shareholder value is in fact not famous in German banks, even though the first view might have led to other results. Therefore, the circumstances for corporate evaluation in the German banking sector are not good. The necessity has not been seen yet by German banks.

3.3.3 Section 3: Question according to Corporate Evaluation

Section 3 as the "heart" of the questionnaire analyzes the usage and the name recognition of the corporate evaluation methods explained above[670]. Question 3.1 asked whether the companies know the approaches. This is shown in the following figure:

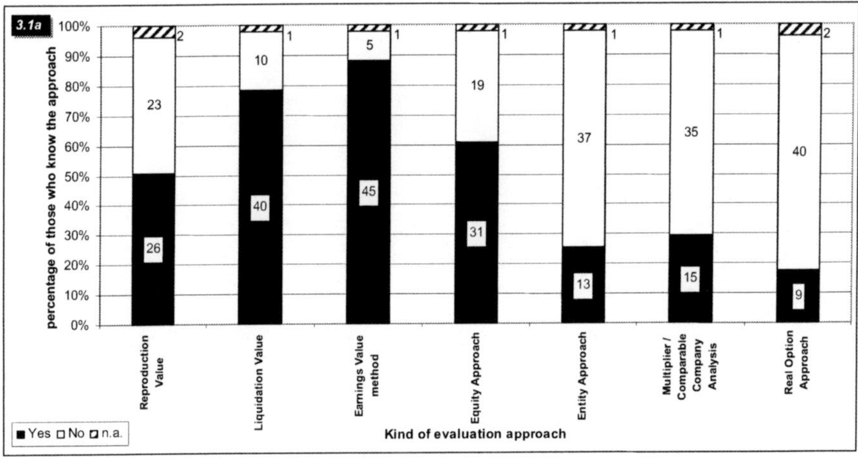

Figure 20:   **Name recognition of evaluation approaches, n = 51[671]**

---

[669]   Cf. questions 2.2, 2.3 and figure 17.
[670]   Cf. section 2.2.
[671]   Author's own figure based on the survey. n.a. = no answer.

The earnings value method is known in more than 80% of the banks. The second famous approach is the liquidation approach. On the one hand, this surprises, as theory has shown that this method is not optimal to value a company[672]. But on the other hand it has to be stated that evaluating the bank's value by a liquidation method is quite simple. It is disappointing that the multiplier approach is only known in 15 banks. Further, the equity approach is only at number three, even though theory has shown that it is the best approach for valuing banks. The low presence of the real option approach is not surprising. In a traditional sector like banking, this approach is not used very often.

The majority mentions the earnings value approach. But how do the answerers value it? This was quantified in the second part of question 3.1[673]. The banks were asked to give marks from 1 (best) to 4 (worst). It was intention that no middle category could be chosen in order to get clearer results. Figure 21 visualizes the results:

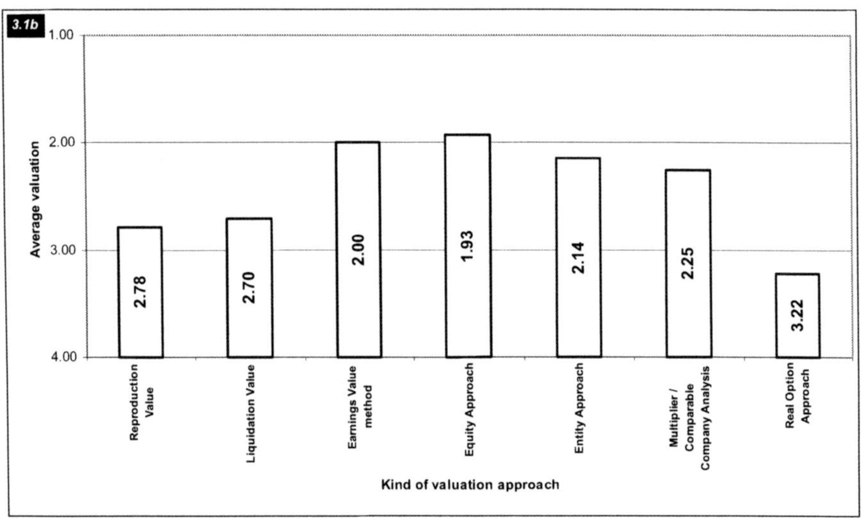

Figure 21:   Valuation of the approaches, n = 51[674]

The marks given show quite a different result. The equity approach is valued more favourably than the earnings value approach, even though the number of those who know the earnings

---

[672] Cf. section 2.2.1.

[673] Only those who know the approach were asked to value it. Sometimes, no valuation was given; sometimes a valuation was given without knowing the approach. As it seems that the answerers missed up "usage" with "knowledge", all answers in this part were counted, independent from the first part of question 3.1.

[674] Author's own figure based on the survey. n differs in relation to the valued variable as not all banks valued every approach.

value approach is higher. It is interesting that the entity approaches get such a good mark, as it is not useful for banks[675]. This might have two reasons: On the one hand, the question was not specialized on the banking sector. In other sectors, the entity approach might be useful. On the other hand, only one bank[676] recognized and mentioned that this approach is not optimal for banks. The author expected more of those comments. This is another hint that most of the German banks do not concentrate on corporate evaluation.

Real option approach, reproduction and liquidation approach got relatively bad marks. So the best approaches in theory get the best marks in practice – with the exception of the entity approach. This general result has to be treated as positive.

Question 3.2 deals with the central aspect of the survey: does the bank evaluate its own value? The result can be summarized as follows:

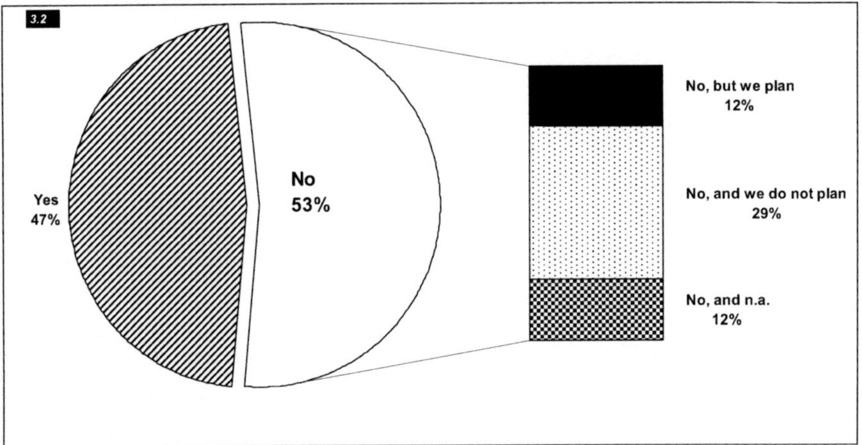

Figure 22:   **Evaluation of the own value, n = 51**[677]

About half of the banks evaluate their own value. This has to be considered positive. Even if a shareholder value-oriented management often is not implemented in the core processes[678], the prerequisites were created. Adding the 12% of those that plan to evaluate their own value leads to a contingent of 59%. Corporate evaluation is more important in the German banking sector than the first questions might have indicated – but the development is at its beginning. Analyzing the 47% positive answers according to the bank type leads to the following result:

---

[675] Cf. section 2.3.1.3.
[676] Bank No. 3, a big bank.
[677] Author's own figure based on the survey.
[678] Cf. section 3.3.2.

Kind of Bank	Number answered	Number with evaluation	Percentage
Big Bank	2	2	100.00%
Bank	7	3	42.86%
Geno	21	12	57.14%
Geno special.	3		
Mortgage Bank	2	1	50.00%
Savings Bank	16	6	37.50%
Sum	**51**	**24**	**47.06%**

Table 17:   Evaluation of the own value according to the bank type[679]

The two big banks evaluate their own value. This is quite logical, as they are stock-listed and thus have to fulfill other criteria. Private banks show a ratio of about 50%. The rate of the Genos is a bit higher, 12 of 21 evaluate their own value. The savings bank sector shows a lower result as only 6 of 16 banks evaluate the corporate value.

The result of 47% is fairly good, but further improvement is still possible. As an integrated bank controlling requires the value of a bank[680], those banks which say "no" now will probably evaluate their value in the future. Another aspect has to be mentioned. Several methods of evaluating the risk covering mass exist in practice. Since the implementation of the MaRisk[681], this has to be done by German banks[682]. If the models of risk covering mass evaluation are based on a present value approach[683], parts of them can be used for a corporate evaluation as well. Perhaps, banks do not know that they can recycle these aspects – and that they do a kind of corporate evaluation in practice.

As from now, sector 3 had to be answered only by those 24 banks that evaluate their value. Question 3.3 asked, for how many years the own value was quantified.

---

[679] Author's own table based on the survey. Without clearing houses as no clearing house answered the questionnaire.
[680] Cf. *Thaller* (2005), p. 144.
[681] Abbreviation for Mindestanforderungen an das Risikomanagement.
[682] Cf. *BaFin* (2005a), AT 4.1.
[683] As done in *Reuse* (2006), pp. 427.

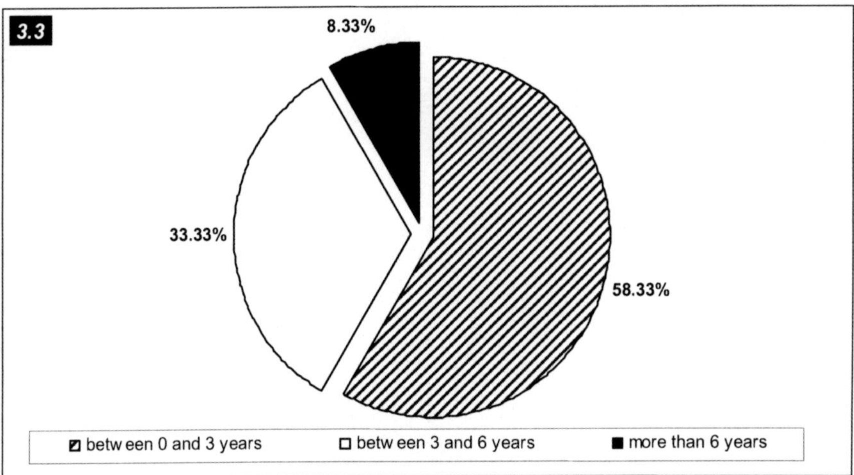

Figure 23:   Age of corporate evaluation, n = 24[684]

The majority of 58% mentioned a time frame of 0 – 3 years. This again leads to the conclusion that methodology and theory have just established and that extensions will occur in the future. Only 2 companies have evaluated their own value for more than 6 years[685]. These companies have an integrated bank controlling and the most important controlling method is the present value[686]. A qualitative but not quantitative significant thesis is that quantifying the own value will lead to an implicit shareholder value management during time.

The next question deals with the frequency of corporate evaluation. This is shown in figure 24:

---

[684] Author's own figure referring to the survey.
[685] Including one big bank and one Geno.
[686] Cf. questions 2.1 and 2.2, concerning bank 3 and 611.

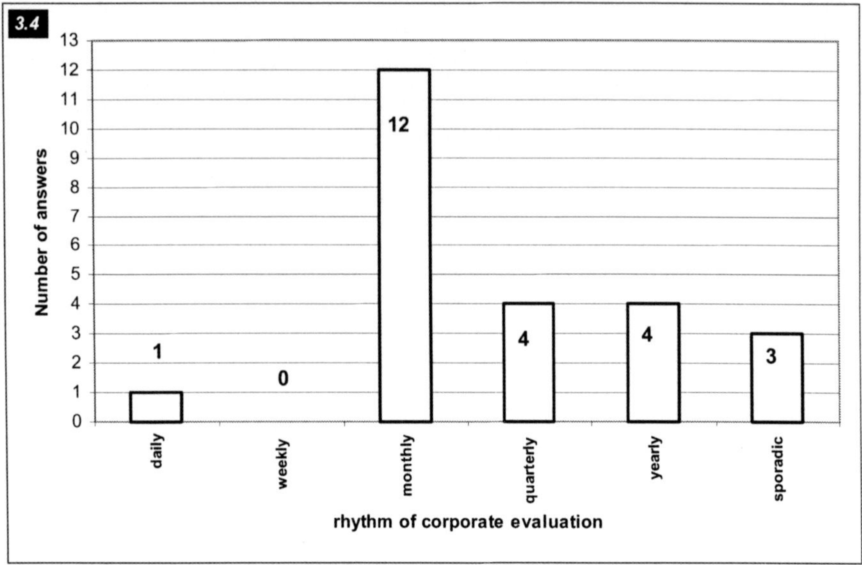

Figure 24:   Frequency of corporate evaluation, n = 24[687]

The result is interesting. About 12 of the 24 banks that evaluate their value (50%) do this monthly. This leads to two conclusions. First: those banks that evaluate their own value do it very thoroughly. Second, the method of corporate evaluation seems to be integrated into a monthly process. This may be the risk cover mass evaluation process. So implicitly banks do corporate evaluation – perhaps without knowing it.

This is verified by question 3.5 which asked for the reason for the corporate evaluation. The result is unequivocal:

---

[687] Author's own figure referring to the survey.

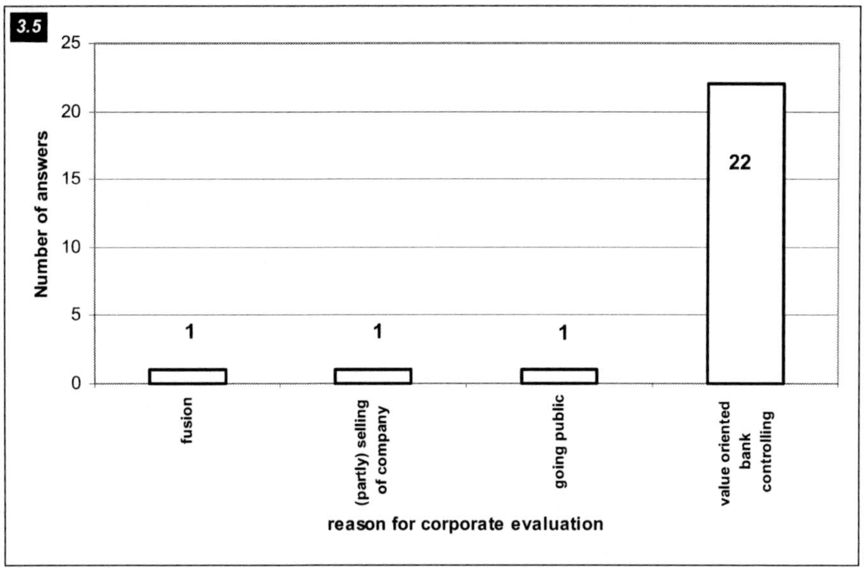

Figure 25:   Reasons for corporate evaluation, n = 24[688]

In total, 22 banks use the value for the value-oriented bank controlling. This does not fit the questions in sector 2, in which the priority of management was rather defined as optimizing the income statement. The answers, however, lead to the conclusion that a shareholder value management is under construction. At least in a second controlling workflow, the present value-oriented ideas become famous. Further, the approaches for a bank evaluation seem to be used implicitly.

Question 3.6 deals with the used approach. All theoretical approaches[689] that were asked in question 3.1 are available. The result can be shown as follows:

---

[688]   Author's own figure based on the survey. 24 banks gave 25 answers as double answers were possible.
[689]   Cf. section 2.2.

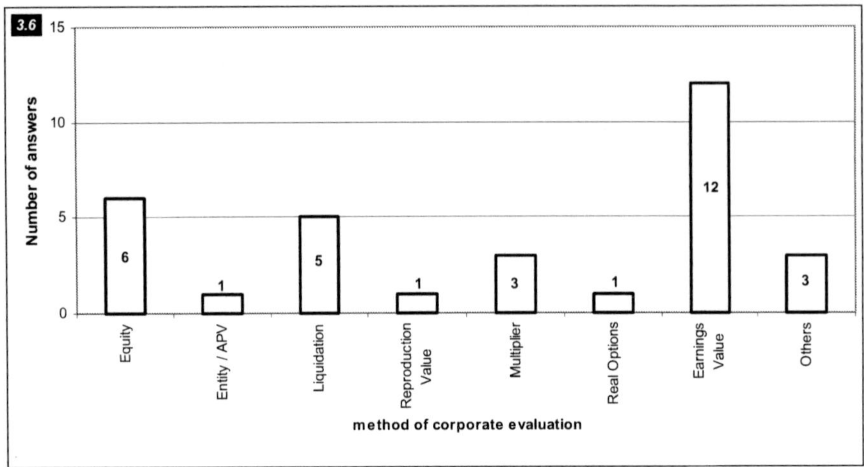

Figure 26:   Used approach for corporate evaluation, n = 24[690]

The most often used approaches are the earnings value method and the equity approach. This is consistent with the theoretical conclusion that these approaches fit best to a bank. The entity approach was only used once – so the aspect that it is normally not useful for banks is has been proven in practice as well. It is wondering at a first glance that the liquidation approach is used in 5 banks. This has to be differentiated. It appears that not every bank was able to structure its approach into the right category. Even the three "other" approaches show aspects of the equity approach. Two of them mention the present value[691]. Inherently, the usage of an equity approach is much higher than expected.

Question 3.7 asked for the implementation of intangible assets[692]. The result was very disappointing. Only one bank implements this factor into its evaluation, the others do not. This shows that the methods of corporate evaluation in the German banking sector just focus on monetary aspects. Immaterial hidden reserves are not considered, so the real value of the banks is not quantified. This leads to a marketing problem of German banks. Their brand name is very high, even in the savings bank pillar[693], but the banks are not able to communicate this in the right way. In the author's opinion, this lack of information led to the high merger rates in the past.

---

[690] Author's own figure based on the survey. 24 banks gave 32 answers, as double answers were possible.
[691] Banks 410 and 611.
[692] A structure of intangible assets can be found in *Aschoff* (1978), p. 40 and *Scholz* (2004), p. 24.
[693] For the value of "Sparkasse" cf. *Schulz/Weissenberger* (2003), p. 5; *Feldmann* (2004) and *Drost/Telgheder* (2006).

Question 3.8 as the last point of this sector deals with the process of the gathered information. Does management base any decisions on the results or not? This is shown in figure 27:

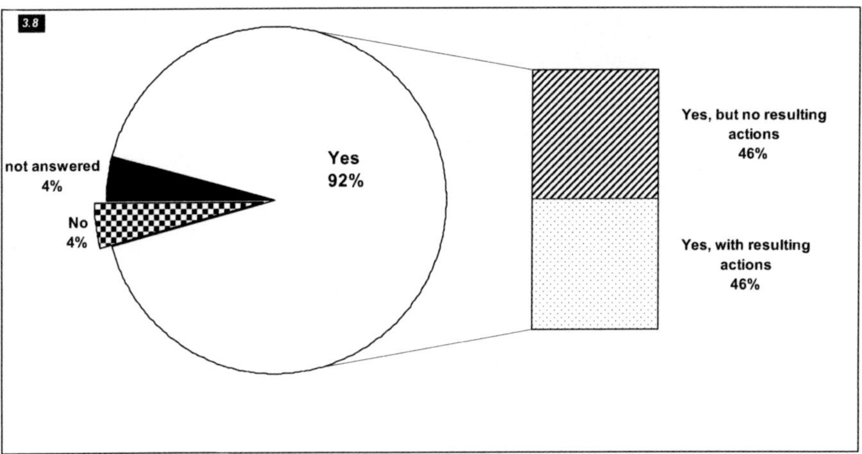

Figure 27:   Knowledge about the results, n = 24[694]

The result is positive. 92% of the banks state that the management knows about the results – and even 46% base their decisions on these results. Shareholder value based management seems to be under construction and in the testing phase. It will increase fast in the future.

Accordingly, the main information coming out of sector 3 is that corporate evaluation in the German banking sector is making progress. Many banks seem to use the right tools implicitly and the very young evaluation process will extend in the future.

3.3.4 Section 4: Individual Corporate Evaluation

The main gimmick of the questionnaire was that banks can get an individual corporate evaluation. The data required for this is difficult to evaluate and often top secret. So, it would be interesting to see, how many of the interviewees want to have an individual evaluation:

---

[694] Author's own figure referring to the survey.

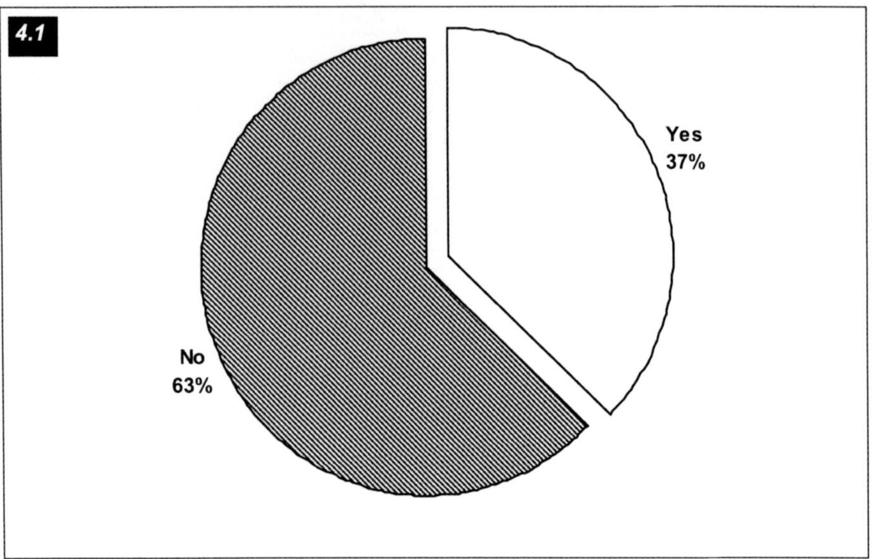

Figure 28:   Interest in an individual corporate evaluation, n = 51[695]

In total, 19 banks (37%) wanted to have such an evaluation. Only 5 of them do this already on their own. Hence, the demand for a corporate evaluation tool is very high in the market. The detailed analysis of the data is not done here, as section 5 of this dissertation quantifies the values of the banks according to the given data[696].

3.3.5 Section 5: Final Amendments

The last three questions deal with general aspects. First, the additional comments have to be mentioned[697]. Free amendments are done very seldom; just 7 comments could be stated[698]. One interviewee was enthusiastic about the questions because of the economic knowledge[699]. Another bank mentioned that more questions according to intangible assets should be done[700]. Other constructive comments were not made.

The last two questions deal with the possibility of mentioning the name of the bank[701] and the wish to get the results[702]. Only 4 banks agreed to mention the names. One of these 4 banks

---

[695] Author's own figure based on the survey.
[696] Cf. section 5.
[697] Cf. question 5.3.
[698] Cf. question 4.2.
[699] Bank 381.
[700] Bank 750.
[701] Cf. question 5.2.
[702] Cf. question 5.3.

wanted to have an individual corporate evaluation. This supports the argumentation that banks offered sensible data – getting so much responses has to be treated as a success. Further, 40 of 51 banks (78%) want to have the results of the survey. This is a high ratio. The conclusion is that those banks that answered the survey are very interested in this topic.

3.4 Extended Analysis

3.4.1 Comparison with Existing Surveys

The survey of the author was surely not the first one done in the German banking sector. Several others have been done, but they were often created for another purpose.

The most important survey was created by the **BaFin**[703] in September 2005[704]. This survey was done in the German banking sector in order to quantify the interest rate risk of the yield book. The advantage is that the BaFin asked detailed questions according to the yield book. As a wish of the BaFin has a nearly obligatory character, 1,202 of the 2,052 addressed banks[705], that is 58.6%, answered the questionnaire[706]. The empirical quantification of the cash flows was done in this survey[707]. Gliding averages for the variable liability side are evaluated empirically[708]. As the main purpose was to measure the risk of maturity transformation, only the parameters for the value of the yield book and the sensitivity according to interest rate shocks were discussed, but not the value of the yield book itself. Nevertheless, the parameters for the gliding averages will be used in section 5.

The **DSGV** goes one step further. Twice a year, a so called present value-oriented comparison in the savings bank sector is done. Every savings bank has to report its yield book cash flow and present value. The DSGV compares them and evaluates the risk of the maturity transformation. Gliding averages are set by using the parameters of each individual savings bank. The advantage is that the present value of a yield book is reported by using a standardized yield book definition. The disadvantage is that no statements according to other parameters are done and that the comparison is restricted to the yield book. [709]

Baetge/Heumann did a current survey in 2006 that discusses the reporting duties according to shareholder value-oriented numbers[710]. The main result is that investors demand a value-

---

[703] Abbreviation for Bundesanstalt für Finanzdienstleistungen.

[704] Cf. *BaFin* (2006).

[705] Nearly the same target group as used in the author's survey.

[706] Cf. *BaFin* (2006), p. 2, p. 4.

[707] For the detailed structure of the evaluation cf. *BaFin* (2005b) and *BaFin* (2005c).

[708] Cf. *BaFin* (2006), p. 8.

[709] Own argumentation, as only internal sources could be mentioned.

[710] Cf. *Baetge/Heumann* (2006), pp. 345 – 350.

oriented controlling in order to quantify the value of the company. These aspects are discussed in a very orderly and structured manner. But this survey was not restricted to banks. The return ratio of 11.5% shows[711] that even professional surveys do not receive very high return ratios.

Höhmann did a study in 1998 which was rather an examination than a survey[712]. He examined the annual reports of 17 stock-listed German banks and did a linear extrapolation of the historical annual reports in order to prognosticate the annual surplus of the future. The results seemed to be reliable, the coefficient of determination r^2 was nearly always higher than 0.70[713].

Ernst & Young asked German banks in 1996 according to the implementation of shareholder value[714]. As mentioned above, 80% of the banks refused to answer the survey. The concept was considered as very critical in German banks in 1996[715].

In 2003, **Grimmer** did an analysis of the status quo of controlling in the banking sector[716], in which the dualism of optimizing the income statement and present value was analyzed. In 2003, the shareholder value was worth less then profitability or earnings[717]. This result fits to the actual survey. Even the importance of earnings, balance sheet growth and CIR was the same as in the author's survey[718]. This proves again that the author's study is representative. Grimmer's work was very structured and exact according to the value-oriented numbers/ratios, but questions according to the corporate evaluation were not given, as the main purpose was another one.

The author's survey thus shows several new aspects that have not been raised in the past in this combination:
- Connecting value-oriented numbers with the real evaluation of the bank's value.
- Asking for the name recognition of several corporate evaluation approaches.
- Quantifying the usage in the German banking sector.
- Offering an individual corporate evaluation[719].

Accordingly, this survey leads to additional information compared to the existing surveys or investigations.

---

[711] Cf. *Baetge/Heumann* (2006), pp. 348.
[712] Cf. *Höhmann* (1998), p. 129, p. 140.
[713] Cf. *Höhmann* (1998), pp. 180.
[714] Cf. *Ernst & Young* (1997).
[715] Discussed in *Kirsten* (2000), pp. 49.
[716] Not restricted to the German banking sector, cf. *Grimmer* (2003), pp. 199.
[717] Cf. *Grimmer* (2003), p. 202.
[718] Cf. *Grimmer* (2003), p. 205.
[719] Done in section 5.

3.4.2 Scoring Model for the Quality of Value Based Management

Last, a qualitative scoring model should be set up that values the quality of corporate evaluation respectively the value-oriented bank controlling. Therefore, several questions of the survey are scored with different numbers. This is shown in the following table:

Question		Valuation		Explanation
2.1	Integrated bank controlling	Yes Partly No	4 2 0	An integrated bank controlling is an important factor for a shareholder value-oriented controlling. The more importance an integrated bank controlling has, the better a shareholder value-oriented management is implemented. Indirectly, a necessity for corporate evaluation is given.
2.2	Income statement vs. present value	Present value IS[720]	8 0	Shareholder value management wants sustainable growth of the company's value, not only a high annual surplus. In order to prevent short term oriented management, the values 0 and 8 are given.
2.3	Usage of controlling numbers *a) – n)* *9 of 14*	Yes No *Per number*	2 0	The more value-oriented controlling numbers are in use, the better it is for a corporate evaluation. So the usage of a shareholder value-oriented number is scored with a 2. In sum, 18 points are possible.
3.2	Evaluating the value	Yes we will No	8 2 0	The evaluation of the own value is the central question. So it is scored with 8. A 2 is given, if it is planned to do an evaluation.
3.3	Age of evaluation	0 – 3 Y 3 – 6 Y > 6 Y	1 2 4	The longer an evaluation is done, the higher the experience and the added value for the controlling are. As shown above, the two companies with more than 6 years show value-oriented numbers.
3.4	Frequency	Daily Weekly monthly quarterly yearly sporadic	6 5 4 3 2 1	The more often the value is evaluated, the better it is. So the scores beside are given.
3.5	Reason	VBM[721] Rest	4 0	If the evaluation is done voluntarily, the only reason can be a value based management. Therefore a 4 is given.
3.6	Approach	Equity Entity Liquid. Reproduction CCA Real Option Earnings val. others	8 2 2 2 6 2 8 6	As equity and earnings value are those which fit best to a bank, an 8 is given for them. Suboptimal approaches were valued with 2 – 6. Their usage is added, so that 36 points are available for this question.
3.7	Intangible assets	Yes No	6 0	Whenever the implementation of intangible assets is done, a real shareholder value-oriented management exists. So the existence of such an approach is valued with 6.
3.8	Information	Nice to know Deciding Not known	2 4 0	The evaluation of a bank's value only makes sense, if the management acts on the basis of this information. So the evaluation on the left side is defined.
Sum[722]			98	

Table 18:   **Definition of the scoring model**[723]

---

[720] Abbreviation for Income Statement.
[721] Abbreviation for Value Based Management.
[722] Question 3.6 is added completely.
[723] Author's own table.

These scores can only be an indicator of a qualitative measurement of the quality of the management. An application of these scorings on the sample leads to the following results:

Place	Bank No	Scoring	Kind of bank	Employees	Balance Sheet Sum
1	3	68	Big Bank	more than 3,000	more than 25,000
2	750	64	Geno	between 250 and 500	between 1,000 and 2,500
3	173	56	Mortgage Bank	between 0 and 100	more than 25,000
4	611	54	Geno	between 100 and 250	between 500 and 1,000
5	449	49	Geno	between 500 and 1,000	between 2,500 and 5,000
6	381	46	Savings Bank	between 500 and 1,000	between 2,500 and 5,000
7	700	45	Geno	between 100 and 250	between 500 and 1,000
8	191	43	Big Bank	more than 3,000	more than 25,000
9	616	43	Geno	between 500 and 1,000	between 5,000 and 10,000
10	400	42	Savings Bank	between 1,000 and 2,000	between 5,000 and 10,000
11	211	41	Savings Bank	between 250 and 500	between 1,000 and 2,500
12	489	41	Geno	between 0 and 100	between 0 and 500
13	476	40	Geno	between 0 and 100	between 0 and 500
14	637	39	Geno	between 0 and 100	between 0 and 500
15	118	38	Bank	between 100 and 250	between 1,000 and 2,500
16	124	38	Bank	between 100 and 250	between 1,000 and 2,500
17	346	38	Savings Bank	between 250 and 500	between 2,500 and 5,000
18	675	38	Geno	between 0 and 100	between 0 and 500
19	684	36	Geno	between 0 and 100	between 0 and 500
20	338	33	Savings Bank	between 500 and 1,000	between 2,500 and 5,000
21	410	33	Savings Bank	between 500 and 1,000	between 2,500 and 5,000
22	591	31	Geno	between 100 and 250	between 0 and 500
23	607	31	Geno	between 0 and 100	between 0 and 500
24	333	28	Savings Bank	between 1,000 and 2,000	between 5,000 and 10,000
25	417	26	Savings Bank	between 1,000 and 2,000	between 5,000 and 10,000
26	657	24	Geno	between 250 and 500	between 1,000 and 2,500
27	739	22	Geno	between 100 and 250	between 500 and 1,000
28	488	20	Geno	between 100 and 250	between 0 and 500
29	10	18	Bank	between 0 and 100	between 500 and 1,000
30	487	18	Geno	between 100 and 250	between 0 and 500
31	495	18	Geno	between 0 and 100	between 0 and 500
32	551	18	Geno	between 0 and 100	between 0 and 500
33	159	16	Geno special.	between 0 and 100	between 0 and 500
34	388	16	Savings Bank	between 100 and 250	between 500 and 1,000
35	695	16	Geno	between 0 and 100	between 0 and 500
36	710	16	Geno	between 100 and 250	between 0 and 500
37	51	14	Bank	between 1,000 and 2,000	more than 25,000
38	100	14	Bank	between 2,000 and 3,000	between 5,000 and 10,000
39	268	14	Savings Bank	between 250 and 500	between 1,000 and 2,500
40	311	14	Savings Bank	between 500 and 1,000	between 1,000 and 2,500
41	11	12	Bank	between 100 and 250	between 500 and 1,000
42	285	12	Savings Bank	between 250 and 500	between 1,000 and 2,500
43	398	12	Savings Bank	between 2,000 and 3,000	between 10,000 and 25,000
44	621	12	Geno	between 100 and 250	between 1,000 and 2,500
45	395	10	Savings Bank	between 100 and 250	between 500 and 1,000
46	164	8	Geno special.	between 0 and 100	between 0 and 500
47	185	8	Mortgage Bank	between 100 and 250	between 10,000 and 25,000
48	277	8	Savings Bank	between 1,000 and 2,000	between 5,000 and 10,000
49	22	6	Bank	between 0 and 100	between 0 and 500
50	160	6	Geno special.	n.a.	between 0 and 500
51	365	6	[anonymous]	between 0 and 100	between 0 and 500

Figure 29:   **Scoring point values, n = 51**[724]

---

[724]   Author's own figure based on the results of the scoring model.

The scoring point values show different results. The first place belongs to one of the two big banks. As this bank is stock listed in the DAX[725], its profile offered many aspects that are valued with high scoring points. The second big bank is at rank 8. This is consistent, as the bank does not really quantify its own value – even not per share price.

In total, shareholder value based management is not very famous in Germany. As the maximal scoring point value is 98, the best bank only reached 68 points and the average is about 27. However, it is surprising that small Genos and savings banks are amongst the top 10. The size seems to have no influence on the corporate evaluation accordingly. This is shown at the example of the rather small Genos, which evaluate their value most often[726].

The scoring system combines the "hard" corporate evaluation factors with the "soft" shareholder value aspects. It cannot be a quantitatively proven system, but the qualitative results seem to be reliable. One of the big banks is number 1, and those banks that show weaknesses in bank controlling have a low scoring. Therefore, this model is a first judgment tool, to score the quality of value based management in German banks. It can be used to interpret, whether the management of a bank is value-oriented or not.

3.5 Conclusions from the Survey

3.5.1 Summing up the Main Results of the Questionnaire

In a qualitative way, the survey is representative, as proven by many argumentations. The results can be summarized as follows:

On the one hand, it has been shown that shareholder value-oriented management is not yet famous in the German banking sector. Even though many banks say that they do so, they act periodically. Further, the usage of controlling variables focuses on the "old" periodic variables. The same can be stated for to the given marks. Periodic variables get better marks than value-oriented ones. Value based management is not really accepted in practice.

On the other hand, the knowledge about the corporate evaluation approaches seems to be there, even though a misunderstanding according to the entity approach might exist. The positive aspect is that despite of a differing controlling, many banks evaluate their own value. As this tendency is very young, the outlook for the next years is positive. Many banks will switch from the classical periodic view to the shareholder value approach. Last, the survey led to

---

[725] Abbreviation for Deutscher Aktienindex.
[726] Cf. section 3.3.3, table 17.

high interest. Many banks want to have the results – and 19 of 51 banks want to have an individual corporate evaluation.

3.5.2 Practical Impulses for a New Evaluation Model

Some aspects have to be discussed here. First, in some questions the risk cover mass was discussed indirectly[727]. Based on a present value approach the banks can quantify the present value of the assets in order to define, what risks can be taken[728]. Implicitly, the knowledge is there. Without knowing, many banks evaluate their own value. Techniques, methods and models are available in practice. As presented above, a new model for valuating a bank must be simple and known. The more parts of the model come from existing processes or systems, the more efficient and accepted the new model will be. So the demands on a new model are to use as much of the existing methods as possible and to keep it simple. Banks sometimes do not have the know-how even to distinguish between the kinds of approach. The easier a new approach is, the more easily it will be accepted.

---

[727] Cf. question 3.6.
[728] Cf. *Reuse* (2006), pp. 426.

4 Development of a New Corporate Evaluation Approach for Banks

4.1 The Main Idea of the Presented Approach

The results of the survey have shown that corporate evaluation in the German banking sector is not very famous. Even classically existing methods are not in use in most of the banks[729]. The reason for this is often high complexity of the approaches and the fact that shareholder value is not very important for non-stock listed companies[730].

An approach that will be accepted by the banks has to be simple. A big advantage would be, if at least parts of the model were used in practice, perhaps for another purpose. The main idea of this individualized approach of a bank evaluation is as simple as brilliant: Why not take existing parts of methods or models that are used for bank controlling? Combining and adjusting them would lead to a new model of corporate evaluation. Therefore, the evaluation of a new model has to be done as follows: First, the existing models or methods that could be used have to be defined. In the second step, they have to be modified and arranged. Last, all additional parts that are really new have to be defined and put together into a new model.

The model shall be as simple as possible. As shown above[731] the complexity will be low, if not all cash flows are considered and the discounting factor is low. The central methodical assumption is: every additional expected earning that can be generated has to be discounted with a risk-adjusted yield as it is insecure. The best idea is to implement only those cash flows that are nearly risk free or risk adjusted. As a consequence, the discounting factor is nearly risk free as well and the CAPM, which was criticized previously[732] can be avoided in a very elegant way.

---

[729] Cf. section 3.3.3.
[730] Cf. section 3.3.
[731] Cf. section 2.3.4.
[732] Cf. sections 2.3.2 and 2.3.3.

4.2 Definition of the Model

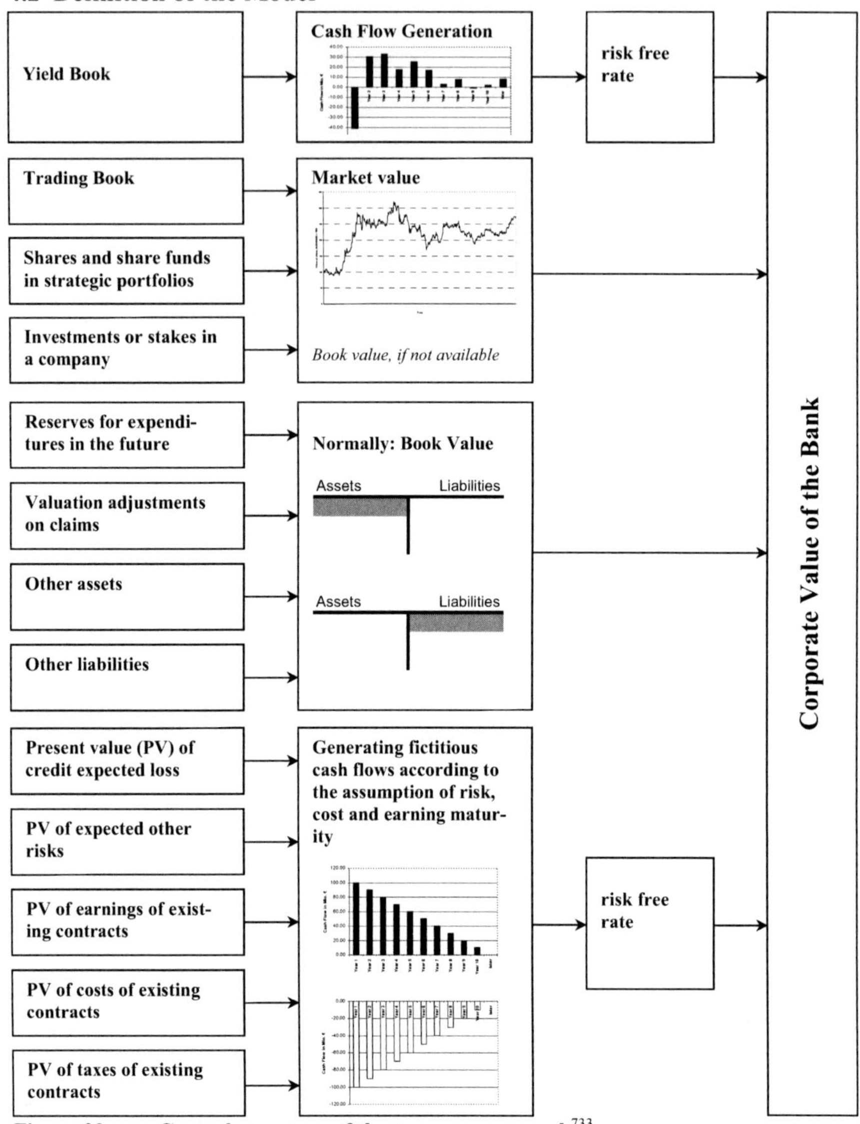

Figure 30:   Central structure of the treasury approach[733]

---

[733] Author's own figure, expanding the main ideas of *Goebel/Schumacher/Sievi* (1997), p. 389; *Behr/Dörner* (2001), p. 24; *Fingerhut* (2001), p. 14; *Schierenbeck* (2001b), p. 18; *Parchert/Markus* (2002), p. 22, p. 44; *Weinzirl* (2002), pp. 95; *Bimmler/Mönke* (2003), p. 31 – 33; *Friedag/Klassen/Robers* (2003), p. 36; *Biehsmann* (2004), p. 11; *Gröning* (2004), pp. 343; *Dietzel* (2005), pp. 7; *Giesecke/Kühne* (2005), pp. 134; *Thaller* (2005), pp. 144 – 152; *Böhm-Dries* (2006), p. 6; *Dauber/Pfeifer* (2006), pp. 232; *Hortmann/Seide* (2006), p. 317; *Münchow/Biehsmann* (2006), p. 8, p. 24 and *Reuse* (2006), p. 428.

The idea of the used theoretical aspects is not really new. Several authors developed a present value-oriented risk covering mass model[734] implementing the market interest rate and the cash flow generation approaches[735]. The core aspect of the model is to use these central ideas and modify them. This new model is defined as the **treasury approach**. It can be set up as shown in figure 3.:

The idea is to divide a bank into several value centres, similar to what Behm[736] and Vettiger[737] suggest. The reason is that the market interest rate method presented above[738] and discussed in Schierenbeck[739] and Rolfes[740] offers the possibility of separating the margin of customer transfers from the maturity transformation[741]. All other approaches that do not offer this possibility, show wrong assumptions according to the author's opinion.

This approach follows the main argumentations offered above[742]. They can be summarized as follows:

1. Only the **existing contracted transfers** are considered[743].

2. No new deals with customers, no treasury results and no results of the trading book are implemented in this approach, as everybody else can generate them without having to buy the bank[744].

3. According to this, only the costs and other earnings deriving from existing transfers are transformed into cash flows and are discounted[745]. Taking the total value of all costs and earnings of the future would be too much.

4. As a consequence, only risk free cash flows exist. They can be discounted at a risk free rate.

---

[734] Cf. *Goebel/Schumacher/Sievi* (1997), p. 389; *Behr/Dörner* (2001), p. 24; *Fingerhut* (2001), p. 14; *Schierenbeck* (2001b), p. 18; *Parchert/Markus* (2002), p. 22, p. 44; *Weinzirl* (2002), pp. 95; *Bimmler/Mönke* (2003), p. 31 – 33; *Friedag/Klassen/Robers* (2003), p. 36; *Biehsmann* (2004), p. 11; *Gröning* (2004), pp. 343; *Dietzel* (2005), pp. 7; *Giesecke/Kühne* (2005), pp. 134; *Thaller* (2005), pp. 144 – 152; *Böhm-Dries* (2006), p. 6; *Dauber/Pfeifer* (2006), pp. 232; *Hortmann/Seide* (2006), p. 317; *Münchow/Biehsmann* (2006), p. 8, p. 24 and *Reuse* (2006), p. 428.

[735] Cf. section 4.1.2.1.

[736] Cf. *Behm* (1994), p. 59, pp. 83 – 85.

[737] Cf. *Vettiger* (1996), pp. 126 – 135.

[738] Cf. section 2.3.1.

[739] Cf. *Schierenbeck* (2001a), pp. 43, pp. 70.

[740] Cf. *Rolfes* (1999), p. 12 – 18, pp. 270.

[741] Cf. *Rolfes* (1999), p. 13.

[742] Cf. section 2.4.

[743] Cf. *Reuse* (2006), p. 427.

[744] In contrast to the approaches of a present value-oriented risk covering mass, cf. *Reuse* (2006), pp. 427.

[745] Cf. *Parchert/Markus* (2002), p. 22 and *Bimmler/Mönke* (2003), p. 31.

At last, adding all assets, liabilities, present value of costs, earnings and taxes could be defined as the present value of a bank. During the following sectors, the evaluation of these parts of a bank's value will be discussed in a more detailed way.

4.2.1 Yield Book

The most important part of a bank's balance sheet of is the so-called **yield book**[746]. It lists all parts of the balance sheet, on which a bank receives or pays interests[747]. This could be credits, bonds, current accounts, deposits, savings, emitted bonds or even derivate instruments[748]. All these transactions are transformed into cash flows[749].

4.2.1.1 Definition of Cash Flow

The most simple way is the most effective one: why not take the cash flows that could be derived from the market yield method? Every loan, bond, deposit and savings generate cash flows[750] which are much more exact than those that are derived from the profit and loss account[751]. Further, this evaluation is done for the strategic treasury management as well[752] – the requirement that existing controlling approaches should be integrated into the new model, is fulfilled. The result is that the present value of every financial asset can be quantified in a very sophisticated but easy and exact way. Normally, the exactness of cash flows in an earnings value method decreases over the considered time period[753]. However, when discounting the cash flows of all financial transfers that occur in the balance sheet, the exactness stays the same[754]. This may be visualized by the following figure, which represents the transactions of the example above[755]. In this fictitious example, a credit and an emitted bond will be transferred into cash flows. The credit and the bond may be due completely after 10 years. So the cash flows could be set up as follows:

---

[746] Cf. *Drosdzol/Hager* (2005), p. 124 and *Hortmann/Seide* (2006), p. 317.
[747] For example discussed in *Bellarz* (2002), p. 534; *Jakob* (2002), p. 340 and *Menninghaus* (2001), pp. 1148.
[748] Cf. *Hortmann/Seide* (2006), p. 317 and *Reuse* (2006), p. 409.
[749] Cf. *Everding/Meier* (2001), pp. 16 and *Wimmer* (2006), p. 317.
[750] Done in *Schierenbeck* (2001a), p. 109, p. 220.
[751] Cf. *Sonntag* (2001), pp. 113 – 114.
[752] Cf. *Reuse* (2006), pp. 407.
[753] Cf. *Börner/Lowis* (1997), pp. 100.
[754] Cf. *Vitt* (2002), p. 554.
[755] Cf. figure 5, section 2.3.1.1.

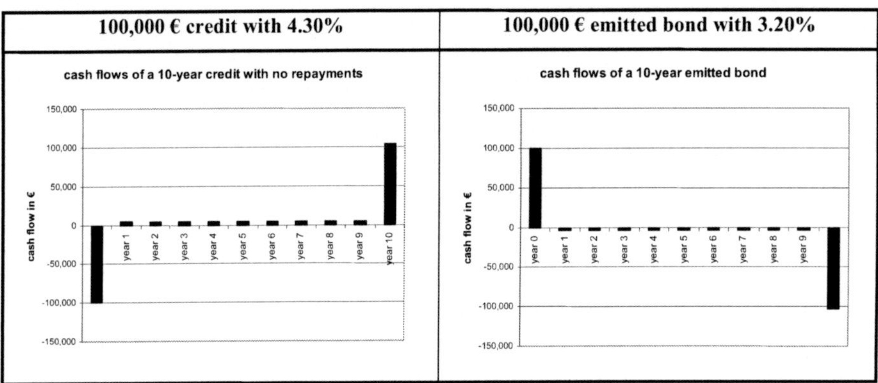

Figure 31:   **Cash flows of the loan and of the emitted bond**[756]

After the payout, the credit consists of 10+1 payment: 10 interest payments and the final redemption rate. The bond shows 10+1 cash flows as well: 10 interest payments, the last together with the repayment[757].

But the balance sheet consists of many positions that do not have an interest fixing. Examples are customer's savings, current deposits and liabilities on current accounts[758]. As a consequence, a fix cash flow cannot be evaluated. To solve this problem, fictitious cash flows have to be defined. Sievi evaluated a system that offered the possibilities to do this at the end of the nineties[759]. He called this the theory of a gliding average[760]. Variable positions at a certain moment result from transactions in the past. Savings of 10,000 Euro might have been deposited 10 years ago and might last 10 years. This happens every year. As consequence, savings would stay in the bank for different times, as the following figure shows:

---

[756] Author's own figure based on the argumentations of *Bauch* (1998), pp. 447 and *Weinzirl* (2002), pp. 92.

[757] Similar done in *Weinzirl* (2002), p. 92.

[758] Cf. *Hortmann/Seide* (2006), p. 318. Further, Schierenbeck structures these positions into several categories. Cf. *Schierenbeck* (2001a), p. 98, p. 109.

[759] Cf. *Sievi* (1999), pp. 31 and *Sievi* (n.Y. a), chapter 2 pp. 6. Widened for example in *Böttrich/ Drosdzol/Hager/Schleicher* (2004), pp. 28.

[760] Cf. *Sievi* (1995), pp. 224.

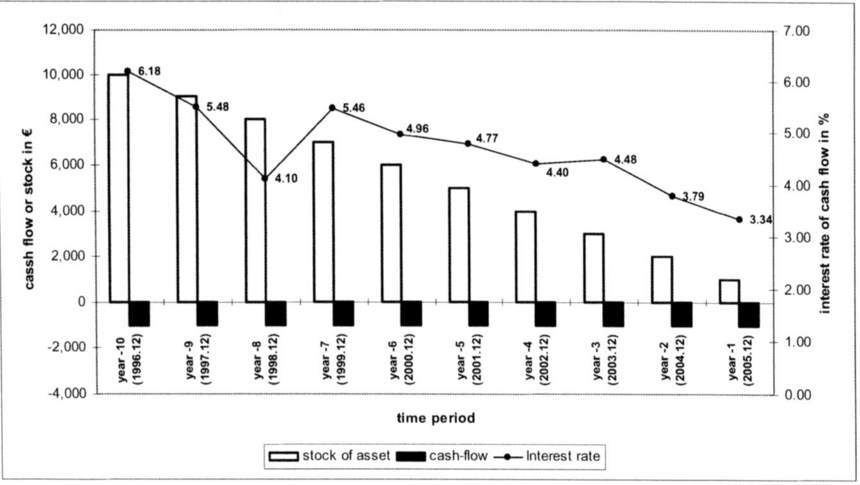

Figure 32:   Gliding 10Y-maturity mixing and the related cash flows 2005.12[761]

The first tranche rests one year in the balance sheet after having stayed 9 years, the corresponding market yield is 5.48%. The second cash flow lasts two years and has a market yield of 4.10% and so forth. The cash flows of such a position could be defined as described according to figure 31[762]. So if it is known, how long a product stays in the bank on average, the related cash flows can be generated. It is very important to point out that "staying" means leaving the money in the bank without wanting another interest rate[763]. Hence, the fictitious interest fixing is the period, on which a discounted interest margin could be calculated[764]. The related market rate for the net interest margin is the average of the above mentioned interest rates: 4.70%[765].

Thus, building up a cash flow implies a fictitious interest fixing. But how can the average lasting period of a product be defined? Sievi answers this, too. His theory is based on one assumption: even though the bank offers customers a variable interest rate, it is not changed very often. The savings are the best examples: even though the interest market has shown a high volatility in the past, the interest rates offered to the customers were always about one percent. Sievi's theory is that the less volatile an interest rate is, the longer the fictitious cash

---

[761] Author's own figure without interest rate cash flows based on *Rolfes* (1999), p. 255 and *Schierenbeck* (2001a), p. 106. For data cf. *Bundesbank* (2006c).
[762] A detailed example can be found in *Crecelius* (2006), pp. 266.
[763] Cf. *Sievi* (n.Y. a), chapter 2, p. 7.
[764] Cf. *Sievi* (1999), p. 32.
[765] Done similar in *Parchert/Markus* (2002), p. 26.

flows stay in the balance sheet and lead to a constant margin[766]. On the one hand, a bank changes the interest rate exactly at the point, at which the customer would close the transaction, if he did not get a better interest rate[767]. Many savings banks and Genos face this situation at the moment as the market is saturated. On the other hand, a bank wants to generate a constant interest margin[768]. Combining these two aspects, a complex mathematical algorithm[769] could be set up that tries to define the mixture of the gliding maturities, which would have led to a constant margin in the past[770]. The results of this algorithm at the example of the product "classical savings" are shown in the following figure. The product might consist of 100 €.

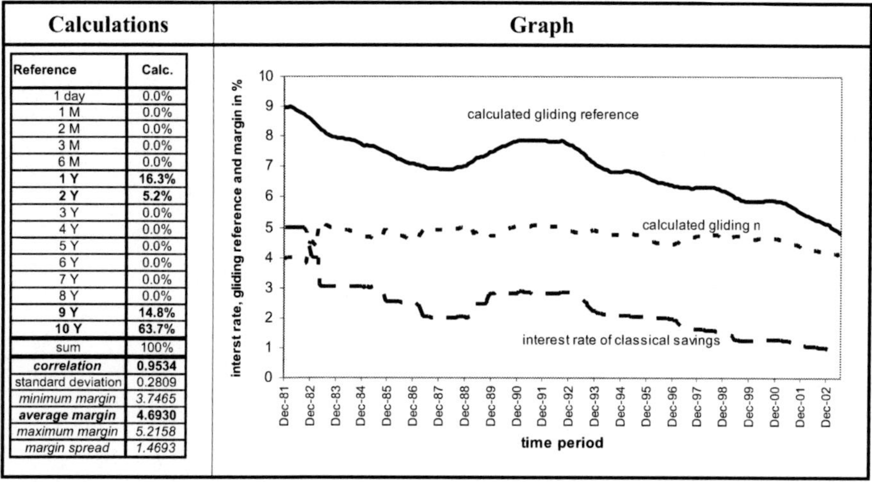

Reference	Calc.
1 day	0.0%
1 M	0.0%
2 M	0.0%
3 M	0.0%
6 M	0.0%
1 Y	16.3%
2 Y	5.2%
3 Y	0.0%
4 Y	0.0%
5 Y	0.0%
6 Y	0.0%
7 Y	0.0%
8 Y	0.0%
9 Y	14.8%
10 Y	63.7%
sum	100%
correlation	0.9534
standard deviation	0.2809
minimum margin	3.7465
average margin	4.6930
maximum margin	5.2158
margin spread	1.4693

Figure 33:   **Example of evaluating a gliding average** [771]

Describing this approach in detail would go beyond the scope of this dissertation[772]. Only the transformation into cash flows is important for a bank evaluation. In this example the cash flows[773] are set as follows[774]:

---

[766] Cf. *Sievi* (n.Y. a), chapter 2, pp. 12 and *Sievi* (n.Y. b), chapter 8, p. 1.

[767] Cf. *Sievi* (n.Y. a), chapter 2, p. 7.

[768] Cf. *Sievi* (1999), p. 32; *Böttrich/Drosdzol/Hager/Schleicher* (2004), p. 29 and *Lüders/Herrmann/Sternberg* (2005), p. 234.

[769] Done in the tool ProVari 4.3.1 of *ifb AG*.

[770] Examples can be found in *Goebel/Schumacher/Sievi* (1998a), pp. 332 and *Drosdzol/Hager* (2005), pp. 126.

[771] Author's own figure based on calculations of the Tool ProVari 4.3.1 from *ifb AG*. For the data of the savings cf. *Bundesbank* (2006d). Capital market data as mentioned above. A similar figure can be found in *Drosdzol/Hager* (2005), p. 136.

[772] For further details cf. *Sievi* (1999), pp. 31 – 39.

[773] Only considering repayment cash flows, no yield cash flows.

[774] Done similar in *Schierenbeck* (2001a), pp. 106 and *Parchert/Markus* (2002), p. 26.

- 16.3% within 1 year (12 tranches, 1.36 € per cash flow)
- 5.2% within 2 year (24 tranches, 0.22 € per cash flow)
- 14.8% within 9 years (108 tranches, 0,14 € per cash flow)
- 63.7% within 10 years (120 tranches, 0,53 € per cash flow)[775]

The correlation of 0.95 and the small standard deviation of the margin indicate that the probability that customers react as predicted is relatively high.

The gliding parameters should come from the internal controlling and should be investigated as described above. They reflect the individual interest rate policy of a bank[776]. Just two factors have to be kept in mind: the longer the gliding average is and the higher the interest margin is, the more (less) assets (liabilities) would be worth[777]. The calibration of these parameters has a strong influence on the present value of the related assets[778].

Last, it has to be mentioned that every asset of a bank that reacts sensitively to interest changes, can be transformed into cash flows – even bond-funds, if the structure of the fund is known. The same can be done with swaps and interest caps, even though they are not be shown in the balance sheet[779].

4.2.1.2 Definition of Discounting Rate

The next step is to discount the cash flows. Taking a nearly risk free rate fits with the cash flow definition[780]. Therefore, the normal spot rates are not used[781]. Derived from the spot rates[782], the so-called zerobond discounting factors[783] are applied onto the cash flows[784]. While classical discounting methods use one yield for all cash flows[785], the zerobond discounting factors are used consistently to the maturity[786]. Every cash flow is discounted with the interest rate of the related maturity[787]. Normally, the zerobond yield is a little bit higher

---

[775] Rounding differences may occur. A similar but more detailed description can be found in *Lüders/Herrmann/Sternberg* (2005), p. 236.
[776] Cf. *Sievi* (n.Y. b), chapter 8, p. 1.
[777] Cf. *Schierenbeck* (2001a), pp. 158.
[778] Cf. *Dauber/Pfeifer* (2006), pp. 233.
[779] For the definition and the structure of a swap cf. *Rolfes* (1999), pp. 74.
[780] Cf. Section 4.1.2.
[781] Cf. *Rolfes/Dartsch* (1998), pp. 67.
[782] Done in *Rolfes* (1999), pp. 49 – 51.
[783] Zdf = zerbond discounting factor.
[784] Cf. *Kotissek* (1987); *Marusev* (1988); *Grabiak/Kotissek/Küsters/Marusev* (1998) and *Biermann/Grosser* (1999), pp. 203.
[785] Cf. for example *Drukarczyk* (1996), p. 9.
[786] The reason for this is discussed in *Rolfes* (1999), p. 52.
[787] Cf. *Wiedemann* (2002), p. 1416.

than the spot rate[788] because the assumption of reinvestment of interest payments is done[789]. The following figure shows the zerobond discounting factors and the related interest rates and yields that will be used in this dissertation: [790]

December 31st 2005	1 day	1 M	2 M	3 M	6 M	1 Y	2 Y	3 Y	4 Y	5 Y	6 Y	7 Y	8 Y	9 Y	10 Y
interest rate in %	2.420	2.401	2.445	2.488	2.637	2.710	2.850	2.940	3.010	3.070	3.130	3.180	3.230	3.270	3.310
zerobond discounting factor	0.9999	0.9980	0.9961	0.9938	0.9870	0.9736	0.9453	0.9166	0.8879	0.8593	0.8306	0.8023	0.7742	0.7470	0.7201
(zerobond) yield in %	2.420	2.401	2.445	2.488	2.637	2.710	2.852	2.944	3.016	3.079	3.143	3.196	3.250	3.294	3.339

Table 19: **Interest rates and zerobond rates per December 31ˢᵗ, 2005**[791]

Using these zerobond yields, the above mentioned cash flows of the loan and the bond can be accumulated[792] and discounted[793] to the net present value of the fictitious bank[794], as the following figure shows:

Discounting the credit: 100,000 €, 4.80%, yearly payment rates									
	1 Y	2 Y	3 Y	4 Y	5 Y	6 Y	7 Y	8 Y	9 Y	10 Y
cash-flows	4,300	4,300	4,300	4,300	4,300	4,300	4,300	4,300	4,300	104,300
discounting factor	0.9736	0.9453	0.9166	0.8879	0.8593	0.8306	0.8023	0.7742	0.7470	0.7201
present value	4,187	4,065	3,942	3,818	3,695	3,571	3,450	3,329	3,212	75,104

108,372

Discounting the credit: 100,000 €, 4.80%, yearly payment rates									
	1 Y	2 Y	3 Y	4 Y	5 Y	6 Y	7 Y	8 Y	9 Y	10 Y
cash-flows	-3,200	-3,200	-3,200	-3,200	-3,200	-3,200	-3,200	-3,200	-3,200	-103,200
discounting factor	0.9736	0.9453	0.9166	0.8879	0.8593	0.8306	0.8023	0.7742	0.7470	0.7201
present value	-3,116	-3,025	-2,933	-2,841	-2,750	-2,658	-2,567	-2,478	-2,390	-74,312

-99,070

Present value of the bank   **108,372** + **-99,070** = **9,303**

Figure 34: **Present value of yield book cash flows**[795]

The present value of the bank is positive, even though the difference between the two book values would be zero. The reason is that the assets have a present value higher than the book value and the liabilities have a present value that is lower than the book value[796]. This refers

---

[788] Cf. *Rolfes* (1999), p. 55.

[789] Cf. *Schierenbeck* (2001a), pp. 162.

[790] For detailed evaluation of this approach cf. *Rolfes* (1999), pp. 49 and *Schierenbeck* (2001a), pp. 161. During this dissertation, all zerobond discounting factors are calculated with an Excel-macro-program in Visual Basic.

[791] Author's own figure, for market data cf. *Bundesbank* (2006a) and *Bundesbank* (2006b).

[792] For the entire bank, normally a so-called mapping is done. Cf. *Sievi* (1998), pp. 7 – 15.

[793] Bid and ask differences of a yield curve are not discussed here. Cf. *Schierenbeck* (2001a), pp. 220 for further details.

[794] Similar done in *Reuse* (2006), pp. 414.

[795] Author's own figure based on own calculations. Values in €.

[796] Argued in *Schierenbeck* (2001a), pp. 163.

to the central assumption of the market yield method: Customers pay more for assets than they would pay on the market and receive less for their savings than the market would pay[797].

	Assets	**Liabilities**
Effect	present value > book value *if:* customer yield > market yield	present value < book value *if:* customer yield < market yield
Profit and loss view	The bank receives more interest payments on the loan than the market would pay for a risk free bond. So if the bank issues a 10y bond, a margin of 0.94% will last.	The bank pays less interest than the market would. So as mentioned above, 0.12% will be the result per year.
Discounted cash flow view	The difference between the present value of the credit and its book value are the discounted 0.94% for the whole term of the credit.	The difference between the present value of the credit and its book value are the discounted 0.12%.

Table 20:   Periodic view vs. present value view[798]

So assets are worthier than the book value while liabilities are less worth. The sum of these present values represents the yield book value[799].

4.2.2 Further Assets

The next asset that has to be considered is the **trading book**[800]. The present value of the trading book is the actual share price multiplied by the number of shares. Setting up cash flows related to this position is not usual, even though in an ideal case a share might represent the expected cash flows of another company. [801]

Shares and share funds in strategic portfolios are handled similarly[802]. The present value is defined as the current price at the market.[803]

Normally, **investments or stakes in a company** have a book value in the bank's balance sheet. But the present value shall be used if available[804]. Consequently, a corporate evaluation of the company the bank is invested in should be done. Hence, the different methods dis-

---

[797] Cf. *Rolfes* (1999), p. 13 and *Reuse* (2002.12), p. 25.
[798] Author's own figure referring to the sources mentioned above.
[799] Cf. *Hortmann/Seide* (2006), p. 317.
[800] Cf. *Reuse* (2006), p. 428.
[801] Cf. *Hortmann/Seide* (2006), p. 318.
[802] Cf. *Hortmann/Seide* (2006), p. 318.
[803] Cf. *Bimmler/Mönke* (2003), p. 31.
[804] Cf. *Parchert/Markus* (2002), p. 44.

cussed before[805] can be applied here. The result may be that a bank has hidden reserves on the participation. But the result may also be that the book value is much higher than the present value. In case of a company not listed at the stock exchange, the book value is often used[806] in order to prevent a large-scale corporate evaluation for a small part of the bank's assets.

At the end **other assets** have to be quantified. Usually, the most important positions of a bank's portfolio are buildings and branches. They could be calculated with the book value, but if a current market value could be defined, this one would represent the present value of the buildings better[807]. For other assets like accruals and deferrals, the book value is chosen.[808]

4.2.3 Further Liabilities

Typical further liabilities for banks are **reserves for expenditures in the future** and **valuation adjustments on claims**. Often a present value is not available, so the cash flows cannot be taken from the internal controlling. The book value is chosen accordingly[809].

The **equity** is the only part of the balance sheet, which is **not** considered as a liability when defining the bank's value. The present value of the equity is the residual value that results from discounting all other assets and liabilities[810]. It is the value of the bank.

According to the other assets **other liabilities** are quantified with their book value as well. They use to consist only of accruals and deferrals.

4.2.4 Expected Losses of Taken Risk

After having discussed the assets and liabilities in the balance sheet, the risks a bank has in its portfolio have to be discussed. According to the existing assets the credit risk and the operational risk should be mentioned[811], explained and discounted[812].

---

[805] Cf. Section 2.2.
[806] Cf. *Dauber/Pfeifer* (2006), p. 233.
[807] Cf. *Parchert/Markus* (2002), p. 44.
[808] Cf. *Hortmann/Seide* (2006), p. 318 and *Reuse* (2006), p. 428.
[809] Cf. *Reuse* (2006), p. 428.
[810] Cf. *Weinzirl* (2002), p. 44.
[811] For example done in *Feix/Stechmeyer-Emden/Stückler* (2006), p. 106.
[812] Cf. *Bimmler/Mönke* (2003), p. 31.

Generally, the **expected loss of the credit portfolio** is the most important risk[813]. It has to be deducted from the bank's value[814]. Every year some parts of the credit exposure will come to bankruptcy. A correction for these risk premiums should be done. The procedure is as follows[815]: a bank has to define an average of credit losses which will occur in the future. These expected losses are often generated from an ex-post analysis. In the next step, this expected loss has to be divided by the current credit exposure. This relation defines which percentage of a credit exposure will be lost per year[816]. Last, this relation has to be applied on the average credit exposure of the following years, which results from the yield book[817], assuming 0.10% of expected loss. The following figure visualizes this:

	stock of credit portfolio	expected loss cash flows	discounting factor	present value of expected losses
2005-12	1,000,000	-1,000	1.0000	-1,000
2006-12	900,000	-900	0.9736	-876
2007-12	800,000	-800	0.9453	-756
2008-12	700,000	-700	0.9166	-642
2009-12	450,000	-450	0.8879	-400
2010-12	350,000	-350	0.8593	-301
2011-12	250,000	-250	0.8306	-208
2012-12	150,000	-150	0.8023	-120
2013-12	50,000	-50	0.7742	-39
2014-12	25,000	-25	0.7470	-19
2015-12	0	0	0.7201	0
				-4,360

Figure 35:   Present value expected losses[818]

Last, these cash flows have to be discounted. They could be defined as the present value of the expected losses of the current credit exposure. Unexpected losses, which can be quantified with the VaR[819], [820] are not deducted here. They represent all those unexpected factors an investor does not implement into his calculations normally. The expected default risk is the biggest risk banks face today[821], so the evaluation of this number is very important.

---

[813] Defined and explained in *Gröning* (2004), pp. 335.

[814] Cf. *Giesecke/Kühne* (2005), p. 128 and *Hortmann/Seide* (2006), p. 319.

[815] Done in *Dietzel* (2005), p. 10.

[816] Done in *Münchow/Biehsmann* (2006), p. 16.

[817] Visualized in *Biehsmann* (2004), p. 12.

[818] Author's own figure referring to *Dietzel* (2005), p. 10.

[819] Abbreviation for Value at Risk.

[820] For a short overview of the idea of the VaR cf. *Reuse* (2003.10), pp. 25. A special overview for the credit VaR can be found in *Reuse* (2006.07-08), pp. 366 – 371.

[821] Cf. *Adamus/Koch* (2006), p. 144.

Credit risk also occurs in the bond portfolio of a bank. The procedure differs for evaluating the **expected losses of a bond portfolio**. The so-called spread[822] is used. It is defined as the difference between the risk free rate and the risk individual rate, a bond has to be discounted with. It quantifies the expected losses of a bond[823]. First, the bond is discounted with the risk-individual interest rate and after that, with the risk-free rate. The difference of these present values is the present value of the expected losses of the bond portfolio.

Another risk a bank faces is the **operational risk**. It uses to occur, when people make mistakes or machinery does not work in the right way[824]. Even risks resulting from lost legal proceedings are defined as operational risks[825]. The expected losses, which result from this risk category, must be discounted as well[826]. The procedure is similar to the method of discounting expected credit losses[827]. First, the average sum spent onto operational risk has to be quantified. This is difficult enough, as processes have to be transparent in banks in order to define losses from operational risk. After that, the bank has to sum up all its transactions that exist at a certain moment. The yield book and all other assets and liabilities are added. The result is a relation of the expenditures on operational risks according to the sum of all transactions. As these transactions will stay in the bank related to their interest fixings or gliding average, the relation will be applied on a decreasing stock of transactions.

Expected losses are thus implemented into the treasury approach. Hence, the usage of the risk free rate is verified. In this model, the equity investor has no risk, as all risks are deducted with their expected value.

4.2.5 Costs related to Active Transactions

In the next step the costs have to be discounted as well[828]. First of all they have to be divided into several categories in order to define whether they have to do something with existing transfers or future deals[829]. The idea is to discount only the costs that have to do with existing transactions[830]. The following categories of costs could be defined:

---

[822] Cf. *Reuse* (2003.12), pp. 16.
[823] A small part of this difference contains unexpected losses, partly discussed in *Hornbach/Jung* (2001), p. 52. These effects should not be discussed here.
[824] Discussed in *Pfeifer* (2006), pp. 446.
[825] Cf. *Pfeifer* (2006), pp. 446.
[826] Done in *Reuse* (2006), p. 428.
[827] Cf. figure 35.
[828] Cf. *Weinzirl* (2002), p. 44.
[829] Done in *Hortmann/Seide* (2006), p. 319.
[830] Cf. *Biehsmann* (2004), p. 13 and *Giesecke/Kühne* (2005), pp. 134.

Kind of costs	Back office costs	Overhead	Sales services
Description	All costs that deal with the handling of customer's transactions. The best example is the credit department.	All costs that have noting to do with customer's transactions, for example controlling, organization, audit department and other strategic departments including the management board.	All personal staff related to sales. Typically, the employees of the branches and the specialists in investment banking can be mentioned here.
Exists for	Partly for new deals Partly for existing deals	Partly for new deals Partly for existing deals	Only for new deals
Denominator	Sum of customer's transactions	Whole balance sheet sum	---

Table 21:   Categorization of costs [831]

The next sectors describe the way of discounting those costs. It has to be kept in mind that only those costs should be considered, which are related to existing transactions[832]. Costs that only come up when new deals occur must not be discounted, as the related earnings are not considered either.

The next question is how long the costs and earnings may appear.

Back Office costs: The same idea that occurs when discounting risks is used when discounting costs. After defining the part of the overhead costs that belongs to existing contracts, this sum has to be discounted over the time. Back office costs will remain related to the average sum of current accounts deposits and credits generated by fixed maturities or gliding averages[833].

The most important number that has to be figured out is how much percent of the existing costs belong to the existing transactions in the balance sheet. This is solved as follows: the sum of all customers' transactions at a certain moment is compared to the sum, which remains one year later. Dividing these two numbers leads to the factor the current costs have to be multiplied with in order to receive the costs that belong to existing deals. If on 31st December of 2006, 1,000 € customer deals exist and one year later 350 € remain, the factor is 35%. 65% belong to existing deals vice-versa.

Overhead costs (fix costs) have little relation to the daily business of a bank, but they are important as well. The procedure is similar to the back office costs. The only difference is that the whole balance sheet sum is considered when generating the above described multiple as shown in the sector operational risk. The percentage of the overhead costs relating to existing

---

[831]   Author's own figure referring to *Bimmler/Mönke* (2003), p. 31 and *Münchow/Biehsmann* (2006), p. 17.
[832]   Cf. *Dietzel* (2005), p. 11.
[833]   Cf. *Bimmler/Mönke* (2003), pp. 31; *Dietzel* (2005), p. 11 and *Thaller* (2005), p. 147.

deals has to be defined as well[834]. To simplify the model in the practical section[835], the overhead costs can be treated in some way as the back office costs.

Sales services are related to generating new contracts. As a consequence, they have not been considered when discounting costs of existing transactions. The conclusion is that sales forces do not generate additional value for the bank according to existing deals. Surely, they generate earnings with new deals, but this aspect of sales forces is discussed later on[836].

4.2.6 Earnings related to Active Transactions

As several cost aspects that have to be discounted related to active transactions exist, some earning positions have to be considered as well. The procedure is always the same:

1. Defining the earnings per year.
2. Evaluating how long these earnings will last according to the existing balance sheet transactions.
3. Discounting those earnings[837].

A bank has some typical earnings positions that are related to existing transactions. The following table gives a short review and describes how the discounting should be done.

Earning position	Description	Discounting method
Earnings of guarantees	Many customers need guarantees for several purposes. This is strictly related to the existing asset balance sheet transactions.	The earnings of guarantees will decrease related to the decreasing asset transactions in the yield book.
Safe fees	Earnings from safes have a long maturity. They are stable earnings for a bank.	For evaluating this, two figures have to be known: the sum of all current accounts and the average closing rate of accounts. With these two numbers, the earnings can be simulated and discounted.
Earnings of depot accounts	Many customers deal with shares. They need custodianship accounts for this. A yearly fee has to be paid for having such an account.	Similar to the earnings of safes.
Rental income	A bank may have several buildings, which cause earnings as well. These earnings are stable and belong to the existing stock in the balance sheet.	Buildings are depreciated with 4% a year. The earnings will decrease with the same rate.

Table 22:   **The present value of earnings** [838]

---

[834] Cf. *Dauber/Pfeifer* (2006), p. 232.
[835] Cf. section 5.
[836] Cf. section 4.2.8.
[837] Cf. *Dietzel* (2005), p. 10.
[838] Author's own figure.

This detailed information is often not available. As a simplification, a percentage of how much of the earnings belong to existing contracts is estimated and discounted in relation to the whole balance sheet sum deduction[839].

4.2.7 Tax Effect

The tax effect is one of the most important aspects. Taxes are treated as costs; they are discounted according to the deduction of the balance sheet sum. The aim is to quantify the taxes belonging to existing contracts. The procedure is as mentioned above[840]. Usually, all deals of the balance sheet are used to discount the taxes resulting of existing business. Further, a tax rate has to be estimated. If no historical data is available, 40% can be chosen.

4.2.8 Performance Aspects

Last, the performance aspects have to be discussed. The central question is whether they will cause additional earnings. Three sectors have to be considered here:

- Treasury,
- Trading,
- Future deals with customers.

According to the treasury a positioning in a maturity transformation structure does **not** generate additional value. The same aspects mentioned in the previous sections could be used here. As everyone who has access to the capital market would be able to duplicate the maturity transformation portfolio of a bank, the expected earnings do not increase the value[841]. In the long run no one can beat the market, so additional value cannot be generated in this sector[842].

However, another aspect has to be mentioned – the realized earnings of maturity transformation have to be implemented. If a loan is granted and the treasurer decides not to close the position, a realized shareholder value results, if the interest rates decrease[843]. The argumentation according to the liability side is similar. These realized earnings can be found in the present value of the yield book – if the treasurer closes the position today, exactly the present value of the yield book can be realized[844]. The same is done with trading. It does not generate value and can be neglected as mentioned[845].

---

[839] Done in section 5.
[840] Cf. section 4.2.4, figure 35.
[841] Cf. section 2.3.3.1.
[842] Cf. *Sonntag* (2001), p. 81.
[843] Cf. *Bannert* (2000), pp. 6 and *Lach/Neubert/Kirmße* (2002), pp. 8.
[844] Cf. *Lach/Neubert/Kirmße* (2002), p. 18.
[845] Cf. section 2.3.3.2.

The last performance part consists of expected deals with the customers. New loans and new savings will generate additional interest margin in the future. However, they also generate new cost cash flows, which were not considered in the sector above. This is not an individual advantage of a bank, sales people are interchangeable. So this part is set as zero as well.

As only secure cash flows shall be considered, **all** performance aspects are treated as **zero** – otherwise discounting with a risk free ratio is not possible.

4.3 Theoretical Analysis of the Model

4.3.1 Structuring the Model according to Existing Literature

Structuring the model according to the categorization mentioned above[846], a clear allocation is not possible. On the one hand, it is a separate evaluation method, as all parts of the bank are described without the synergies[847]. A classical reproduction or realization approach would be the result. The main argument is that new deals are not considered; only existing contracts are discounted. On the other hand, the (available) assets, liabilities, cost and earnings are transformed into cash flows and thus discounted according to an equity approach. As the yield book implements the refinancing side[848], the cash flow is defined according to the equity approach without the usage of the CAPM. It is not an entity approach, as the paid interests for the liability side are deducted directly in the beginning before discounting; a subtraction of the liability side in the end is not done and the WACC is not used.

As a consequence the presented model is a mixture method, combining the aspects of a separate evaluation approach with those of a risk free equity approach.

4.3.2 Conclusions and Theory-Based Criticism of the Model

The presented model consists of existing approaches and is widened with aspects that are almost not described in literature. The model quantifies the value of a bank more exactly than every other approach. Theoretically, this approach has to lead to a lower value than the equity and earnings value approach, because maturity transformation is not considered as a value center.

The model offers several **advantages**. First, the usage is relatively simple. A bank that practices an integrated bank controlling can offer all required data very easily. Further, the sepa-

---

[846] Cf. section 2.2.
[847] Cf. for example *Thaller* (2005), p. 147 and *Hortmann/Seide* (2006), p. 317. They define the parts used in the model explicitly as a separate evaluation method.
[848] The present value of liabilities is inherently deducted.

rated evaluation has the advantage of showing the real value drivers or even value destroyers in a bank. This helps to manage a bank in a value based management style. Further, the exactness of results is given, as maturities of customer deals help to quantify the value in a balance sheet for the next years. Further, the earnings generated by the treasury are eliminated in an elegant way. Hence, the value of the bank consists of its efforts in the past only. Further, the risk free rate is taken, the CAPM discussion[849] is solved in a very elegant way. Possible risks are discounted as well and subtracted from the value of the bank, so that nearly no rest risk exists[850].

Of course, several **disadvantages** can be mentioned. The first one is data availability. Gliding averages and the other discussed data are only available from the internal strategic controlling, so that the approach can only be applied, if internal data are available. This is very difficult for the standard investor. Standard equity approaches could be done based on the balance sheet and the profit and loss account. But the target group of the bank's value often is the management that wants to do value based management. The management has access to all internal data, so this disadvantage only occurs for external investors.

Every method of corporate evaluation has its critical parameters which influence the value of a bank. The standard equity approaches need an individual discounting factor and forecasted annual surpluses as well as a terminal value. Varying these factors will lead to different values. The presented treasury approach does not need the terminal value or the individual discounting factor. The gliding averages, the percentages of costs belonging to existing transactions and the assumptions of discounting those earnings, risks and costs have strong influence on a bank's value. This has to be kept in mind when interpreting the results deriving from this approach.

Further, synergies are not directly implemented. The simple addition of the value parts is unable to consider synergies. But it can be argued that these synergies are inherently quantified in the existing present value, as they must have led to higher contribution margins in the end.

Last, missing intangible assets[851] might lead to an undervaluation of the value. However, as only one bank implements this factor into its evaluation model[852], this idea is not quantified in this dissertation. Defining the other parts of a bank is more important in the beginning. Intangible assets are important as well, but they have to be added in an extension of the presented model. The advantage is that they can be added simply – the model is open enough to offer this possibility.

---

[849] Cf. section 2.2.2.

[850] Despite from the unexpected loss, the VaR. Discussed in *Münchow/Biehsmann* (2006), p. 26.

[851] For example human capital and value of a brand. A structure of intangible assets can be found in *Aschoff* (1978), p. 40 and *Scholz* (2004), p. 24.

[852] Cf. question 3.7 of the survey.

5 Quantifying the Value of German Banks

Taking into consideration the theoretical and practical results of sections 2 and 3 and the new model coming out of section 4, the value of German banks shall be analyzed in this section. The model developed by the author and other, existing approaches of corporate evaluation will be applied on those banks that asked for a corporate evaluation.

5.1 Central Idea of the Empirical Corporate Evaluation

The central idea is relatively simple. The survey was the best way to address banks. Section 4 of the questionnaire contains all data that are necessary for a corporate evaluation[853]. Hence, linking the survey to 5 standardized corporate evaluation models is the real new fact.

As the questionnaire was standardized in this part as well, the harmonization work was out-sourced to the banks, as they had to quantify the numbers defined in the survey. Based on these harmonized data, a structured corporate evaluation is possible. For the banks, answering the questions in section 4 took a bit more time than answering the other questions[854], but it has to be kept in mind that a complete evaluation was done based on these data.

As the system is standardized, not all specialties of all banks can be considered. Simplified assumptions and the quality of given data might lead to differences between the 5 used approaches. However, the general conclusions will be of general interest.

5.2 Detailed Evaluation for One Bank

Every bank offered several data. In this section, the detailed procedure from the data evaluation process up to the application of the approaches and presentation of the results will be done. Therefore, a calculation sheet is developed which evaluates the value for every bank by the same process. A macro, developed by the author, filled the evaluation sheet and inserted the results into another table database. The structure of the evaluation sheet will be explained at the example of bank 365, a classical small bank[855]. This bank offered data with a high quality; almost no adjustments were required.

---

[853] Cf. appendix 3, questions 4.2 – 4.5.
[854] The author tested it: About an hour of concentrated work has to be reserved.
[855] Anonymity was required by the answering bank. So no further details can be mentioned.

5.2.1 Required Data

5.2.1.1 General Data

First, some general data have to be defined. The yield structure as presented above[856] will be used here to develop the present values in the classical way and to define the zerobond discounting factors. Further, a minimum tax rate of 40% is defined[857]. The spreads evaluated in the survey[858] will be used as well for some evaluation approaches. If a bank does not offer an own spread, the average spread of its banking group will be used.

5.2.1.2 Specific Data based on the Empirical Study

In the next step, the bank individual data have to be analyzed. Balance sheet sum, employees and some other basic factors resulting from other sections of the questionnaire are presented. For some evaluation approaches, several other, often more detailed data are necessary. Question 4.2 of the survey discussed the classical income statement data.

---

[856] Cf. section 4.2.1.2, table 19. For market data cf. *Bundesbank* (2006a); *Bundesbank* (2006b).
[857] Assumption. Many banks in Germany pay about 40% taxes, depending on the "Gewerbesteuerhebesatz". Analyzed for example in *Reuter/Blees* (2006).
[858] Cf. section 3.3.1, table 14.

	Year -2	Year -1	Year 0	Ø Prog.
+ Interest Earnings	18.400	17.700	17.000	16.900
- Interest Expenditures	-9.100	-7.900	-7.600	-7.700
+/- Derivates				
= Net interest yield	**9.300**	**9.800**	**9.400**	**9.200**
+ Fees	1.600	2.100	1.900	2.000
- Personal Expenditures	-4.400	-4.700	-4.500	-4.800
- Non-Personal Expenditures	-2.900	-3.000	-2.800	-2.700
+/- other			-0.500	-0.100
= Result before valuation	**3.600**	**4.200**	**3.500**	**3.600**
+/- Provisions for lost loans	-1.100	-1.700	-0.800	-1.000
+/- Depreciation of Bonds			-0.100	-0.100
= Earnings before taxes	**2.500**	**2.500**	**2.600**	**2.500**
- taxes	-0.900	-0.900	-1.100	-1.000
= Result of operating business	**1.600**	**1.600**	**1.500**	**1.500**
+/- §340f HGB	-0.800	-0.500	-0.400	-0.400
= Balance sheet earnings	**0.800**	**1.100**	**1.100**	**1.100**

Check:

	Year -2	Year -1	Year 0	Ø Prog.
= Balance sheet earnings	0.800	1.100	1.100	1.100
	O.K.	*O.K.*	*O.K.*	*O.K.*

Tax Rate	36.00%	36.00%	42.31%	40.00%

Table 23:   **Income statement data at the example of bank 365**[859]

The recent three years and, if available, an average prognosis for the following years had to be inserted by the banks. The four years are requested in order to verify the sustainability of the income parts and to adjust the prognosis year if necessary. Nevertheless, no changes of the forecasted income statement had to be done, growth assumptions were always realistic for all banks. It has to be kept in mind, that no growth rate according to this eternal annual surplus is prognosticated. Further, no inflation adjustments will be done.

The detailed data of the income statement were used to quantify extraordinary effects. But this is not as simple as it seems to be. The income statement had to be put into a standardized format that might differ from the bank's own annual report. This format divides the income statement into sustainable income and those earnings or costs that are no cash flows[860]. This led to several complications in the banks. Very often, a correction of the values had to be made. Several inconsistencies were found and the author had to communicate with the banks in order to verify the data.

---

[859] Author's own figure based onto question 4.2 of the survey.
[860] Despite the depreciation. Therefore, a simplified assumption will be done.

Question 4.3 requested information from the balance sheet. According to the income statement, the balance sheet has to be structured in a certain form as well. The definition of the yield book as presented above[861] and the differentiation into fix and variable positions was requested. Further, the yield of the balance sheet position and the average rest maturity was asked in order to build up a yield book cash flow, if this one is not given in the second part of question 4.3. The requested balance sheet structure is as follows:

Assets					Liabilities				
Position		Value	Ø Yield	Ø Maturity	Position		Value	Ø Yield	Ø Maturity
Yield Book	Customer Deals fix	178.10	5.220%	4.00	Yield Book	Customer Deals fix	123.40	2.850%	2.50
Yield Book	Customer Deals variabel	41.30	8.200%	0.50	Yield Book	Customer Deals variabel	109.70	0.960%	3.40
Yield Book	Depot A	61.50	3.610%	5.00	Yield Book	Emissions	34.30	4.490%	4.00
Other Assets		52.90			Other Liabilities		53.50		
Shares		8.30			Equity		21.20		
		342.10					**342.10**		

Table 24: Balance sheet data at the example of bank 365[862]

The definition of the yield book and other assets and liabilities can be recognized. The difficulties that were stated according to the income statement occurred again. Some of the banks did not know how to structure the balance sheet positions. Most difficulties occurred when analyzing the average maturity of the balance sheet positions. Very often a second contact had to be made by the author in order to verify the data[863].

Thereafter, the cash flow of the yield book – corrected by the value corrections and the cash position – was requested. 13 of the 19 banks that asked for a corporate evaluation offered the yield book cash flow as well. In these cases, the average maturity was only used to generate fictitious cash flows of costs and earnings. In the 6 other cases it was used to generate a fictitious yield book cash flow as well.

Questions 4.4 deals with the costs. It was asked, how much percent of the costs belong to existing business and new deals. Question 4.5 asked which part of the fees belongs to existing transactions. These percentages will be used in the treasury approach.

It becomes clear that using the earnings value method and the equity approach are only based on the income statement data. Cash inflows and cash outflows coming out of a balance sheet

---

[861] Cf. section 4.2.

[862] Author's own figure based onto question 4.2 of the survey.

[863] Often, the standard factors of the BaFin survey were used in the end. Cf. *BaFin* (2006), p. 8.

will not be analyzed here.[864] The other questions aim at the treasury approach only. The data are more complex, but the results might be better as well.

5.2.2 Setting up the Approaches

Five approaches are used to quantify the value: net asset value, earnings value, equity approach, treasury approach and multiplier approach[865]. After having inserted all given data into the Excel-database, they are calculated in the evaluation sheet of the database.

5.2.2.1 Net Asset Value Approach / Substance Value

The most simple approach is to mention the equity of a bank[866], a classical substance value. As all banks were requested to insert their equity including the §340 reserves[867], the real economic capital, including hidden reserves[868] and excluding certain forms of secondary loan funds is quantified. This is the book value of the company, a floor for all other approaches. For example, the book value of bank 365 is about 21.20 Mio. €.

5.2.2.2 Multiplier Approach

Next the multiplier method as the external benchmark approach shall be applied ono all banks. When using the CCA, the first step is to define a possible peer group. As the value of German banks has to be quantified, a comparison with stock listed German banks should lead to a fair value. The comparable companies should show a good mixture of the German market and they have to be listed on the German stock exchange. Defining strategies and policies of each bank of a peer group would go beyond the scope of this dissertation, so it is not discussed here. The author decided to chose the following companies:

---

[864] Cf. section 5.3.

[865] Cf. section 2.2 and section 4.

[866] For example done in *Yegge* (1996), p. 51.

[867] For the character and definition of the reserves cf. §340 *HGB*.

[868] §340f reserves are not clearly mentioned in an annual report, so they can be treated as hidden.

- Aareal Bank[869]
- Comdirect[870]
- Deutsche Postbank[871]
- Hypo Real Estate[872]
- IKB Deutsche Industriebank[873]
- Deutsche Bank[874]
- Hypovereinsbank (HVB)[875]
- Commerzbank[876]

This peer group might represent almost all kinds of German banks. Direct banks, classical private banks and a former state-owned enterprise, the Postbank can be found in the group. In order to get a better overview, the share price development of the last three years (January 2nd, 2003 – December 31st, 2005) will be presented. The share prices were indexed to 100 on January 3rd, 2003[877] and combined with the lognormal daily yields that could be derived from the historical share price development. Together with the DAX the following development can be visualized:

	02/01/2003	02/01/2004	03/01/2005	30/12/2005
Aareal Bank	100.00	197.98	199.35	258.63
Comdirect	100.00	254.21	242.42	268.01
Postbank			144.19	215.87
Hypo Real Estate		177.50	264.12	375.31
IKB	100.00	151.25	174.17	208.33
Deutsche Bank	100.00	139.41	137.86	171.70
HVB	100.00	138.73	128.80	195.65
Commerzbank	100.00	193.17	187.80	317.32
DAX	100.00	129.42	138.21	174.18

Figure 36:   Development of the indexed share prices of the peer group[878]

---

[869] Cf. *S-Investor* (2006aa – ab).
[870] Cf. *S-Investor* (2006ba – bb).
[871] Cf. *S-Investor* (2006ca – cb).
[872] Cf. *S-Investor* (2006da – db).
[873] Cf. *S-Investor* (2006ea – eb).
[874] Cf. *S-Investor* (2006fa – fb).
[875] Cf. *S-Investor* (2006ga – gb).
[876] Cf. *S-Investor* (2006ha – hb).
[877] Postbank's prices are only available till June 23rd, 2004, Hypo Real Estate till October 6th, 2003. They are indexed on the DAX-price guilty on that day.
[878] Author's own figure based on data of *Reuters* (2006) and own calculations.

The development of each share differs. Some of them beat the DAX, others even underperform it. This leads to the conclusion that some of the banks might have problems. It turns to be true, when considering the recent last annual reports. The Aareal Bank for example had to build many corrections for lost loans. The annual surplus was negative in 2005[879].

Further, the important fundamental data have to be analyzed and a share price analysis has to be done. The following table gives an overview of the chosen comparable companies and the data which are basis for the CCA. All annual accounts are per December 31st, 2005. The chosen date to do the CCA is December 31st, 2005 as well. Fundamentals were taken directly from the S-Investor[880], while the share price analysis bases on data of Reuters[881].

---

[879] Cf. *S-Investor* (2006ga).
[880] Cf. *S-Investor* (2006aa – hb).
[881] Cf. *Reuters* (2006).

All data per December 30th, 2005. Values in Mio. €	Aareal Bank	Comdirect	Deutsche Postbank	Hypo Real Estate Holding	IKB Deutsche Industriebank	Deutsche Bank	Hypo-vereinsbank	Commerz-bank	DAX			
reference number	DE0005408116	DE0005428007	DE0008001009	DE0008027707	DE0008063306	DE0005140008	DE0008022005	DE0008032004	DE0008469008			
share price per Dec 30th, 05	32.07	7.96	49.00	43.98	25.00	81.90	25.61	26.02	5,408.26			
shares outstanding (May 29th, 06	42,755,159	141,000,000	164,000,000	134,072,175	88,000,000	514,535,270	750,699,140	656,812,557	---			
market cap. = corporate value	1,371	1,122	8,036	5,896	2,200	42,140	19,225	17,090	---			
Index	MDAX	MDAX	MDAX	MDAX	MDAX	DAX	DAX	DAX	---			
Risk — Volatility — 12 months	23.33%	25.01%	20.03%	24.79%	17.16%	17.61%	22.45%	22.29%	12.08%			
Volatility — 24 months	31.79%	31.40%	18.11%	25.29%	16.04%	19.55%	25.27%	22.72%	14.01%			
Volatility — 36 months	32.55%	39.01%	18.11%	27.47%	14.60%	26.33%	40.13%	33.12%	20.57%	Beta		
Beta — 12 months	0.7295	0.8424	0.6010	0.8632	0.4415	1.1814	0.8602	1.0981	1.0000	0.8272		
Beta — 24 months	0.6872	0.9632	0.5160	0.8002	0.4393	1.0947	0.9692	1.0712	1.0000	0.8176		
Beta — 36 months	0.4696	0.7563	0.5165	0.8220	0.2243	1.0893	1.3410	1.1543	1.0000	0.7967		
Correlation — 12 months	0.3779	0.4071	0.3625	0.4208	0.3109	0.8106	0.4631	0.5955	1.0000			
Correlation — 24 months	0.3029	0.4299	0.3600	0.4433	0.3836	0.7847	0.5374	0.6607	1.0000			
Correlation — 36 months	0.2967	0.3988	0.3600	0.4333	0.3159	0.8510	0.6873	0.7169	1.0000			
Perform — daily lognormal yield 03.01.2003 - 30.12.2005	0.12%	0.13%	0.14%	0.22%	0.10%	0.07%	0.09%	0.15%	0.07%	50 year Ø		
p.a. yield 03.01.2003 - 30.12.2005	31.01%	32.18%	33.80%	53.78%	23.95%	17.64%	21.90%	37.69%	18.11%	9.60%		
Fundamentals 2005 — annual surplus	-55	34	492	359	143	3,529	642	1,165				
net interest revenue	419	64	1,675	685	442	6,001	5,885	3,172				
sum of balance sheet	39,186	3,367	140,280	152,460	38,303	992,161	493,523	444,861				
economic equity	997	565	4,980	3,066	2,289	28,672	12,976	12,375				
common share equity	128	141	410	402	225	1,420	2,252	1,705				
equity ratio	2.5	16.8	3.6	2.0	6.0	2.9	2.6	2.8				
net interest spread	1.069%	1.902%	1.194%	0.449%	1.154%	0.605%	1.192%	0.713%				
net income before valuations	168	44	693	520	313	5,132	3,469	1,632				
number of employees	3,217	638	9,523	1,233	1,438	63,427	61,251	33,056	Average	Median	r2	
Multiples 2005 — net interest revenue	3.27	17.53	4.80	8.61	4.98	7.02	3.27	5.39	6.86	5.18	0.8127	
sum of balance sheet	0.0350	0.3334	0.0573	0.0387	0.0574	0.0425	0.0390	0.0384	0.080	0.041	0.9924	
economic equity	1.38	1.99	1.61	1.92	0.96	1.47	1.48	1.38	1.52	1.48	0.9963	
net income before valuations	8.16	25.67	11.60	11.34	7.04	8.21	5.54	10.47	11.00	9.34	0.9356	

Table 25: **Fundamentals of the peer group**[882]

---

[882] Author's own table based on data of *Reuters* (2006) and *S-Investor* (2006aa – hb).

In the next step, those fundamentals that might be able to be used in a CCA have to be defined. As a bank shows another structure as other companies, multiples like turnover or EBIT are not suitable for banks. New multiples have to be defined:

Possible Multiple	Explanation	Usage
Annual surplus	The easiest number to get is the annual surplus. But the question, whether it can be used as a comparable multiple should be answered with no, as taxes and other effects cover up the sustainable earnings.	*No*
Total net revenue before provisions for lost loans	Apart from some other small corrections, the total net revenue before provisions for loan losses is a figure that represents the sustainable earnings. It may vary over the years, too. But if it becomes negative, the bank is really worth nothing. As a consequence it is tested, whether it can be used for the CCA.	*Yes*
Net interest revenue	Even though the scope of the yield book differs from bank to bank, the largest part of the balance sheet consists of deals, which lead to the net interest revenue. So this might be a good multiple as well.	*Yes*
Sum of balance sheet	This figure represents the size of the bank. Even though it might be "tuned" by window dressing, it is a stable value to compare banks.	*Yes*
Common share equity	Banks normally have a low equity ratio. But the more equity they have, the more they are worth. But taking the common share equity into account would not be enough, as reserves derived from §340f HGB often build up a great part of the equity. So this value cannot be used.	*No*
Economic equity	Going one step further, the economic equity including all these visible reserves may be a good multiple. So it is analyzed here.	*Yes*
Number of employees	Even though the size of a bank could be represented by this figure, it is not suitable for all types of banks. Different structures lead to a different number of employees.	*No*

Table 26:   Evaluation of new multiples[883]

These four multiples show significant dependencies between the market value of the bank and the basis variable. This can be visualized as follows, containing average, median and coefficient of determination r^2:

---

[883] Author's own table.

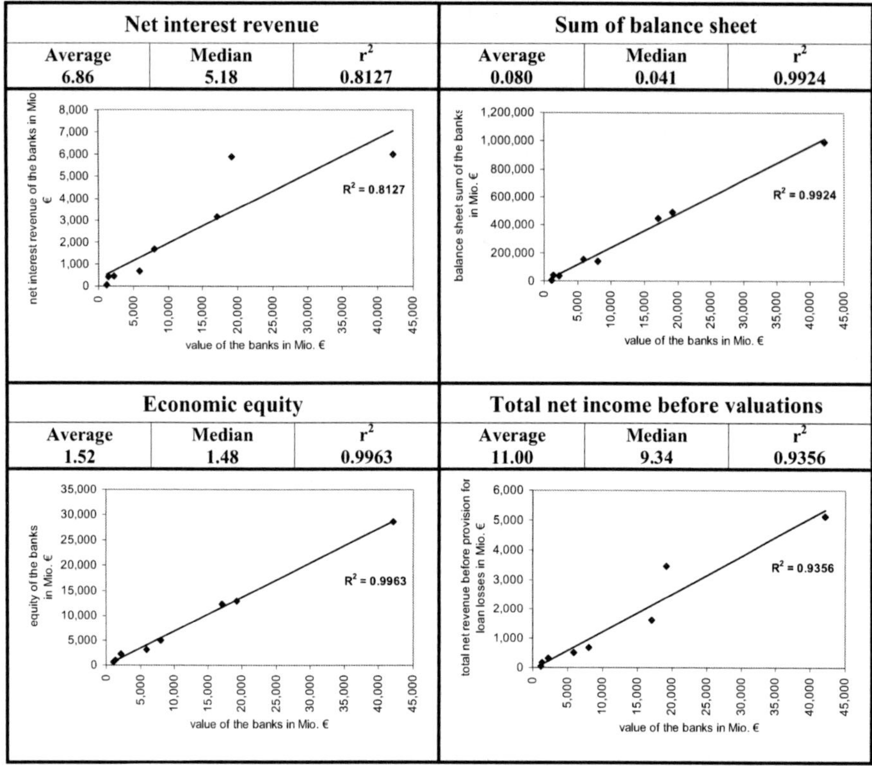

Figure 37:   Definition of the multiples for the CCA[884]

These multiples differ partially from those which would be used usually. Adamus/Koch define Market/Book, Price/Earnings and Price/AuM.[885] The first one is called economic equity multiple in this dissertation. It is consistent in its definition. Koch evaluated an r^2 of 0.86 in 2004[886]. However, the Price/Earnings ratio is defined in a different manner in this dissertation. Adamus/Koch subtract the value corrections. The author does not do this, as significant dependencies between the bank's value and the earnings do not exist, if value corrections are implemented. Koch evaluated an r^2 as well – it was only 0.58, when using the price/earnings ratio[887]. The last ratio, the Price/AuM is not used here, as it is only suitable for investment

---

[884]   Author's own figure.
[885]   Cf. *Adamus/Koch* (2006), p. 157.
[886]   Cf. *Koch* (2004), p. 134.
[887]   Cf. *Koch* (2004), p. 132.

banks, as Adamus/Koch admit[888]. The balance sheet multiple, offering a good r^2 in this dissertation, is not considered in Adamus/Koch however.

These multiples are applied on every bank. The average of the four multiples coming out of the multiplier approach is defined as the bank's value. For example, a value of 40.47 Mio. € can be stated for bank 365:

	Banks's value	**Multiple**	**Value of bank**
net interest revenue	9.20	6.86	63.09
sum of balance sheet	335.000	0.08	26.87
economic equity	21.20	1.52	32.31
total net income bef. valuation	3.60	11.00	39.61
			40.47

Table 27:   Multiplier approach at the example of bank 365[889]

It is obvious that the net interest revenue of the savings bank would lead to a higher value than the other multiples might define. The strengths of the savings banks are customer deals in the balance sheet while the economic equity is lower than in the peer group.

After having presented the equity of the bank in section 5.2.2.1 and after having done the external analysis of the bank in this section, three internal approaches will be presented.

5.2.2.3 Earnings Value Approach

The earnings value approach is the first internal approach applied on the banks. Only the sustainable parts of the income statement shall be used[890]. Following this, the given data of the income statement have to be corrected by the non-sustainable values[891]. First, all other and extraordinary results are treated as non-sustainable. Further, the tax payments are modified. The tax ratio has to be paid only onto the sustainable income as well. Value corrections for lost loans remain uncorrected – expected losses will always occur in future and are often deducted in current literature[892]. As the usage of a nearly risk free ratio will be favoured, all ex-

---

[888]   Cf. *Adamus/Koch* (2006), p. 157.
[889]   Author's own figure based onto the evaluation sheet.
[890]   Cf. *Schierenbeck* (1998), p. 395. For a detailed analysis of the evaluation of the relevant earnings cf. *Schell* (1988), pp. 92.
[891]   For example done in *Ballwieser* (2004), pp. 24.
[892]   Cf. *Copeland/Koller/Murrin* (2002), p. 505. This problem will be discussed later on again. Cf. section 5.2.2.4.

pected risks have to be deducted. Thereafter, the sustainable income after taxes can be quantified. For bank 365, it looks as follows:

Position	Ø Prog.	Explanation
+ Interest Earnings	16.900	*Sustainable income of the yield book*
- Interest Expenditures	-7.700	*Sustainable expenditure of the yield book*
+/- Derivates		*Sustainable income of the yield book*
+ Fees	2.000	*Sustainable income*
- Personal Expenditures	-4.800	*Sustainable expenditures*
- Non-Personal Expenditures	-2.700	*Sustainable expenditures*
+/- other expenditures/earnings		*Set as zero - no sustainable income!*
+/- Provisions for lost loans	-1.000	*Have to be deducted as they minimize the sustainable income*
+/- Depreciation of Bonds	-0.100	*Considered, even though the sustainablity may be discussable.*
= Earnings before taxes	**2.600**	
- taxes	-1.040	*Minimum tax rate: 40%. Adjusted taxes of the data given.*
= Result of operating business	**1.560**	

Yield	3.310%
Spread	0.158%
Discounting factor	**3.468%**
Terminal Value	**44.98**

Table 28:   Earnings value approach at the example of bank 365[893]

While the net interest yield remains unchanged, other expenditures and the building of §340f reserves are eliminated, as they cannot be considered as sustainable income. After that, the tax rate resulting from the average tax rate of the last years, at least 40% is applied on this corrected result[894].

Further, the question of the discounting rate has to be discussed. As all risks as expected loss and depreciation for bonds are deducted, the remaining income is almost risk-free as well. Only the market risk remains, so that the discounting rate is defined as the 10Y market yield[895] plus the related spread. For bank 365, the earnings value is about 44.98 Mio. € – twice as much as the net asset value.

5.2.2.4 Equity Approach

Discussing the equity approach leads to other assumptions and accordingly to other results. The cash flow is setup as requested in current literature[896]. Cash inflows and cash outflows coming out of the customer deals are not considered here, as they cannot be quantified by the

---

[893] Author's own figure based onto the evaluation sheet. Cf. table 23 for the average tax rate of bank 365.
[894] Cf. *Reuter/Blees* (2006).
[895] Following the argumentation *of Adolf/Cramer/Ollmann* (1989b), pp. 552.
[896] Cf. *Börner/Lowis* (1997), pp. 106; *Copeland/Koller/Murrin* (2002), pp. 504; *Koch* (2004), pp. 128 and *Adamus/Koch* (2006), pp. 154.

data given[897]. It has to be kept in mind that the presented approaches are only simplifications; a more exact valuation would require much more data.

In order to receive a cash flow resulting from the income statement[898], several adjustments had to be done. All those expenditures and earnings that are no cash flows have to be corrected. This is done in the following table:

Position	Ø Prog.	Explanation
+ Interest Earnings	16.900	*Treated as 100% cash flow*
- Interest Expenditures	-7.700	*Treated as 100% cash flow*
+/- Derivates		*Treated as 100% cash flow*
+ Fees	2.000	*Treated as 100% cash flow*
- 85% Personal Expenditures	-4.080	*Assumption - 15% are no cash flow*
- 85% Non-Personal Expenditures	-2.295	*Adjusted by depreciation. Assumption: 15% of given non-personal expenditures*
+/- other expenditures/earnings		*Set as zero - no sustainable income!*
+/- Provisions for lost loans		*Set as zero - no cash flow*
+/- Depreciation of Bonds		*No cash flow - set as zero*
= Cash Flow before taxes	4.825	
- taxes	-1.040	*According to Earnings Value Approach*
= Result of operating business	3.785	

Yield	8.32%
Terminal Value	45.49

Table 29:   Equity approach at the example of bank 365[899]

Net interest earnings are treated as a cash flows. Some small aspects that are no cash flows might exist, for example discounts of loans that are spread over the years. However, these effects are only marginal; they shall not be considered here. Also fees are treated as 100% cash flow, even though some of them might be no cash flow. Personal expenditures and non-personal expenditures on the other side are corrected. It was assumed that 15% of the personal expenditures are used for pension obligations. They stay in the bank and cause no cash outflow. The same is done with the non-personal expenditures. 15% are treated as depreciations that cause no cash outflow as well.

However, the most important factor that has to be discussed is the value correction position. As value corrections are no cash outflows[900], they are not considered in this calculation[901]. But this topic has to be treated very critically, as literature does not finally answer the question, but tends to neglect the value corrections[902]. On the one hand, it is no cash flow in the

---

[897] Only balance sheet data was requested in the survey, no changes between two years. A complete example is given in *Koch* (2004), p. 129.

[898] As for example done in *Koch* (2004), p. 129.

[899] Author's own figure based onto the evaluation sheet. Yield as per share price analysis based on CAPM.

[900] Cf. *Copeland/Koller/Murrin* (2002), pp. 504.

[901] Following *Koch* (2004), pp. 128 and *Adamus/Koch* (2006), pp. 15.

[902] Beneath Koch and Adamus/Koch, Börner/Lowis do so as well. Cf. *Börner/Lowis* (1997), pp. 106.

beginning. On the other hand, some future expected cash inflows[903] might be lost. These cash flows cannot be anticipated[904]. The presented equity approach assumes that these lost yield cash flows are considered in the income statement prognosis in form of a lower interest yield. The value corrections can be neglected as redemption payments or other capital cash flows are in general not considered in this model[905]. It has to be kept in mind that as soon as these capital cash flows are inserted into the model, the value corrections have to be implemented as well.

In case of a bond, this problem does not occur. Depreciation in this case is only a time effect[906], so it is considered as zero[907]. In the last step, the evaluated taxes of the earnings value approach are deducted[908]. They are completely taken as cash outflows. It has to be kept in mind that the taxes must not differ to the earnings value approach, as they are not calculated on the basis of a cash flow, but on the basis of sustainable earnings.

The resulting returns to discount are much higher than the earnings value approach[909]. According to this, a risk adjusted discounting rate has to be used. The 10Y market yield is combined with the CAPM approach – even though it is often criticised in theory[910]. The share price history of the DAX and the peer group presented above[911] lead to an average beta of 0.7967 and a DAX yield of 18.11%[912].

But this DAX yield has to be considered very critical as it only represents 3 years. While betas can be stable during time[913], the market yields show a high volatility. Between 1948 and 2003, the one year yield varied between -43.9% and 161.3%[914]. Taking the average of three years would not lead to the right results. So the average of the last 50 years, 1953 – 2003 was chosen to evaluate the CAPM ratio. The yield is about 9.60%[915]. This fits to current literature. While Behm[916] states a market yield of 10.07% in 1994[917], Rolfes[918] offers 11.7% in 1997[919].

---

[903] Interest cash flows and payback cash flows.
[904] Cf. *Copeland/Koller/Murrin* (2002), p. 505.
[905] Börner/Lowis for example deduct value corrections. Cf. *Börner/Lowis* (1997), pp. 110.
[906] All bonds are paid back at 100%, if no default occurs.
[907] Cf. *Strutz* (1993), pp. 87.
[908] Deprecations and value corrections have a tax effect. Cf. *Copeland/Koller/Murrin* (2002), pp. 504.
[909] Cf. section 5.2.2.3.
[910] Cf. section 2.2.2.
[911] Cf. section 5.2.2.2, table 25.
[912] Presented in detail during the multiplier approach. Cf. section 5.2.2.2.
[913] Shown and summarized in *Grimmer* (2003), p. 159.
[914] Cf. *Deutsches Aktieninstitut* (2004), p. 1.
[915] Cf. *Deutsches Aktieninstitut* (2004), p. 1.
[916] Cf. *Behm* (1994).
[917] Time period: 1970 – 1992.
[918] Cf. *Rolfes* (1997), pp. 95 – 118.
[919] Time period: 1954 – 1995.

Nevertheless, the evaluated betas fit with those of Rolfes. Deutsche Bank gets a beta of 1.12 in Rolfes work, the own calculations offer 1.08. The same can be stated according to the Commerzbank. Rolfes offers 1.04, the own calculations lead to 1.15. So the betas evaluated at a three year average can be used in this analysis.

Together with the 10Y market yield, a CAPM yield of 8.32% can be stated[920].

A beta correction as requested by many authors[921] is not done, as Adamus/Koch had proven empirically that there is no dependency between leverage and beta[922]. An unadjusted beta can be used accordingly.

The central question that has to be answered is why the discounting rates in the earnings value approach and the equity approach differ. This is explained as follows: while the earnings value approach consists of secure and sustainable earnings only (all measurable risks are deducted), the equity approach is based on some insecure cash flows, as the value corrections are not deducted. Accordingly, the discounting factor must be higher.

5.2.2.5 Treasury Approach

Last, the treasury approach is applied on the banks. The assumption to prove is that the value coming out of it must be a little bit smaller compared to the other approaches[923]. This can be explained as follows: Future maturity transformation is not worth anything, as worked out above[924]. Hence, the expected additional earnings that are inherent quantified in the earnings value method or the equity approach are set as zero in the treasury approach.

Further, only secure cash flows are discounted in the treasury approach. The fact that the sum of the cash flows is smaller than in the equity approach is compensated by using a complete risk free rate to discount the cash flows. If it can be proven in practice that the value based on the treasury approach is smaller than in the other approaches, the treasury approach will be verified.

First of all, the present value of the yield book is defined. In the cases the bank offered it, the discounting was relatively simple, as only some corrections according to the yield book definition had to be done. If the cash flow was not given, a simplified approach based on the av-

---

[920]　$i_{CAPM} = 3.31\% + (9.60 - 3.31\%)*0.7967 =$ **8.32%**

[921]　A beta adjustment as requested in *Kirsten* (2000), pp. 158 is not done in this dissertation.

[922]　Cf. *Adamus/Koch* (2006), pp. 155.

[923]　Cf. section 4.3.2.

[924]　Cf. section 4.2.8.

erage maturity date was evaluated. Multiplying the average maturity with the factor 2 leads to a gliding average. Taking that as a fact, the cash flows were set up as follows[925]:

Assets - Customer Deals Fix								
Year	Date	Value	Repayment	Yield	Yield CF	Cash Flow	ZDF	PV
	31/12/2005	178.10		5.22%				
1	31/12/2006	155.84	22.26	5.22%	8.72	30.98	0.9736	**30.16**
2	31/12/2007	133.58	22.26	5.22%	7.55	29.82	0.9453	**28.19**
3	31/12/2008	111.31	22.26	5.22%	6.39	28.65	0.9166	**26.27**
4	31/12/2009	89.05	22.26	5.22%	5.23	27.49	0.8879	**24.41**
5	31/12/2010	66.79	22.26	5.22%	4.07	26.33	0.8593	**22.63**
6	31/12/2011	44.53	22.26	5.22%	2.91	25.17	0.8306	**20.90**
7	31/12/2012	22.26	22.26	5.22%	1.74	24.01	0.8023	**19.26**
8	31/12/2013	0.00	22.26	5.22%	0.58	22.84	0.7742	**17.69**
9	31/12/2014		0.00	5.22%	0.00	0.00	0.7470	**0.00**
10	31/12/2015			5.22%			0.7201	
11	31/12/2016			5.22%			0.6970	
12	31/12/2017			5.22%			0.6747	

189.50

Table 30:   Simplified cash flow evaluation of fix customer deals of bank 365[926]

With the use of the gliding average, a continuous declining of the asset's volume can be simulated. Interests are paid per assumption at the end of each year, always paid on the annual average. Adding all cash flows lead to the simulated present value of the yield book. The present value of the yield book can be approximated by this approach, but the maturity transformation and interest rate sensitivity differ. It can be used in this model only for quantifying the present value of the yield book. If the real yield book cash flow is given by the bank, it always dominates the simplified approach. In this case the latter is only used for discounting costs and earnings.

With the example of bank 365, the difference is about 2.61%. Even though most of the other banks also have similar small differences, some show higher differences. The problem might be that the given basis data are not exact enough. Bank 365 certainly is one of the best examples to apply the treasury approach.

These results are visualized in the following figure:

---

[925] Cf. table 24 for the basis data. Volume: 188.30 Mio. € , 5.440% yield, Ø maturity 2.96 years, gliding average 5.92 years.

[926] Author's own figure based on the evaluation sheet.

General Data		Given Cash Flow		Simplified approach	
Time	ZDF	Cash Flow	PV	Cash Flow	PV
Day	0.9999	-33.60	-33.60		
Year 1	0.9736	2.40	2.34	31.55	30.71
Year 2	0.9453	12.60	11.91	-11.78	-11.14
Year 3	0.9166	11.10	10.17	-12.11	-11.10
Year 4	0.8879	17.50	15.54	-12.45	-11.05
Year 5	0.8593	11.30	9.71	-12.78	-10.98
Year 6	0.8306	8.10	6.73	11.21	9.31
Year 7	0.8023	7.40	5.94	13.39	10.74
Year 8	0.7742	7.70	5.96	25.16	19.48
Year 9	0.7470	-3.10	-2.32	6.48	4.84
Year 10	0.7201	1.10	0.79	6.26	4.51
later	0.6970	1.80	1.25	0.00	0.00
		44.30	**34.43**	**44.94**	**35.33**

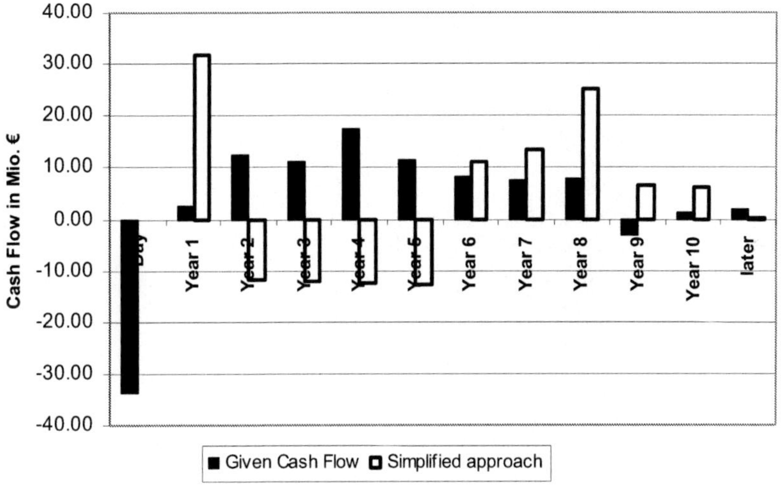

Figure 38: **Cash flow of the yield book – simulated vs. given cash flows**[927]

Thereafter, the value of other assets and liabilities is added. Further, the costs, fees and taxes are discounted according to the rest cash flows of existing business, as explained in section 4:

---

[927] Author's own figure.

Position	Value	Percentage	To discount	Assumption	
Expected Losses Loans	-1.000	0.46%	-1.000	Asset Customer Deals	
Costs	-7.500	40%	-3.000	Whole Customer Deals	
Fees	2.000	60%	1.200	Whole Customer Deals	
Taxes	-1.000	100%	-1.000	Whole Yield Book Deals	40.00%

General Data			Aggregations			Cash Flow				Present Value			
Year	Date	ZDF	Assets Customer Deals	Whole Customer Deals	Whole Yield Book	Expected Losses	Costs	Fees	Taxes	Expected Losses	Costs	Fees	Taxes
	31/12/2005		219.40	452.50	548.30	-1.00	-3.00	1.20	-1.00				
1	31/12/2006	0.9736	155.84	348.13	433.49	-0.71	-2.31	0.92	-0.79	-0.69	-2.25	0.90	-0.77
2	31/12/2007	0.9453	133.58	285.05	359.98	-0.61	-1.89	0.76	-0.66	-0.58	-1.79	0.71	-0.62
3	31/12/2008	0.9166	111.31	221.98	286.46	-0.51	-1.47	0.59	-0.52	-0.47	-1.35	0.54	-0.48
4	31/12/2009	0.8879	89.05	158.90	212.95	-0.41	-1.05	0.42	-0.39	-0.36	-0.94	0.37	-0.34
5	31/12/2010	0.8593	66.79	95.83	139.44	-0.30	-0.64	0.25	-0.25	-0.26	-0.55	0.22	-0.22
6	31/12/2011	0.8306	44.53	57.43	90.61	-0.20	-0.38	0.15	-0.17	-0.17	-0.32	0.13	-0.14
7	31/12/2012	0.8023	22.26	22.26	45.00	-0.10	-0.15	0.06	-0.08	-0.08	-0.12	0.05	-0.07
8	31/12/2013	0.7742	0.00	0.00	12.30	0.00	0.00	0.00	-0.02	0.00	0.00	0.00	-0.02
9	31/12/2014	0.7470			6.15				-0.01				-0.01
10	31/12/2015	0.7201			0.00				0.00				0.00
11	31/12/2016	0.6970											
										-2.60	-7.30	2.92	-2.66

Table 31:   Present value of fees, costs and taxes of bank 365[928]

The expected losses are determined by the asset customer deals. The discussion of the value corrections[929] leads to the conclusion that they must be deducted, as capital cash flows and redemptions are considered as well.

The costs and fees factor given for existing business (40% and 60%) are deducted according to the whole customer deals, while the taxes are discounted according to the whole yield book sum development. The presented model is simplified here, as a differentiation into overhead and back office would have been too complex for a questionnaire.

Last, all value parts of the treasury approach are added. This is shown in figure 39:

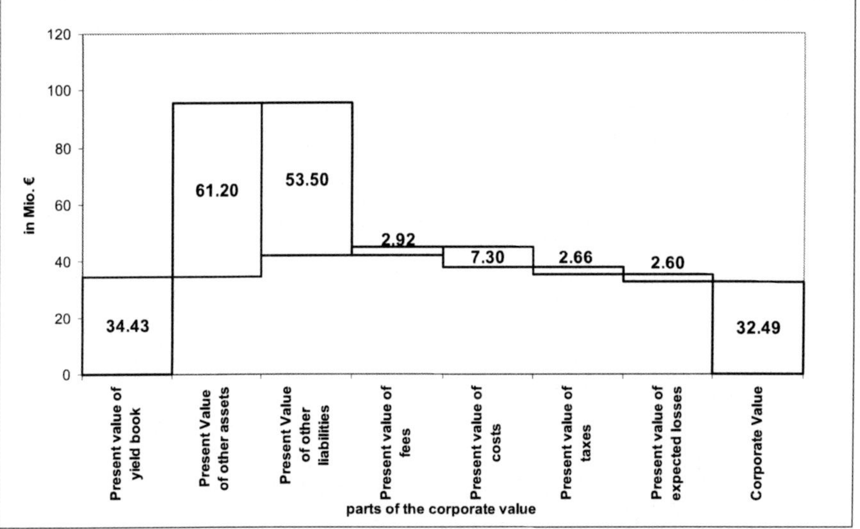

Figure 39:   **Treasury approach at the example of bank 365**[930]

The resulting value is about 32.49 Mio. €, it is a lower than in the equity and earnings value approach. The advantage of the treasury approach is that the parts of the bank's value can be structured and added. The main value part is the yield book, as the all purpose banks do most of their business in it.

---

[929] Cf. section 5.2.2.4.
[930] Author's own figure.

5.2.3 Summing up the Results

Figure 40 aggregates the results. The requested result is optimal. The treasury approach offers a lower value than the equity and the earnings value approach. Further, the other two internal approaches offer almost the same value while the multiplier approach is a little bit higher. For sure, this example represents one of the banks that offered the best data quality. As to the other banks, the results differ and are often not as good as in this example. This is shown in the following section.

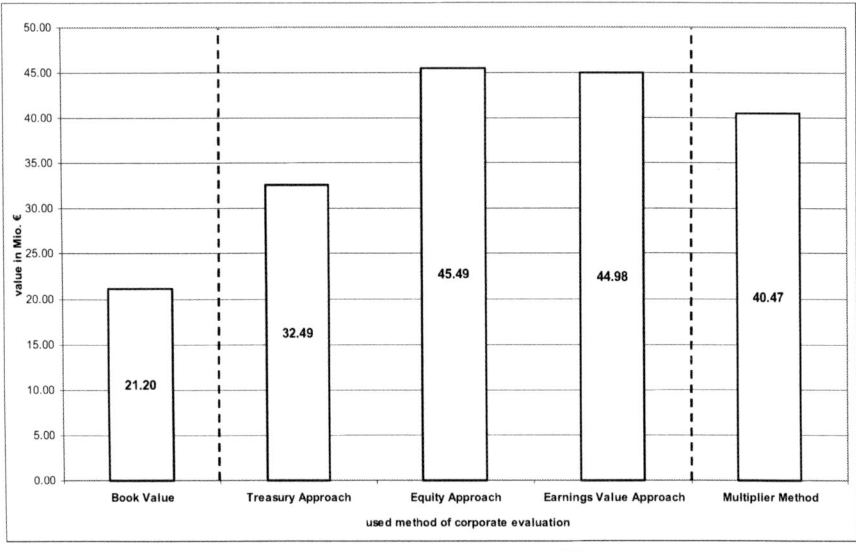

Figure 40:   Value of bank 365 based on all approaches[931]

5.3 General Evaluation for all Banks

5.3.1 Structuring the Banks

In total, 19 banks wanted to have an individual evaluation. This is about 37.25% as mentioned above[932]. The next step is to have a closer look onto the related banks. A corporate evaluation was done for the following banks:

---

[931] Author's own figure.
[932] Cf. section 3.3.4.

Type of Bank	Number of answered surveys	Wanting an Evaluation	Percentage
Big Bank	2		
Bank	7	3	42.86%
Clearing House			
Geno	21	8	38.10%
Geno special.	3	2	66.67%
Mortgage Bank	2	1	50.00%
Savings Bank	16	5	31.25%
Sum	**51**	**19**	**37.25%**

Table 32:   Structure of the banks with an interest in a corporate evaluation[933]

It is not surprising that the two big banks did not fill out the questions due to the fact that they treat internal data as very sensitive. The other results lead to the conclusion that the interest in a corporate evaluation exists in all banking groups. But the type of bank which should be interested in a corporate evaluation, the savings bank sector, only offers a ratio of 31.25%. Even though this is only a conclusion based on a small database, this percentage should be higher in order to grant shareholder value management, considering the actual background of 3 pillar discussion.[934] The result fits with question 3.2 of the survey. Only 37.50% evaluate their own value up to now[935].

Nevertheless it is a success that so many banks offered internal data in order to get a corporate evaluation[936]. The topic seems to be interesting for the banks.

5.3.2 The Corporate Value of the 19 Banks

Using the evaluation sheet presented in detail above leads to the following results for all banks, including bank 365:

---

[933] Author's own figure based on the evaluation sheet.
[934] Cf. section 1.1.
[935] Cf. section 3.3.3, table 17.
[936] Every bank gets its own evaluation sheet in a *.pdf format as a result of the corporate evaluation.

Data of the banks		Absolute Results				
Number	Name of the Bank	Equity Value	Treasury Approach	Equity Approach	Earnings Value Approach	Multiplier Method
11	Bank 11	29.00	67.18	69.67	56.46	53.72
22	Bank 22	15.00	18.69	35.33	49.67	28.67
51	**Bank 51**	**1,500.00**	**4,671.62**	**3,720.74**	**6,473.83**	**3,450.20**
159	Bank 159	10.00	13.87	28.70	22.82	22.31
160	**Bank 160**	**5.20**	**6.31**	**13.16**	**11.53**	**9.56**
185	**Bank 185**	**513.00**	**498.11**	**1,019.12**	**1,900.29**	**985.59**
277	Bank 277	393.00	575.33	722.17	1,004.09	687.29
311	Bank 311	232.26	200.99	250.72	354.94	288.33
346	Bank 346	160.84	218.14	342.80	117.24	282.61
365	Bank 365	21.20	32.49	45.49	44.98	40.47
398	Bank 398	726.00	1,059.76	1,360.18	1,577.65	1,301.97
476	Bank 476	11.00	39.89	21.06	14.69	22.15
488	Bank 488	33.21	48.10	78.70	83.64	62.12
489	Bank 489	14.30	21.02	28.24	25.64	26.45
607	Bank 607	15.26	30.38	30.41	29.48	28.94
621	Bank 621	83.00	137.39	99.15	86.47	122.17
637	Bank 637	20.76	17.36	28.26	37.93	31.39
695	Bank 695	22.20	28.90	51.56	38.15	42.21

Table 33:   Results of the corporate evaluation for all banks, n = 19[937]

It is interesting to see that the results often do not fit as optimal as in bank 365. Sometimes, relatively big differences can be found between equity approach and earnings value method. Certainly, one reason is that the assumptions are generalized for all banks. This might not fit for specialized banks. Further, the data quality is not optimal, even though many banks were contacted a second or third time. The author had to adjust several data in order to keep consistency in data – another indication that there is not a huge experience in German banks with respect to corporate evaluation. Otherwise the necessary data would have been available directly.

5.3.3 Interpreting the Results

It would make no sense to analyze the results according to the type of banks, as the sample is too small and the results are considered to be too volatile. But analyzing the sum of all banks, differentiated into the five approaches, is useful. In total, the above mentioned volatile effects should be much lower. Setting the equity book value as 100% and generating an average of all banks leads to the following figure:

---

[937] Author's own figure based on the evaluation sheet. Specialized banks (not defined as all purpose banks) are marked bold in the table.

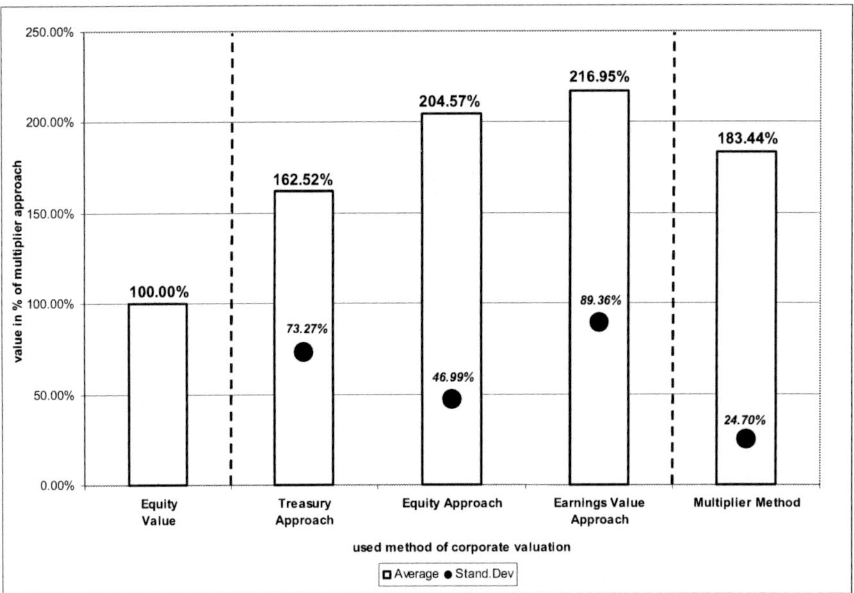

Figure 41:   **Indexed value of all banks based on all approaches, n = 19**[938]

The value generated by all other approaches is higher than the equity value. This is a good indication for the validity of the data. Analyzing the approaches in detail leads to the following results: The multiplier method generates a value that is 183.44% of the equity on average – with a standard deviation of only 24.70%. The internal approaches lead to higher standard deviations. This implies that the multiplier approach is better than the other models, as the results are very stable. But this has to be seen critical. The multiplier approach is only an external approach. It does not consider internal aspects and can thus be treated as a first hint only. Further, corporate values react more sensitive to internal data changes. A higher volatility is normal.

The equity approach, often discussed as the best model in theory, leads to the lowest standard deviation and a corporate value of about twice the equity. The earnings value approach leads to nearly the same result but with a higher standard deviation. Both approaches state that the bank is worth about 205% - 215% of the equity. This is very interesting, as this result is higher than the 183.44% coming out of the multiplier approach, based on the stock-listed German big banks. A possible conclusion is that smaller banks in Germany have a higher value than the stock-listed companies – but no one considers this. This is the main problem in

---

[938]   Author's own figure.

the German banking sector. Genos and savings banks represent themselves under value, even though many hidden reserves and a high potential of growth are given in these sectors. However, the banks do not realize this. Both shareholder value based management and the evaluation of the own value belong together. Nevertheless, both are not realized completely in practice. Most investors think that the major stock listed banks have the highest value – but this is not the fact. A missing brand management or a better shareholder value management might help to increase in particular the value of Genos and savings banks.

Last, the verification of the treasury approach is also given – even though the underlying data are not reliable in a quantitative way. This leads to a higher standard deviation compared to earnings value and equity approach. The treasury approach reacts more sensitively to changes in the parameters than the other approaches. But the value of the bank is lower when using the treasury approach, even though a real risk free ratio is used. The reason is that the expected result of maturity transformation is set as zero. Therefore, the value of the banks generated by the treasury approach must be lower than in the other approaches. This is a fact – the value is about $1/4^{th}$ lower when using the treasury approach. This verifies the quality of the approach; it is proven by the practical application. It is interesting to see that the resulting value is even lower than the value resulting from the multiplier approach. A conclusion can be that even the market has not recognized that maturity transformation is worth nothing regarding the question of corporate value.

5.4 Empirical Evaluation of Internal Multiples

Last, some further multiples can be defined. These multiples differ from above[939], as they are not based on the market price but onto the fictitious price coming out of internal approaches. Leaving the specialized banks out of this analysis[940], the table 34 offers some additional results, compared to those of the external based multiplier approach. The multiples remain almost constant – and the effects discussed in section 5.3.3 are visible in this table as well: While the equity multiple and the balance sheet multiple lead to a higher value, net interest revenues and income before valuation lead to a lower one. This can be interpreted as follows: The stock listed peer group has a higher equity, a higher balance sheet sum and lower value corrections. However, the net interest revenue seems to be higher in small companies – using the brand and market power. The underestimation of the banks in the market according to the net interest yield leads to the conclusion that the balance sheet and its earnings are still the most important and strategic success factor. Genos and savings banks offer a relatively high rate.

---

[939] Cf. section 5.2.2.2.
[940] Banks 51, 160 and 185 have special functions and cannot be treated similar to other all purpose banks.

The defined multiples[941] can be used in practice accordingly. It is really new that multiples resulting from internal approaches are evaluated in order to apply them onto other banks. However, it is interesting to see that these multiples do not differ very much from the external multiplier analysis. Multiples resulting from both, internal and external analysis, will lead to an objectified value. But the usage of the multiples has to be seen critical. They will only lead to reliable results, if real comparable companies are used. The value coming out of such an analysis will only quote a value that offers no hints according to the value parts of the bank. The real value drivers of a bank cannot be controlled with this approach. No hints for the management can be generated. A value based management is not possible when using this approach. A multiplier approach thus can only be a first orientation value. Therefore, the classical approach or in best case the treasury approach have to be used. The latter fits best to a value based management, as the value parts are quantified best.

---

[941] 4 external and 4 internal multiples.

Results		Equity Multiple			Balance sheet sum Multiple			Net interest revenue			Net income before valuation			Ø Multiple
Ratios	Average	1.8354			0.1145			4.8002			13.1384			4.9721
	Multiples	1.5970	1.9884	1.9209	0.0978	0.1232	0.1225	4.1268	5.1467	5.1270	11.8754	14.1074	13.4324	
	Standard deviation	42.00%	24.33%	33.17%	35.79%	20.29%	38.41%	33.07%	15.56%	37.97%	72.90%	54.22%	47.68%	
Bank No	Name	Treasury Approach	Equity Approach	Earnings Value Approach	Treasury Approach	Equity Approach	Earnings Value Approach	Treasury Approach	Equity Approach	Earnings Value Approach	Treasury Approach	Equity Approach	Earnings Value Approach	
11	Bank 11	2.3165	2.4025	1.9469	0.0940	0.0974	0.0790	4.8681	5.0488	4.0914	39.5176	40.9845	33.2122	
22	Bank 22	1.2457	2.3555	3.3111	0.0788	0.1491	0.2096	3.7372	7.0665	9.9334	5.3389	10.0950	14.1906	
51	Bank 51													
159	Bank 159	1.3865	2.8701	2.2822	0.0670	0.1387	0.1103	2.7731	5.7402	4.5645	6.6026	13.6671	10.8678	
160	Bank 160													
185	Bank 185													
277	Bank 277	1.4639	1.8376	2.5549	0.1064	0.1336	0.1857	4.1691	5.2331	7.2760	8.2190	10.3167	14.3441	
311	Bank 311	0.8654	1.0795	1.5282	0.0905	0.1128	0.1597	3.6412	4.5421	6.4301	9.1154	11.3707	16.0971	
346	Bank 346	1.3563	2.1313	0.7289	0.0860	0.1352	0.0462	3.5629	5.5990	1.9149	9.1594	14.3938	4.9228	
365	Bank 365	1.5324	2.1456	2.1216	0.0970	0.1358	0.1343	3.5311	4.9443	4.8890	9.0239	12.6355	12.4940	
398	Bank 398	1.4597	1.8735	2.1731	0.0883	0.1133	0.1315	4.1888	5.3762	6.2358	8.3053	10.6597	12.3640	
476	Bank 476	3.6260	1.9145	1.3353	0.2157	0.1139	0.0794	7.9140	4.1785	2.9143	19.5714	10.3334	7.2070	
488	Bank 488	1.4484	2.3695	2.5184	0.1040	0.1701	0.1807	3.6853	6.0291	6.4078	7.4305	12.1559	12.9195	
489	Bank 489	1.4701	1.9750	1.7931	0.0891	0.1197	0.1086	3.6246	4.8693	4.4209	9.1402	12.2791	11.1483	
607	Bank 607	1.9910	1.9927	1.9321	0.1044	0.1045	0.1013	4.2192	4.2230	4.0944	16.8767	16.8918	16.3776	
621	Bank 621	1.6553	1.1945	1.0418	0.0981	0.0708	0.0618	6.2449	4.5067	3.9305	15.2653	11.0164	9.6079	
637	Bank 637	0.8359	1.3609	1.8269	0.0629	0.1024	0.1375	2.5667	4.1785	5.6095	7.5167	12.2370	16.4277	
695	Bank 695	1.3017	2.3224	1.7185	0.0843	0.1504	0.1113	3.1756	5.6656	4.1923	7.0482	12.5748	9.3049	
Ratios as per multiplier approach		1.5238			0.0802			6.8580			11.0038			4.8665
Difference: + internal approaches are higher		20.45%			42.73%			-30.01%			19.40%			

Table 34: **Multiples resulting from the applied internal approaches**[942]

6 Critical Discussion and Outlook

6.1 Summary of the Main Results

Summing up the results of this dissertation leads to the following aspects: First, the theoretical status quo was defined. Existing approaches of corporate evaluation cannot be used directly for banks. The entity approach for example is not useful in the banking sector as it does not consider the fact that banks earn money with the liability side.

When analyzing the existing approaches of bank evaluation it becomes clear that several aspects remain unsolved in theory, even though many authors offered possible solutions. However, these statements differ. Crucial aspects are the discounting rate, the procedure of integrating value corrections and the consideration of maturity transformation. The latter is the most contested one. Many authors implement these additional earnings into their present value approaches, others do not. The author of this dissertation follows Sonntag in his argumentation not to implement maturity transformation results. Everyone has access to the capital market and can build up maturity positions. Hence, this value can be generated independent of the fact whether the bank that does maturity transformation is acquired or not.

The impulses for a new model coming out of the existing theory are simplicity and the usage of secure cash flows and thus secure discounting rates in order to prevent the problems coming out of the CAPM.

The status quo of corporate evaluation in the German banking sector was done by the author's survey. This survey can be treated as representative. It offered some real new aspects of corporate evaluation, as current published surveys to this topic do not exist in literature. Two topics were analyzed: the dissemination of shareholder value based management combined with shareholder value-oriented controlling tools and the usage of corporate evaluation methods. The results are very remarkable. Shareholder value based management is not very famous in the German banking sector. Even those banks stating to be shareholder value-oriented prefer periodic oriented values and controlling methods. On the one hand, EVA and RAROC as the most important value-oriented numbers are not used often. Further, they get the worst marks[943]. On the other hand, CIR and annual return get the best marks. It is disappointing to see that the consideration of the own brand is not important for most banks – even though this represents the future of the German banks. This is proven by a scoring model to value the quality of shareholder value based management. The resulting scoring points confirm that shareholder value has no priority in German banks. A maximum rate of 98 points

---

[943] Cf. figure 19.

was possible, but the best bank received only 68 points, the average of all banks was about 27 points.

Nevertheless, it has to be taken as positive that nearly half of the banks quantify their own value. At least the know how and the methods are available in German banks. This is proven by the analysis of the known and used methods. Despite the good mark for the entity approach – only one bank[944] found out that the entity approach is not useful for banks – the theoretically derived approaches were valued similarly in practice. Even though shareholder value is not famous in German banks, many banks stated that they evaluate their value in order to do such a management. At least, the specialists in the banks, the controllers, are on the right way. The main practical impulse for a new model was that existing bank controlling methods as risk covering mass models and market interest rate method should be integrated into a new model. Acceptance would increase and the banks would have much of the needed know how in-house.

The developed treasury approach took all these aspects into consideration. Using the present value extension of the market interest rate method and the gliding average approach, only the cash flows of existing deals and positions are considered. Costs, expected losses, taxes and earnings are subdivided into those that belong to new deals and into those that belong to existing deals. Discounting all those cash flows can be done with a risk free rate. Further, the expected earnings of maturity transformation are not considered in an elegant way. Accordingly, every bank that does integrated bank controlling should be able to apply this approach. Surely, the assumptions are debatable, as some of them react very sensitively to changes. But as no new deals of the future have to be forecasted, the prognosis risk does not occur. This is a very important advantage. Further, the model enables the bank to get management impulses out of it. As it is a mixture between a separate evaluation approach and a discounted cash flow approach, the parts of the bank that generate the most value can be defined. The management thus knows about its critical success factors and about its core competencies. This information is not generated by classical approaches. The parts of the developed model are completely known in theory and even often in practice – but their combination and their usage as a corporate evaluation tool is new.

The model is verified in practice. As 19 banks are valued by the approach, the general result is that earnings value approach and the equity approach generate a higher value on average, even though the treasury approach is the only one that uses a risk free rate. The reason is that the effect of maturity transformation is not considered. The model can be treated as verified in practice, even though the results of the three approaches differ for some banks. This can be explained by several reasons. First, the data quality might be low in some questionnaires.

---

[944] Bank 3, one of the two big banks.

However, the most important conclusion is that the treasury approach only functions with all purpose banks. Specialized banks with a low yield book have to be treated differently; the treasury approach might lead to inconsistent results.

Another result is that the multiplier approach offers better results than expected. If a good peer group is chosen, the results are quite stable. The multiplier approach can be used as a first hint for the value of a bank, if the presented multiples are used. But is has to be kept in mind that only external factors are considered. Only an internal analysis offers impulses for the management. Internal approaches will always be better than an external multiplier approach accordingly.

During the development of the model, the question of integrating intangible assets occurred. The model is flexible and allows the implementation of intangible assets as a further additional component. However, the usage of intangible assets, in particular human resources, was very low in practice. Only one bank stated that the value of human resources is implemented into the corporate value[945]. Further, as mentioned above, the brand and the increase of its value does not seem to be important for German banks. This might have two reasons. On the one hand, the interviewees of the questionnaire nearly always were controllers. Immaterial assets and their valuation are not very famous in controlling. On the other hand, even a financial oriented value based management often cannot be found in practice. Implementing human capital and the brand value would go too far at the moment. But in five or ten years, the situation might change.

Nevertheless, the empiric analysis has evaluated some additional multiples to estimate a bank's value in a quick and simple manner in order to receive a first result. The database of the 19 banks offers supplementary multiples based on internal information. This is really new considering the classical CCA. It is interesting to see that the net interest rate multiple is significantly higher in the internal setup – banks that are not listed at the stock exchange have high hidden values in the balance sheet. This was proven by the comparison of the multiplier approach with the average value[946], too. Equity approach and earnings value method generated a higher value than the multiplier approach.

Finally, the main questions of this dissertation[947] have to be answered. Aggregating all aspects mentioned above leads to table 35.

---

[945] Bank 750, a rather small Geno.
[946] Cf. figure 41.
[947] Cf. section 1.1.

Question	Main Arguments	Status
Do the existing approaches of corporate evaluation lead to the right values?	The main weaknesses of existing methods of corporate evaluation are worked out in section 2.2. The entity approach is not useful for banks and the individual structure of banks including the maturity transformation effect demand another model.	✓
How far is theory in quantifying the value of banks?	The status quo of bank evaluation was worked out and explained in section 2.3. The weaknesses as the implementation of maturity transformation results were discussed. Critical aspects as the definition of relevant cash flow and the discounting yield were presented as well.	✓
What is the practical status quo of corporate evaluation in the German banking sector?	The empirical study of the author answers all question according to the status quo and the integration of value based management. The usage of corporate evaluation and value based management controlling numbers are quantified.	✓
What is the value of a typical German bank?	The application of several corporate evaluation methods including the treasury approach solves this question. Internal and external multiples were defined to quantify the value of a German bank.	✓
Do banks manage their business in a shareholder value-oriented way?	The survey in section 3 answers this question as well. The interlink of value based management and corporate evaluation was analyzed in a detailed way. The result is that a value based management does not occur very often in practice. But quantifying the own value will lead to a value based management during time.	✓

Table 35:   **Answering the central questions of the dissertation**[948]

It can be stated that all questions are answered in a sufficient way. This dissertation expands existing theory, defines the practical status quo and evaluates a new approach to measure the value of a bank.

6.2 Recommendation and Outlook

It has to be stated that the outlook for a value based management in the German banking sector is positive. Many banks evaluate their own value and the controlling tools to apply the treasury approach are available in practice. Even though the methods are very young in practice, management knows about the results. During the next years, corporate evaluation will be established in practice.

The main recommendation is to implement the value of immaterial assets. Classical Genos and savings banks have the biggest brand value, but most of them do not consider this essen-

---

[948] Author's own table.

tial factor in their evaluation process. The recommendation for German banks is to be aware of this central asset they have.

Banks do not have material assets. Their balance sheet consists of customer deals. Getting new deals in the future can only be realized by two strategies: being quality leader or price leader[949]. While banks as DiBa[950] try to get the customer by attractive prices, classical savings banks and Genos can only generate new contribution margins by good services and by the value of the brand that promise competence and sympathy. Therefore the intangible values as the quality of the service, the know-how of the employees and the resulting value of the brand will become the most important value drivers for the quality leader banks in the future. It has to be realized in practice and connected to the shareholder value approach[951]. It will be the job of internal and external marketing to publish these strategies adequately.

The treasury approach extends current theory and existing models. It is the only approach that is able to implement immaterial assets into the corporate value by adding it. As only existing customer deals and no future deals are considered, an addition of the brand value is possible. Only a distinguishing into the part that belongs to existing assets and the part that belongs to future expected earnings has to be done. It has to be kept in mind that in case of implementing immaterial assets, the related costs have to be deducted as well. The dissertation did not implement immaterial assets on purpose. The financial aspects of the treasury approach or similar models have to be accepted in practice first. After that, the treasury approach shall be extended.

Further, an integration of this model into the shareholder value process is necessary. This is not a modification of the model itself; it is a transformation of its usage into the management workflow. As the value drivers and its changes during time can be recognized, a shareholder value-oriented management can react to these changes. Therefore a balanced scorecard should be implemented and integrated with the existing treasury approach. A fixed process has to be setup that leads to impulses and results for the management. In many banks, a balanced scorecard and a evaluation model exist. But they are not connected. Integrating both aspects into this process offers the advantage that management decisions can be backtested. The direct dependency between management decisions and EVA can be measured. Nowadays controlling often offers a highly sophisticated risk/return model, but management does not use it to increase shareholder value. The required process can be modeled as follows:

---

[949] Cf. *Porter* (1996), pp. 62; *Thompson/Strickland* (2003), pp. 151 and *Kotler/Armstrong* (2004), p. 574.
[950] Direktanlagebank.
[951] Cf. *Vogler* (n.Y.), pp. 467.

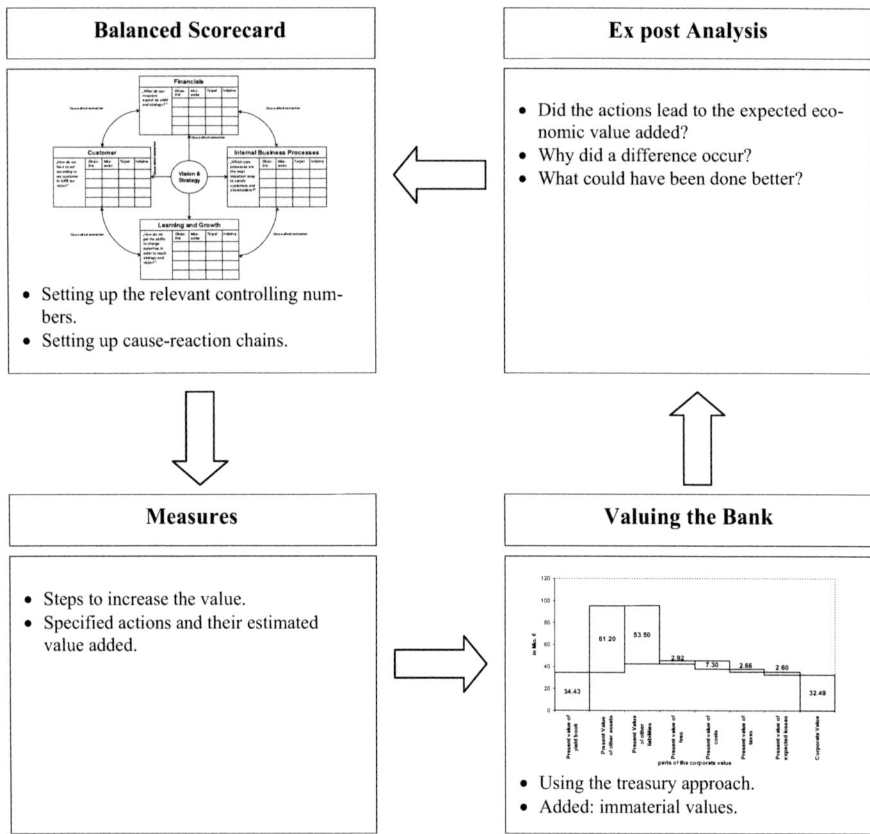

Figure 42:   Integrated shareholder value management process[952]

By sing the above mentioned process, management obliges itself to the bank's strategic aims. The risk of wrong management decisions will be minimized.

Therefore the most important recommendation for the banks is to use evaluation models as the treasury approach and to combine them with the core management processes. German banks are better than their reputation. The immaterial values as customer satisfaction, brand and employees will determine the success of the banks in the future. A value based management is the key to communicate this to customers, employees and to other banks. In this case, unnecessary mergers and fusions can be prevented.

---

[952] Author's own figure.

Appendix

Appendix 1: Survey Letter

Mülheim an der Ruhr, 15.05.2006

Svend Reuse / Hornhof 23 / 45478 Mülheim

«Name»
- «Contactperson» -
«Street»
«Place»

Empirische Analyse zur Unternehmensbewertung im Bankenbereich

«Field_in_Letter»,

haben Sie sich nicht schon oft gefragt, was Ihr Institut wirklich wert ist? Genau diese Frage versuche ich im Rahmen meiner abschließenden Master Dissertation

> *„Corporate Valuation in the German Banking Sector – Definition of the Status Quo, Quantifying the Value of German Banks by existing Approaches and Development of a new Evaluation Model"*

zur Erlangung des Grades „Master of Business Administration (MBA)" zu beantworten. Mit dieser Umfrage möchte ich gerne den Status quo in der deutschen Bankenlandschaft darstellen und ein eigenes Modell zur Unternehmensbewertung im Bankenbereich entwickeln.

Um zu brauchbaren Ergebnissen zu kommen, bin ich auf Ihre Hilfe angewiesen (vgl. auch umseitiges abgedrucktes Begleitschreiben meiner Universität). Deshalb richte ich hiermit meine Bitte an Sie, beiliegenden Fragebogen zu beantworten und an mich zurückzusenden. Die Beantwortung ist aufgrund der Erläuterung der Fachtermini recht einfach und schnell erledigt. Die Beantwortung der Umfrage ist auch für Sie interessant – wenn Sie mir einige wenige Daten Ihres Hauses zur Verfügung stellen, **bewerte ich Ihr Unternehmen** nach klassischen, bereits bestehenden Verfahren und nach meinem selbst entwickelten Ansatz.

Selbstverständlich garantiere ich Ihnen absolute Anonymität Ihrer Antworten! Da die Master Dissertation nur über einen begrenzten Zeitraum geschrieben werden darf, wäre ich Ihnen für eine schnelle Rücksendung sehr dankbar! Die Ergebnisse lasse ich Ihnen nach Fertigstellung gerne zukommen. Sollten Sie weitere Rückfragen haben, stehe ich selbstverständlich unter unten genannten Referenzen zur Verfügung.

In der Hoffnung auf Antwort verbleibe ich

mit freundlichen Grüßen

- Svend Reuse -

<u>Anlagen</u>

SVEND REUSE
BC / DIPL.-BETRIEBSW. (FH) / DIPL.-INFORM. (FH)
HORNHOF 23 • 45478 MÜLHEIM AN DER RUHR•
TELEFON: 0208/84709949 • MOBIL: 0172/2842093
EMAIL: SVEND.REUSE@GMX.DE

Appendix 2: Confirmation Letter of the FOM

**Fachhochschule
für Oekonomie & Management**
University of Applied Sciences

FOM-STUDIENZENTREN
BERLIN | BOCHUM |
BREMEN | DORTMUND |
DUISBURG | DÜSSELDORF |
ESSEN | FRANKFURT A. M. |
GÜTERSLOH | HAMBURG |
KÖLN | MARL | MÜNCHEN |
NEUSS | NÜRNBERG |
SIEGEN

Herrn
Svend Reuse
Hornhof 23
45478 Mülheim

ANRUFE BUNDESWEIT
ZUM CITY-TARIF
Telefon 0180 1810048
Telefax 0180 1810049

POSTANSCHRIFT
Rolandstraße 5-9
45128 Essen

info@fom.de
www.fom.de

Ansprechpartner
Erika Poell
E-Mail
erika.poell@fom.de

Unser Zeichen	Telefon 0201	Telefax 0201	Datum
DS/EP	81004-407	81004-420	2006-04-25

**Matrikelnummer 137186
Studiengang Master of Business Administration (MBA)**

Sehr geehrter Herr Reuse,

gerne bestätigen wir hiermit, dass Sie seit dem 01.09.2004 im Studiengang
Master of Business Administration eingeschrieben sind und das Studium
voraussichtlich im August 2006 abschließen werden.

Mit der Master Thesis wird nachgewiesen, dass während des Studiums alle
erforderlichen Kenntnisse und Fähigkeiten erworben wurden, um selbst-
ständig wissenschaftlich fundierte, integrative Lösungen praxisrelevanter
Probleme zu erarbeiten. Sie kommt im Anspruch und Umfang einer Dip-
lomarbeit gleich. Der wesentliche Unterschied liegt in der Praxisorientie-
rung der Master Thesis, in der in aller Regel konkrete Problemstellungen
aus den Unternehmen bearbeitet werden.

Aktuelle Daten und fundierte Fakten werden für wesentlich erachtet, um eine praxisrelevante und wissenschaftlich wertvolle Arbeit anzufertigen. Eine
gute Recherche im Themengebiet ist hierfür erforderlich. Eine Unterstüt-
zung seitens der angesprochenen Unternehmen wäre daher sehr nützlich.

Mit freundlichen Grüßen
FOM Fachhochschule für
Oekonomie & Management gGmbH
Studienzentrum Essen
Geschäftsleitung

i. V.

Dipl.-Psych. Dagmar Schneider

Erika Poell
Betriebswirtin (VWA)

FOM FACHHOCHSCHULE FÜR
OEKONOMIE & MANAGEMENT
GEMEINNÜTZIGE
GESELLSCHAFT MBH

HOCHSCHULLEITUNG
Prof. Dr. Burghard Hermeier
Rektor
Dr. Harald Beschorner
Kanzler

GESCHÄFTSFÜHRUNG
Klaus Dieter Braun

BANKVERBINDUNGEN
Dresdner Bank AG Essen
Konto 428 051 000
BLZ 360 800 80

National-Bank AG Essen
Konto 121 487
BLZ 360 200 30

Commerzbank AG Essen
Konto 1 231 713
BLZ 360 400 39

St.-Nr. 112/5738/0008

AMTSGERICHT ESSEN
HRB 10896

Appendix 3: Questionnaire addressed to 750 Banks

Svend Reuse
Hornhof 23

45478 Mülheim an der Ruhr

Sie brauchen den Bogen nur zu falten und in einen frankierten Fensterumschlag zu stecken, meine Adresse ist passgenau.

Eine Bitte von mir: Setzen Sie pro Frage bzw. Kategorie nur <u>ein</u> Kreuz – es sei denn, es ist etwas anderes angegeben. Sonst sind die Antworten nur sehr schwer auswertbar.

---

1. Allgemeine Daten zum Kreditinstitut

Dieser Abschnitt hilft mir, die Repräsentativität der Umfrage festzustellen und generelle Aussagen bezüglich eines bestimmten Bankensektors ableiten zu können.

1.1. Wie viele Mitarbeiter hat Ihr Institut?

Anzahl Mitarbeiter: _______________

1.2. Wie groß ist die Jahresdurchschnittsbilanzsumme (JDBS) Ihres Institutes?

JDBS: _______________ Mio. €

1.3. Wie lange existiert das Institut bereits?

☐ seit weniger als 10 Jahren
☐ seit mehr als 10 Jahren
☐ seit mehr als 25 Jahren
☐ seit mehr als 50 Jahren

1.4. Ist Ihr Institut Handelsbuchinstitut?

☐ ja
☐ nein

1.5. Ist Ihr Institut börsennotiert?

☐ ja
☐ nein

1.6. Was zahlen Sie für einen Ø Spread am Geld- und Kapitalmarkt (unbesicherte Papiere)?

Spread: _______________ %

---

2. Fragen zur Banksteuerung

Unternehmenswertermittlung, integrierte Gesamtbanksteuerung und wertorientierte Steuerung sind eng miteinander verbunden. Dieser Abschnitt hat das Ziel, den Status quo der wertorientierten Steuerung festzustellen.

Wertorientiert bedeutet in diesem Zusammenhang primär barwertige Steuerung, aber auch Shareholder Value-orientierte Unternehmensführung.

Gesamtbanksteuerung bedeutet Allokation von Risikokapital auf Risikoklassen, Gesamtbanklimitierung und Ermittlung von Risikotragfähigkeit.

2.1. Verfügt Ihr Haus über eine integrierte Gesamtbanksteuerung?

☐ ja
☐ eine Umsetzung ist nur in Teilbereichen vollzogen
☐ nein

2.2. Welche Steuerungsart hat bei Ihnen den größten Stellenwert?

☐ Optimierung der GuV bzw. der Bilanzwerte
☐ Optimierung aus wertorientierter Sicht

2.3. Welche der folgenden Kennzahlen <u>nutzen</u> Sie zur Unternehmenssteuerung? Wie werten Sie diese?

Kennzahl	Erläuterung	Nut-zung?	Wichtigkeit 1 (hoch) – 4 (gering)			
a) Barwert der Bank	Ziel kann es sein, einen Gesamtbankbarwert zu addieren und dessen Optimierung zu steuern.	☐ ja ☐ nein	1 ☐	2 ☐	3 ☐	4 ☐
b) BE vor oder nach Bewertung	Betriebsergebnis vor oder nach Bewertung. Vor Steuern, aber nach außerordentlichen Positionen.	☐ ja ☐ nein	1 ☐	2 ☐	3 ☐	4 ☐
c) VaR	Value at Risk. Der Verlustwert, der innerhalb einer bestimmten Zeit (z.B. 10 Tage) mit einer bestimmten Wahrscheinlichkeit (z.B. 99%) nicht überschritten wird. Übertragbar auf nahezu alle Risikokategorien.	☐ ja ☐ nein	1 ☐	2 ☐	3 ☐	4 ☐
d) RORAC	Return on risk adjusted capital. Definiert als erwartete Performance durch Value at Risk.	☐ ja ☐ nein	1 ☐	2 ☐	3 ☐	4 ☐
e) RAROC	Risk adjusted return on risk adjusted capital. Vergleich des Ist-RORAC mit dem Ziel-RORAC.	☐ ja ☐ nein	1 ☐	2 ☐	3 ☐	4 ☐
f) EVA	Economic Value added. Definiert als: NOPAT (Net operating Profit after taxes) abzüglich gewichtetem Kapitalkostensatz multipliziert mit dem investierten Kapital. Echte Überrendite über einer am Markt üblichen Rendite.	☐ ja ☐ nein	1 ☐	2 ☐	3 ☐	4 ☐
g) CIR	Cost Income Ratio. Vereinfachend definiert als ordentliche Kosten / ordentliche Erträge.	☐ ja ☐ nein	1 ☐	2 ☐	3 ☐	4 ☐

Kennzahl	Erläuterung	Nut-zung?	Wichtigkeit 1 (hoch) – 4 (gering)			
h) EKR	Eigenkapitalrentabilität. Bezogen auf alle Eigenkapitalbestandteile nach KWG, aber exklusive Nachrangmittel.	☐ ja ☐ nein	1 ☐	2 ☐	3 ☐	4 ☐
i) Bilanz-wachstum	Wachstumsziel in diversen Bilanzpositionen.	☐ ja ☐ nein	1 ☐	2 ☐	3 ☐	4 ☐
j) Marktan-teil	Gegebenenfalls ist Ihr Ziel Expansion um jeden Preis: dann ist der Marktanteil eine zentrale Steuerungsgröße.	☐ ja ☐ nein	1 ☐	2 ☐	3 ☐	4 ☐
k) Wert der Marke	Falls ermittelbar, kann auch eine Steigerung des immateriellen Firmenwertes eine zentrale Steuerungsgröße sein.	☐ ja ☐ nein	1 ☐	2 ☐	3 ☐	4 ☐
l) Deckungs-beitrag	Nettoertrag. Kundenzins bereinigt um Refinanzierung, gegebenenfalls abzüglich Stückkosten und Risikokosten.	☐ ja ☐ nein	1 ☐	2 ☐	3 ☐	4 ☐
m) DB-Barwert	Verbarwertung der oben genannten Größe.	☐ ja ☐ nein	1 ☐	2 ☐	3 ☐	4 ☐
n) Balanced Scorecard	Vierdimensionales Kennzahlen- und Prozesssystem zur ganzheitlichen Unternehmenssteuerung.	☐ ja ☐ nein	1 ☐	2 ☐	3 ☐	4 ☐

3. Fragen zur Unternehmenswertermittlung

Mit diesem Abschnitt soll der Status quo der Unternehmenswertermittlung evaluiert werden. Der Unternehmenswert ist der Kaufpreis, den Ihr Institut zur Zeit am Markt erzielen könnte – natürlich immer unter gewissen Annahmen. Eine Fusion / ein Verkauf ist nur ein Grund der Unternehmenswertermittlung. Zu internen Steuerungszwecken und auch für die Ermittlung der Risikotragfähigkeit ist es schon wichtig, diesen Wert zu kennen.

3.1. Welche Form der Unternehmenswertermittlung <u>kennen</u> Sie? Wie werten Sie diese? Bitte <u>werten</u> Sie diese in der letzten Spalte <u>nur</u>, wenn Sie sie auch kennen.

Bewertungsmethode		Kurze, nicht abschließende Erläuterung	Be-kannt?	Wertung 1 (gut) – 4 (schlecht)			
Substanzwert	*Reproduktionswert*	Wert bei Neuerrichtung eines Unternehmens „auf der grünen Wiese".	☐ ja ☐ nein	1 ☐	2 ☐	3 ☐	4 ☐
	Liquidationswert	Veräußerung des Unternehmens im Liquidationsfall. Keine Berücksichtigung immaterieller Vermögensgegenstände.	☐ ja ☐ nein	1 ☐	2 ☐	3 ☐	4 ☐
Ertragswertverfahren		Verbarwertung zukünftiger nachhaltig erzielbare (!) Erträge des Unternehmens. Steuerzahlungen sind zu berücksichtigen. Diskontierung mit risikofreier Rendite plus Aufschlag.	☐ ja ☐ nein	1 ☐	2 ☐	3 ☐	4 ☐
Discounted Cashflow Ansätze	*Equity Approach*	Verbarwertung der Cashflows des Unternehmens statt der Gewinne. Beim Equity Approach wird mit dem Eigenkapitalkostensatz (z.B. über CAPM – Capital Asset Pricing Model) abgezinst. Hierbei gilt der Cashflow nach Steuern, Zinsen, Tilgung und Investitionen. Der (Bar)Wert des Fremdkapitals ist nicht abzuziehen.	☐ ja ☐ nein	1 ☐	2 ☐	3 ☐	4 ☐

Bewertungs-methode		Kurze, nicht abschließende Erläuterung	Be-kannt?	Wertung *1 (gut) – 4 (schlecht)*			
	Entity Approach	Der Cashflow, der allen Kapitalgebern zusteht, wird mit dem WACC (weighted average costs of capital) abgezinst. Zum Cashflow des Equity Approaches werden Zinsen und Tilgungen addiert. Der Wert des Fremdkapitals ist im Nachgang hiervon abzuziehen. Unter dieser Position wird vereinfachend (!) auch das APV (Adjusted Present Value) Verfahren verstanden.	☐ ja ☐ nein	1 ☐	2 ☐	3 ☐	4 ☐
Multiplikator-verfahren /& Comparable Company Ana-lysis		Analyse von vergleichbaren (börsennotierten) Unternehmen und Ermittlung von Relativkennzahlen. Beispiel: Ein Unternehmen hat nach Analyse der Marktkapitalisierung einen Marktwert, der im Schnitt dem 1,8-fachen Buchwert entspricht.	☐ ja ☐ nein	1 ☐	2 ☐	3 ☐	4 ☐
Real Option Approach		Übertragung des Finanzoptionsmodells auf reale Optionen: Ein Unternehmen hat die Möglichkeit, aber nicht die Pflicht, eine (real existierende) Option auszuüben. Wird oft verwendet, wenn kein positiver Cashflow oder Ertrag zu erwarten ist. Der Wert des Unternehmens entspricht vereinfacht ausgedrückt dem Zeitwert der Option.	☐ ja ☐ nein	1 ☐	2 ☐	3 ☐	4 ☐

3.2. Ermitteln Sie bereits Ihren Unternehmenswert?

☐ ja
☐ nein,
    ☐ wir planen aber, dies in naher Zukunft umzusetzen
    ☐ wir werden dies auch in absehbarer Zeit nicht anstreben

Wenn Sie die Frage 3.2. mit „nein" beantwortet haben, können Sie direkt mit Abschnitt 4 fortfahren. Alle nun folgenden Fragen sind nur dann relevant, wenn Sie bereits Ihren Unternehmenswert ermitteln. Scheuen Sie sich jedoch nicht, den Fragebogen trotzdem einzusenden – natürlich sind auch solche Bögen für die Auswertung sehr interessant!

3.3. Wie lange ermitteln Sie bereits Ihren Unternehmenswert?

☐ seit 0 – 3 Jahren
☐ 3 – 6 Jahren
☐ länger als 6 Jahre

3.4. Wie oft ermitteln Sie Ihren Unternehmenswert?

☐ täglich
☐ wöchentlich
☐ monatlich
☐ vierteljährlich
☐ jährlich
☐ sporadisch

3.5. Was ist bzw. war für Sie der Grund für die Unternehmensbewertung?

☐ Fusion
☐ Unternehmensverkauf (in Teilen)
☐ Börsengang
☐ wertorientierte Unternehmenssteuerung

3.6. Welche(s) Verfahren nutzen Sie? (mehr als ein Kreuz möglich)

- ☐ Equity Approach
- ☐ Entity Approach / Adjusted Present Value
- ☐ Liquidationswert
- ☐ Reproduktionswert
- ☐ Multiplikatoransatz
- ☐ Real Option Approach
- ☐ Ertragswertverfahren
- ☐ Andere: *Bitte kurz erläutern, um was es sich handelt:*

____

____

____

3.7. Implementieren Sie immaterielle Vermögenswerte (z.B. nicht bilanzierbare Firmenwerte oder Human Capital) in Ihren Unternehmenswert?

- ☐ ja
- ☐ nein

3.8. Kennt Ihre Geschäftsleitung die Ergebnisse?

- ☐ ja, die Geschäftsleitung wird regelmäßig hierüber informiert, ein konkreter Handlungsimpuls wird jedoch nicht generiert – „nice to know"
- ☐ ja, die Geschäftsleitung wird regelmäßig hierüber informiert und handelt dementsprechend
- ☐ nein, die Ermittlung ist nur für Fachbereiche interessant

---

4. Unternehmensbewertung Ihres Institutes

Auch wenn Sie Ihren Unternehmenswert bereits kennen sollten – **ich werde dies für Sie aufbereiten, wenn Sie mir entsprechende Daten zur Verfügung stellen.** Diese lasse ich Ihnen dann natürlich zukommen. Selbstverständlich behandele ich diese Detaildaten absolut vertraulich! Bedenken Sie – billiger und vor allem diskreter können Sie hier keine Ergebnisse erhalten! Und: je genauer Ihre Angaben, desto realistischer wird der von mir ermittelte Wert sein.

4.1. Wünschen Sie eine individuelle Unternehmensbewertung?

- ☐ ja
- ☐ nein

Wenn Sie die Frage 4.1. mit „nein" beantwortet haben, bitte ich Sie, direkt mit Abschnitt 5 fortfahren! Allerdings gebe ich zu bedenken, dass Sie gratis eine individuelle Unternehmensbewertung mit einem von mir entwickelten Modell erhalten!

4.2. Daten zur GuV

Hierzu benötige ich von Ihnen die aktuellen Ist-Zahlen der letzten drei Jahre sowie eine Wachstumsprognose für die kommenden Jahre. Ist letztere nicht vorhanden, wird der letzte Jahresabschluss für die Zukunft fortgeschrieben. Alle Angaben bitte in **Mio. €!**

	Jahr -2	Jahr -1	Jahr 0	Ø Prognose Folgejahre
+ Zinsertrag				
- Zinsaufwand				
+/- Derivateergebnis				
+ Provisionsergebnis				
- Personalaufwand				
- Sachaufwand				
+/- Saldo sonstige und a.o. Positionen				
+/- Bewertungsergebnis Kredit				
+/- Bewertungsergebnis Wertpapiere				
- Steuerzahlungen				
+/- §340f HGB				
= Bilanzgewinn				

4.3. Daten zur Bilanz   passend zur GuV aus 4.2

Des Weiteren benötige ich von Ihnen Daten zur Bilanz. Einige dieser Dinge sind bereits von der BaFin per 30.09.2005 im Rahmen der Zinsschockumfrage Basel II bei Ihnen erfragt worden – deshalb handelt es sich primär um bereits bekannte Daten.

Aktiva					Passiva			
	Position	*Volumen in Mio. €*	*Ø Zins in %*	*Ø Rest-Zinsbindung in Jahren*	*Position*	*Volumen in Mio. €*	*Ø Zins in %*	*Ø Rest-Zinsbindung in Jahren*
Zinsbuch	*Kundengeschäft fest*				*Kundengeschäft fest*			
	Kundengeschäft variabel				*Kundengeschäft variabel*			
	Depot A – Bonds				*Eigengeschäft*			
Buchwert sonstige Aktiva & Kasse					Buchwert sonstige Passiva inkl. EWB/PWB			
Aktien und Beteiligungen					Eigenkapital *(ohne Nachrang)*			

Anmerkung zur Ø Rest-Zinsbindung: Zu vergleichen mit der **Duration**. Haben Sie Geschäfte, die in der Regel 10 Jahre laufen und über die Laufzeit gleichverteilt sind, so ist die Ø Rest-Zinsbindung 5 Jahre. Ein gleitender Durchschnitt von 10 Jahren entspricht somit auch einer Ø Rest-Zinsbindung von 5 Jahren. In der Regel führen nur sehr viele endfällige Geschäfte zu größeren Ø Rest-Zinsbindungen als 5 Jahre. Das BaFin bezeichnete diese Größe in seiner Umfrage als „mittlere Laufzeit".

In Ergänzung dazu <u>können</u> Sie mir auch Ihren Gesamtbank-Cashflow zur Verfügung stellen, am besten auf Jahresbänder gemappt und passend zu o.g. Bilanz. Der Cashflow enthält in dieser Definition festverzinsliche und variable Aktiva und Passiva, aber auch Spezialfonds und Derivate. <u>Nicht</u> enthalten sein sollten Wertberichtigungen und Kasse.

Zeitpunkt	Cashflow in Mio. €
Tag 1	
Jahr 1	
Jahr 2	
Jahr 3	
Jahr 4	
Jahr 5	
Jahr 6	
Jahr 7	
Jahr 8	
Jahr 9	
Jahr 10	
Summe Folgejahre	

4.4. Daten zur Kostenverteilung (Personal und Sachkosten)

Des Weiteren benötige ich Daten zur Kostenverteilung. Zentrale Idee ist die **Aufteilung aller Kosten nach der Verursachung: Kosten für Bestandspflege (Stab/Overhead) vs. Kosten für Neugeschäfte (Vertrieb).** Generell gilt: in einer „idealen" Welt sind zumindest die „Vertriebler" (Personalkosten) einer Bank zuständig für Neugeschäfte.

Kostenart	Erläuterung	Prozentsatz
Vertrieb	Zuständig für neue Geschäfte, nicht oder kaum für Bestandsgeschäft.	%
Back Office & Overhead	Zuständig für die Pflege des Bestandsgeschäftes oder für die Stabsmitarbeit. Geht voll als verbarwerteter (negativ wirkender) Kostenbestandteil in den Unternehmensbarwert ein.	%
Σ		100 %

4.5. Daten zur Bestandsprovision

Bitte schätzen Sie: Wie viel Prozent Ihrer Provisionen (vierte Zeile auf Seite 6 oben) sind echte Bestandsprovisionen, die Sie auch erhalten würden, wenn Sie keine Akquise mehr betreiben würden?

Schätzung: _____________%

---

5. Abschließendes

5.1. Wenn Sie noch weitere fachliche Dinge oder Anmerkungen zu diesem Fragebogen haben, so können Sie dies hier zum Ausdruck bringen:

____

____

____

____

5.2. Art und Umfang der Veröffentlichung

Selbstverständlich habe ich Verständnis dafür, dass Sie Ihre Daten absolut vertraulich behandelt wissen wollen. Generell verpflichte ich mich, die von Ihnen erhaltenen Informationen nur **anonymisiert** für meine Master Arbeit zu verwenden, wenn Sie dies wünschen. Allerdings kann eine namentliche Nennung Ihres Institutes partiell sinnvoll sein. Bitte treffen Sie Ihre Wahl:

☐   Sie können den Namen und die Daten meines Institutes in Ihrer Arbeit erwähnen.

☐   Wir möchten nicht, dass der Name unseres Institutes in Ihrer Arbeit auftaucht. Bitte wählen Sie Bezeichnungen wie „Bank «No»" o.ä.

5.3. Kontaktadresse

Nach Vollendung meiner Arbeit stelle ich Ihnen bei Bedarf gerne die Ergebnisse zur Verfügung. Bitte geben Sie doch in diesem Falle Ihre Kontaktadresse oder Email an, an welche ich Ihnen Ihr persönliches Exemplar senden kann.

☐   Bitte senden Sie mir nach Vollendigung die Ergebnisse der Master Dissertation zu.

Name: _____________________________

Straße: _____________________________

Ort: _____________________________

Tel.:   _____________________________

Email: _____________________________

Herzlichen Dank, dass Sie sich die Zeit genommen haben, diesen Fragebogen zu beantworten!

Svend Reuse

Bibliography

Achleitner, P. / Dresig, T. (2000): Unternehmensbewertung, marktorientierte, in: *Ballwieser, W. / Coenenberg, A. / Wysocki, K. von* (ed.): Handwörterbuch der Rechnungslegung und Prüfung, 3rd edition, Stuttgart 2002, column 2432 – 2445.

Adamus, N. / Koch, T. (2006): Bewertung von Banken, in: *Drukarczyk, J. / Ernst, D.* (ed.): Branchenorientierte Unternehmensbewertung, Munich 2006, pp. 131 – 162.

Aders, C. / Schröder, J. (2004): Konsistente Ermittlung des Fortführungswertes bei nominellem Wachstum, in: *Richter, F. / Timmreck, C.* (ed.): Unternehmensbewertung – Moderne Instrumente und Lösungsansätze, Stuttgart 2004, pp. 99 – 116.

Adolf, R. / Cramer, J. / Ollmann, M. (1989a): Die Bewertung von Kreditinstituten – ein Modell zur Ermittlung der Ertragswerte, in: *Die Bank,* Volume 09/1989, Berlin-Cologne 1989, pp. 485 – 492.

Adolf, R. / Cramer, J. / Ollmann, M. (1989b): Die Bewertung von Kreditinstituten – ein Modell zur Ermittlung der Ertragswerte, in: *Die Bank,* Volume 10/1989, Berlin-Cologne 1989, pp. 546 – 554.

Amely, T. / Suciu-Sibianu, P. (2001): Realoptionsbasierte Unternehmensbewertung – ein Praxisbeispiel; in: *Finanzbetrieb,* Volume 3, No. 02.2001, Düsseldorf 2001, pp. 88 – 92.

Aschoff, C. (1978): Betriebliches Humanvermögen – Grundlagen einer Humanvermögensrechnung, Wiesbaden 1978.

Baetge, J. / Heumann, R. (2006): wertorientierte Berichterstattung – Anforderungen des Kapitalmarktes und Umsetzung in der Konzernlageberichterstattung, in: *Der Betrieb,* No. 07 of February 2nd, Düsseldorf 2006, pp. 345 – 350.

BaFin (1999): Zuordnung der Bestände und Geschäfte der Institute zum Handelsbuch und zum Anlagebuch (§ 1 Abs. 12 KWG, § 2 Abs. 11 KWG), circular letter 17/99, reference number I 3 – 1119 – 3/98, Berlin, December 12th, 1999, http://www.bafin.de/rundschreiben/95_1999/rs17_99.htm [accessed on September 3rd, 2006].

BaFin (2005a): Rundschreiben 18/2005 – Mindestanforderungen an das Risikomanagement, Bonn 2005, available from: http://www.bafin.de/rundschreiben/89_2005/051220.htm [accessed on September 3rd, 2006].

BaFin (2005b): Vorgaben zur Umfrage "Ausmaß der Zinsänderungsrisiken im Anlagebuch", accompanying document of the survey, Bonn-Frankfurt 2005.

BaFin (2005c): Umfrage zu Zinsänderungsrisiken im Anlagebuch – Häufig gestellte Fragen (FAQ) und deren Antworten, accompanying document of the survey, Bonn-Frankfurt 2005, available from:
http://www.bundesbank.de/download/bankenaufsicht/pdf/umfrage/FAQ_umfrage.pdf
[accessed on September 3rd, 2006].

BaFin (2006): Zinsänderungsrisiko im Anlagebuch Informationsveranstaltung für die Verbände der Kreditwirtschaft – Präsentation der Ergebnisse der Umfrage, Bonn-Frankfurt, January 27th, 2006.

Ballwieser, W. (1988): Unternehmensbewertung bei unsicherer Geldentwertung, in: *Zeitschrift für betriebswirtschaftliche Forschung*, Volume 40, Düsseldorf 1988, pp. 798 – 812.

Ballwieser, W. (1997): Eine neue Lehre der Unternehmensbewertung?, in: *Der Betrieb*, Volume 50, Düsseldorf 1997, pp. 185 – 191.

Ballwieser, W. (1998): Unternehmensbewertung mit Discounted Cash Flow-Verfahren, in: *Die Wirtschaftsprüfung*, Volume 51, Düsseldorf 1998, pp. 81 – 92.

Ballwieser, W. (2001): Unternehmensbewertung, Marktorientierung und Ertragswertverfahren, in: *Wagner, U.* (ed.): Zum Erkenntnisstand der Betriebswirtschaftslehre am Beginn des 21. Jahrhunderts, commemorative publication, Loitlsberger-Berlin 2001, pp. 17 – 31.

Ballwieser, W. (2003): Unternehmensbewertung durch Rückgriff auf Marktdaten, in: *Heintzen, M. / Kruschwitz, L.* (ed.): Unternehmen bewerten, Berlin 2003, pp. 13 – 20.

Ballwieser, W. (2004): Unternehmensbewertung – Prozeß, Methoden und Probleme, Stuttgart 2004.

Ballwieser, W. (2005): Verbindungen von Ertragswert- und Discounted-Cashflow-Verfahren, in: *Peemöller, V.H.* (ed.): Praxishandbuch der Unternehmensbewertung, Herne-Berlin 2005, pp. 363 – 373.

Bamberger, B. (1999): Unternehmensbewertung in Deutschland: Die zehn häufigsten Bewertungsfehler; in: *Matschke, M.J. / Sieben, G. / Schildbach, T.* (ed.): Betriebswirtschaftliche Forschung und Praxis, Volume 1999-06, Herne-Berlin, June 1999, pp. 653 – 670.

Bankenverband (2006): Anzahl der Banken und ihrer Zweigstellen in den einzelnen Banken, Berlin 2006, available from:
http://www.bankenverband.de/pic/artikelpic/062006/774-Bankstellen-BGr-0606.pdf
[accessed on September 3rd, 2006].

Bannert, T. (2000): Integriertes Treasury-Management – Bilanzstruktursteuerung mit kombinierten barwertig/periodischen Konzepten, in: *Zeitschrift für das gesamte Kreditwesen,* edition 18/2000, Frankfurt 2000, also available from: http://www.zeb.de/zeb/download/leistungen_riskmanagement/praxis_integrierte_zinsbuchsteuerung.pdf [accessed on September 3rd, 2006].

Banz, R. (1981): The Relationship between Return and Market Value of Common Stock, in: *Journal of Financial Economics,* Rochester 1981, Volume 9, pp. 3 – 18.

Bartetzky, P. / Oesterhelweg, O. (2002): Hat die Fristentransformation Einfluss auf den Wert einer Bank?, in: *Sparkasse* 11/2002, Berlin 2002, pp. 508 – 512, also available from: http://www.finius-group.net/downloads/fachartikel/FRISTENT.pdf [accessed on July 15th, 2006].

Bartke, G. (1978): Grundsätze ordnungsgemäßer Unternehmensbewertung – Zur Entwicklung und zum Stand der Diskussion über die Unternehmensbewertung, in: *Zeitschrift für betriebswirtschaftliche Forschung,* Volume 30, Düsseldorf 1978, pp. 238 – 250.

Bauch, J. (1998): Positive Erfahrungen mit dem Barwertkonzept, in: *Betriebswirtschaftliche Blätter* No. 9/1998, Berlin 1998, pp. 447 – 453.

Bausch, A. (2000): Die Multiplikator-Methode – Ein betriebswirtschaftlich sinnvolles Instrument zur Unternehmenswert- und Kaufpreisfindung in Akquisitionsprozessen?; in: *Finanzbetrieb,* Volume 2, No. 7 / 8, 2nd edition, 07./08.2000, Düsseldorf 2000, pp. 448 – 459.

Becker, G. M. / Seeger, N. (2003): Internationale Cash Flow-Rechnungen aus Eigner- und Gläubigersicht, Hochschule für Bankwirtschaft / HfB, working paper No. 48, Frankfurt 2003, available from: http://www.hfb.de/Dateien/Arbeits48e.pdf [accessed on September 3rd, 2006].

Beer, A. / Goj, W. (2002): Zinsrisikomanagement mit Ablaufbilanz und Barwertmethode, Stuttgart 2002.

Behm, U. (1994): Shareholder-Value und Eigenkapitalkosten von Banken, Bern 1994.

Behr, B. / Dörner, H. (2001): Steuerung des Zinsbuchrisikos mit dem Barwertkonzept, in: S-Management, No. 41, Stuttgart 2001, pp. 21 – 28.

Beisel, W. / Klumpp, H.-H. (1991): Der Unternehmenskauf, 2nd edition, Munich 1991.

Bellarz, S. (2002): Strategien im Zinsbuch, in: *Eller, R. / Gruber, W. / Reif, M.* (ed.): Risikomanagement und Risikocontrolling im modernen Treasury-Management, Stuttgart 2002, pp. 521 – 576.

Bellinger, B. / Vahl, G. (1992): Unternehmensbewertung in Theorie und Praxis, 2nd edition, Wiesbaden 1992.

Benninga, S. Z. / Sarig, O. H. (1997): Corporate Finance; A Valuation Approach, New York 1997.

Berekoven, L. / Eckert, W. / Ellenrieder, P. (2004): Marktforschung – Methodische Grundlagen und praktische Anwendung, Wiesbaden 2004.

Bertsch, A. (2002): Zinsswaps im Jahresabschluss und der Steuerbilanz, in: *Eller, R. / Gruber, W. / Reif, M.* (ed.): Risikomanagement und Risikocontrolling im modernen Treasury Management, Stuttgart 2002, pp. 449 – 473.

BFH (1991): Judgement of 1991-03-06, II R 18/88 BStBl II 1991, pp. 558.

Bhandari, L. (1988): Debt/Equity Ratio and Expected Common Returns: Empirical Evidence, in: *Journal of Finance*, Volume 43, no place 1988, pp. 507 – 525.

Biehsmann, J. (2004): Barwertige Risikotragfähigkeitsermittlung und Ableitung von Limiten, presentation at the ifb SparkassenDIALOG, Cologne, September 23rd, 2004.

Biermann, B. / Grosser, K. (1999): Taschenlexikon Finanzmathematik / Statistik, Stuttgart 1999.

Bimmler, M. / Mönke, R. (2004): Sockel der Gesamtbanksteuerung, in: *Bankpraxis + Geschäftspolitik* No. 3/2004, Berlin 2004, pp. 31 – 34, also available from: http://www.ifb-group.com/html/download/fachartikel/2004/BI_04_03Risikotragfaehigkeit.pdf [accessed on September 3rd, 2006].

Black, F. (1993): Beta and Return, in: *Journal of Portfolio Management*, Volume 8, New Hope 1993, pp. 5 – 20.

Black, F. / Jensen, M. / Scholes, M. S. (1972): The Capital Asset Pricing Model: Some Empirical Tests, in: *Jensen, M.* (ed.): Studies in the Theory of Capital Markets, no place 1972, pp. 79 – 124.

Black, F. / Scholes, M. S. (1973): The pricing of options and corporate liabilities, in: *Journal of Political Economy*, Volume 81, Chicago 1973, pp. 637 – 654.

Bleymüller, J. / Gehlert, G. / Gülicher, H. (1996): Statistik für Wirtschaftswissenschaftler, 10th edition, Munich 1996.

Böcking, H. J. / Nowak, K. (1999): Marktorientierte Unternehmensbewertung - Darstellung und Würdigung der marktorientierten Vergleichsverfahren vor dem Hintergrund der deutschen Kapitalmarktverhältnisse, in: *Finanzbetrieb*, Volume 1, No. 8, Düsseldorf 1999, pp. 169 – 176.

Böhm-Dries, A. (2006): Risikokapitalallokation in Kreditinstituten, presentation at the ifb SparkassenDIALOG, Cologne, June 29th, 2006.

Born, K. (2003): Unternehmensanalyse und Unternehmensbewertung, 2nd edition, Stuttgart 2003.

Börner, C. / Lowis, S. (1997): Ein Rahmenmodell für die Umsetzung des Shareholder-value-Konzepts bei Banken, pp. 87 – 133, no place 1997, available from: http://www.econbiz.de/archiv/k/uk/ibank/rahmenmodell_umsetzung_sv.pdf [accessed on September 3rd, 2006].

Börsig, C. (1993): Unternehmenswert und Unternehmensbewertung; in: *Zeitschrift für betriebswirtschaftliche Forschung*, Volume 45, No. 1, Düsseldorf 1993, pp. 79 – 91.

Böttrich, U. / Drosdzol, A. / Hager, P. / Schleicher, H. (2004): Optimierung gleitender Durchschnitte für die barwertige Zinsbuchsteuerung, in: *Betriebswirtschaftliche Blätter*, Volume 53, No. 01/2004, Berlin 2004, pp. 28 – 31.

Brealey, R. A. / Myers, S. C. (1996): Principles of Corporate Finance, 5th edition, New York 1996.

Bretzke, W.-R. (1975): Das Prognoseproblem bei Unternehmensbewertung, Düsseldorf 1975.

Bretzke, W.-R. (1976): Zur Berücksichtigung des Risikos bei der Unternehmensbewertung, in: *Zeitschrift für betriebswirtschaftliche Forschung*, Volume 28, No. 2, Düsseldorf 1976, pp. 153 – 165.

Breuer, W. (2001): Unternehmensbewertung: Equity-, Entity- und APV-Ansatz, in: *WISU – Das Wirtschaftsstudium*, No. 11/01, Düsseldorf 2001, pp. 1511 – 1515.

Buchner, R. (1981): Grundzüge der Finanzanalyse, Munich 1981.

Buffet, W. (n.Y.): "Price is what you pay. value is what you get.", cited on: http://www.brainyquote.com/quotes/quotes/w/warrenbuff149692.html [accessed on September 3rd, 2006].

Bundesbank (2005): Verzeichnis der Kreditinstitute und ihrer Verbände sowie der Treuhänder für Kreditinstitute in der Bundesrepublik Deutschland, Frankfurt 2005, available from: http://www.bundesbank.de/download/bankenaufsicht/pdf/ verzeichnis_kreditinstitute_2006.pdf [accessed on September 3rd, 2006].

Bundesbank (2006a): Histories wt03400 – wt 3409: capital market rates per December 31st, 2005, Frankfurt 2006, available from: http://www.bundesbank.de/statistik/statistik_zeitreihen.php?func=list&tr=www_s300 _it03b [accessed on September 3rd, 2006].

Bundesbank (2006b): Histories st0304, st0310, st0316, st0325, st0343: money market rates per December 31st, 2005, Frankfurt 2006, available from: http://www.bundesbank.de/statistik/statistik_zeitreihen.php?func=list&tr=www_s11b _gmt [accessed on September 3rd, 2006].

Bundesbank (2006c): History wz9826: yield curve (Svensson-method) / stock-listed bonds of Germany/ 10.0 years maturity, Frankfurt 2006, available from: http://www.bundesbank.de/statistik/statistik_zeitreihen.php?func=row&tr=wz9826 [accessed on September 3rd, 2006].

Bundesbank (2006d): History su0022: Average yield for normal 3 month savings, available from: http://www.bundesbank.de/statistik/statistik_zeitreihen.php?func=row&tr=su0022 [accessed on September 3rd, 2006].

Casey, C. (2003): Unternehmensbewertung anhand von Discounted Cash Flow-Modellen – Ein methodischer Vergleich der verschiedenen Verfahren, habilitation at University of Wien, Wien 2003.

Claus, J. / Thomas, J. (2001): Equity Premia as Low as Three Percent? Evidence from Analysts' Earnings Forecast for Domestic and International Stock Markets, in: *Journal of Finance*, Volume 56, no place 2001, pp. 1629 – 1666.

Coenenberg, A. G. / Sautter, M. T. (1988): Strategische und finanzielle Bewertung von Unternehmensakquisitionen; in: *Die Betriebswirtschaft*, Volume 48, No. 6, Stuttgart 1988, pp. 691 – 710.

Coenenberg, A. G. / Schultze, W. (2002): Unternehmensbewertung: Konzeptionen und Perspektiven, in: *Die Betriebswirtschaft*, Volume 62, No. 6, Stuttgart 2002, pp. 597 – 621, also available from: http://www.wiwi.uni-augsburg.de/bwl/coenenberg/download/beitraege/ub_dbw.pdf [accessed on September 3rd, 2006].

Copeland, T. E. / Koller, T. / Murrin, J. (1994): Valuation. Measuring and Managing the value of Companies, 2nd edition, New York 1994.

Copeland, T. E. / Koller, T. / Murrin, J. (1998): Unternehmenswert. Methoden und Strategien für eine wertorientierte Unternehmensführung, 2nd edition, Frankfurt 1998.

Copeland, T. E. / Koller, T. / Murrin, J. (2002): Unternehmenswert – Methoden und Strategien für eine wertorientierte Unternehmensführung, 3rd edition, Frankfurt 2002.

Crasselt, N. / Tomaszewski, C. (1999): Unternehmerische Flexibilität bei strategischen Akquisitionen – Einsatzmöglichkeiten von Optionspreismodellen; in: *Controlling*, Volume 11, No. 11, Munich-Frankfurt 1999, pp. 517 – 524.

Crecelius, J. (2006): Quantifizierung und Steuerung der Zinsänderungsrisiken des Anlagebuches, in: *Becker, A. / Gruber, W. / Wohlert, D.* (ed.): Handbuch MaRisk, Frankfurt 2006, pp. 265 – 276.

Csoport, P. / Linner, F. (2002): Shareholder Value: Instrument zur Nutzenmaximierung des Managements? – Eine kritische Betrachtung, Zürich 2002, available from: http://www.isb.unizh.ch/publikationen/pdf/workingpapernr32.pdf#search=%22share holder%20value%20shareholder%20wealth%22 [accessed on September 3rd, 2006].

Daske, H. / Gebhardt, G. / Klein, S. (2004): Estimating the Expected Cost of Equity Capital Using Consensus Forecasts. Working paper No. 124 of *Finance & Accounting*, Johann Wolfgang Goethe-University, Frankfurt 2004.

Dauber, M. / Pfeiffer, G. (2006): Rahmenbedingungen des Risikomanagements, in: *Pfeifer, G. / Ullrich, W. / Wimmer, K.* (ed.): MaRisk Umsetzungsleitfaden: Neue Planungs-, Steuerungs- und Reportingpflichten gemäß Mindestanforderungen an das Risikomanagement, Heidelberg 2006, pp. 221 – 284.

Deutsches Aktieninstitut (2004): DAX-Renditen seit 1948, Stand: 31. Dezember 2003, Frankfurt 2004, available from: http://www.dai.de/internet/dai/dai-2-0.nsf/LookupDL/ 909195F9F5C9400CC1256E2E00311DE4/$File/DAX-Renditedreieck_2003.pdf# search=%22dax%20rendite%22 [accessed on September 3rd, 2006].

Die Welt (2003): Europäische Banken stehen kurz vor einer Welle von Fusionen und Übernahmen, Berlin, September 24th, 2003, available from: http://www.welt.de/data/2003/09/24/172764.html [accessed on September 3rd, 2006].

Dietzel, M. (2005): Ergänzung der barwertigen Zinsbuchsteuerung: Ableitung einer Risikotragfähigkeit und Überleitung zur GuV, presentation at the ifb SparkassenDIALOG, Cologne, September 8th, 2005.

Dillman, D. A. (1978): Mail and telephone surveys – The total design method, New York 1978.

Drosdzol, A. / Hager, P. (2005): Abbildung variabel verzinslicher Produkte im Zinsbuch-Cashflow, in: *Wiedemann, A. / Lüders, U.* (ed.): Integrierte Rendite-/ Risikosteuerung, Montabaur 2005, pp. 123 – 139.

Drost, F. M. / Telgheder M. (2006): Wer darf die Marke Sparkasse nutzen?, in *Handelsblatt* No. 129, July 7th, Düsseldorf 2006, p. 23, also available from: http://www.emissionshaus.com/kc/deutsch/news/pressespiegel.db?item=18470 [accessed on September 3rd, 2006].

Drukarczyk, J. (1996): Unternehmensbewertung, Munich 1996.

Drukarczyk, J. (2003): Unternehmensbewertung, 4th edition, Munich 2003.

Drukarczyk, J. / Honold, D. (1999): Unternehmensbewertung, DCF-Methoden und der Wert steuerlicher Finanzierungsvorteile, in: *ZBB*, Volume 11, no place 1999, pp. 333 – 349.

Eisenmann, S. / Höfele, O. (n.Y.): Die Anwendung der Discounted Cashflow Varianten Equity, APV und WACC auf Kapital- und Personengesellschaften, available from: http://www.cashflow.de/download/white_papers/DiscountedCashflow.pdf [accessed on September 3rd, 2006].

Eller, R. (1996): Zinsswaps – Produktbeschreibung, Pricing und Bewertung, in: *Eller, R.* (ed.): Handbuch derivativer Instrumente, Stuttgart 1996, pp. 401 – 418.

Entrop, O. / Scholz, H. / Wilkens, M. (2002): Zum Einfluss der Fristentransformation auf den Wert einer Bank, in: *Sparkasse* No. 08/2002, Berlin 2002, pp. 360 – 364, also available from: http://www.ku-eichstaett.de/Fakultaeten/WWF/Lehrstuehle/LFB/ download/HF_sections/content/fristentransformation_entrop_scholz_wilkens.pdf [accessed on September 3rd, 2006].

Ernst & Young (1997): Entwicklung des Sharholder-value-Ansatzes – eine Umfrage bei Bankvorständen. Presentation of results of the former Gesellschaft für Bankrevision, today Ernst and Young, Bern 1997.

Ernst, D. / Thümmel, R. C. (2000): Realoptionen zur Strukturierung von M&A-Transaktionen; in: *Finanzbetrieb*, Volume 2, No. 11, Düsseldorf 2000, pp. 665 – 673.

Everding, M. / Meier, C. (2001): Barwertige Ermittlung des Zinsänderungsrisikos, in: S-Management, No. 41, Stuttgart 2001, pp. 16 – 20.

Ewert, R. / Wagenhofer, A. (2000): Rechnungslegung und Kennzahlen für das wertorientierte Management, in: *Wagenhofer, A. / Hrebicek, G.* (ed.): Wertorientiertes Management, Stuttgart 2000, pp. 3 – 64.

Fama, E. / French, K. (1992): The Cross-Section of Expected Stock Returns, in: *Journal of Finance*, Volume 47, no place 1992, pp. 427 – 465.

Fama, E. / MacBeth, J. (1973): Risk, Return and Equilibrium: Empirical Tests, in: *Journal of Political Economy*, Volume 81, Chicago 1973, pp. 607 – 636.

Feix, M. / Stechmeyer-Emden, K. / Stückler, R. (2006): Integration von Risiken und Risikotragfähigkeit, in: *Becker, A. / Gruber, W. / Wohlert, D.* (ed.): Handbuch MaRisk, Frankfurt 2006, pp. 103 – 116.

Feldmann, K. (2004): Achtung Marke! For *Sparkasse* 12/04, no place 2004, IconValueAdded, available from: http://www.icon-added-value.com/deutsch/presse/pdf/2005/marken_geben_flanken.pdf [accessed on September 3rd, 2006].

Fingerhut, T. (2001): Controlling im genossenschaftlichen Bankensektor, Paderborn December 14th, 2001, available from: http://wiwi.uni-paderborn.de/bwl3/de/Rahmen_re/download/material/gast/fingerhut14122001.pdf [accessed on September 3rd, 2006].

Fischer, E. O. (1999): Die Bewertung riskanter Investitionen mit dem risikolosen Zinsfuß, in: *Albach, H.* (ed.): Innovation und Investition, Zeitschrift für Betriebswirtschaft No. 1/99, Wiesbaden 1999, pp. 25 – 42.

Fischer, H. (1989): Bewertung beim Unternehmens- und Beteiligungskauf; in: *Hölters, W.* (ed.), Handbuch des Unternehmens- und Beteiligungskaufs, 2nd edition, Cologne 1989, pp. 51 – 176.

Franke, D. (2004): Die 1.000 größten Banken der Welt: Wieder auf Kurs, in: *Die Bank*, Berlin-Cologne, November 2004, available from: http://www.die-bank.de/printArtikel.asp?artID=361 [accessed on September 3rd, 2006].

Freiburg, M. / Timmreck, C. (2004): Fundamentalmultiples, in: *Richter, F. / Timmreck, C.* (ed.): Unternehmensbewertung, moderne Instrumente und Lösungsansätze, Stuttgart 2004, pp. 381 – 396.

Frère, E. / Reuse, S. (2006): Kriterien und Aufbau eines effizienten Anreizsystems im Bankenbereich, in: Controller Magazin, Volume 31, No. 05/2006, Offenburg and Wörthsee/München, September 2006, pp. 484 – 492.

Friedag, U. / Klassen, S. / Robers, M. (2003): Barwertige Zinsbuchsteuerung gemäß VR-Control, in: *Bankpraxis + Geschäftspolitik* 10/2003, Berlin 2003, pp. 34 – 39, also available from: http://www.ifb-group.com/html/download/fachartikel/2003/BI0310_ifb.pdf [accessed on September 3rd, 2006].

Funk, J. (1995): Aspekte der Unternehmensbewertung in der Praxis; in: *Zeitschrift für betriebswirtschaftliche Forschung*, Volume 47, No. 5, Düsseldorf 1995, pp. 491 – 514.

Gaughan, P. A. (2002): Mergers, Acquisitions and Corporate Restructurings, 3rd edition, New York 2002.

Gebhardt, W. R. / Lee, C. M. C. / Swaminathan, B. (2001): Toward An Implied Cost of Capital, in: *Journal of Accounting Research*, no place 2001, Volume 39, pp. 135 – 176.

Gerling, C. (1985): Unternehmensbewertung in den USA, Bergisch Gladbach-Cologne 1985.

Giesecke, K. / Kühne, J. (2005):Von der Zinsbuch- zur Gesamtbanksteuerung, in: *Eller, R.* (ed.): Gesamtbanksteuerung und qualitatives Aufsichtsrecht, Stuttgart 2005, pp. 105 – 139.

Gode, D. / Mohanram, P. (2002): Inferring the Cost of Capital Using the Ohlson-Juettner Model, working paper, University of New York.

Goebel, R. / Schumacher, M. / Sievi, C. (1997): Bilanzstrukturen mit Performance-Konzept steuern (I), in: *Betriebswirtschaftliche Blätter* No. 8/97, Berlin 1997, pp. 385 – 390.

Goebel, R. / Schumacher, M. / Sievi, C. (1998a): Bilanzstrukturen mit dem Performance-Konzept steuern, in: *Betriebswirtschaftliche Blätter* No. 7/98, Berlin 1998, pp. 332 – 339.

Goebel, R. / Schumacher, M. / Sievi, C. (1998b): Bilanzstrukturen mit dem Performance-Konzept steuern (II), in: *Betriebswirtschaftliche Blätter* No. 7/98, Berlin 1998, pp. 340 – 347.

Göllert, K. / Ringling, W. (1999): Die Eignung des Stuttgarter Verfahrens für die Unternehmens- und Anteilsbewertung im Abfindungsfall, in: *Der Betrieb*, Volume 52, Düsseldorf 1999, pp. 516 – 519.

Göppl, H. (1980): Unternehmungsbewertung und Capital-Asset-Pricing-Theorie; in: *Die Wirtschaftsprüfung*, Volume 33, No. 9, Düsseldorf 1980, pp. 237 – 245.

Grabiak, S. / Kotissek, N. / Küsters, H. / Marusev, A. W. (1988): Die moderne Marktzinsmethode im Tagesgeschäft der Banken, in: *Zeitschrift für das gesamte Kreditwesen*, Volume 41, Frankfurt 1988, pp. 787 – 790.

Gramlich, D. / Peylo, T. (2000): Portfolio Selection auf Basis des Value-at-Risk, in: *Matschke, M.J. / Sieben, G. / Schildbach, T.* (ed.): Betriebswirtschaftliche Forschung und Praxis, No. 5/2000, Herne-Berlin 2000, pp. 507 – 526.

Grill, W. / Perczynski, H. (1998): Wirtschaftslehre des Kreditwesens, Bad Homburg 1998.

Grimmer, U. (2003): Gesamtbanksteuerung – Theoretische und empirische Analyse des Status Quo in der Bundesrepublik Deutschland, Österreich und der Schweiz, dissertation at university of Essen 2003, available from: http://www.ub.uni-duisburg.de/ETD-db/theses/available/duett-08162003-010019/unrestricted/grimmerdiss.pdf [accessed on September 3rd, 2006].

Gröning, J. (2004): MaK aus Sicht der Kreditpraxis, in: *Gröning, J. / Hoock, R. / Lammer, M. / Maifarth, M. / Renz, S. / Schneider, A. / Struwe, H. / Totzek, A. / Wannhoff, J. / Weis, D.* (ed.): MaK-Praktikerhandbuch, 2nd edition, Heidelberg 2004, pp. 317 – 394.

Günther, T. (1995): Zur Notwendigkeit des Wertsteigerungsmanagements, in: *Högner, K. / Pohl, A.* (ed.): Wertsteigerungs-Management – das Shareholder-value-Konzept: Methoden und erfolgreiche Beispiele, Munich 1995, pp. 13 – 58.

Hachmeister, D. (2000): Der Discounted Cash Flow als Maß der Unternehmenssteigerung, 4th edition, Frankfurt 2000.

Hackmann, A. (1987): Unternehmensbewertung und Rechtsprechung, Wiesbaden 1987.

Hafner, R. (1993): Unternehmensbewertung als Instrument zur Durchsetzung von Verhandlungspositionen, in: *Matschke, M.J. / Sieben, G. / Schildbach, T.* (ed.): Betriebswirtschaftliche Forschung und Praxis, No. 45, Herne-Berlin 1993, pp. 79 – 89.

Harter, W. / Franke, J. / Hogrefe, J. / Seger, R. (2002): Fachbegriffe Börsen und Wertpapiere, 8th edition, Stuttgart 2002.

Hayn, M. (2003): Bewertung junger Unternehmen, 3rd edition, Herne-Berlin 2003.

Heinrich, M. (2002): Einsatz derivativer Instrumente im Treasury Management, in: *Eller, R. / Gruber, W. / Reif, M.* (ed.): Risikomanagement und Risikocontrolling im modernen Treasury Management, Stuttgart 2002, pp. 568 – 590.

Heinzel, D. (2002): Geschäfte in neuartigen Produkten oder neuen Märkten (Produkteinführung eines Kuponswaps), in: *Eller, R. / Gruber, W. / Reif, M.* (ed.): Risikomanagement und Risikocontrolling im modernen Treasury Management, Stuttgart 2002, pp. 404 – 448.

Helbing, C. (1998): Unternehmensbewertung und Steuern, 9th edition, Düsseldorf 1998.

Herter, R. N. (1992): Berücksichtigung von Optionen bei der Bewertung strategischer Investitionen; in: *Controlling*, Volume 4, No. 6, Munich-Frankfurt 1992-11/12, pp. 320 – 327.

Hetzel, H. (1988): Stichtagsszins oder zukünftiger Zins zur Ertragswertermittlung im Rahmen der Unternehmensbewertung, in *Betriebs-Berater*, Volume 43, Frankfurt 1998, pp. 725 – 728.

HGB (2006): Handelsgesetzbuch, available from: http://www.gesetze-im-internet.de/bundesrecht/hgb/gesamt.pdf [accessed on September 3rd, 2006].

Hillmer, M. (2002): Strategische Asset Allocation und Umsetzung in Portfolio-/Fondslösungen, in: *Eller, R. / Gruber, W. / Reif, M.* (ed.): Risikomanagement und Risikocontrolling im modernen Treasury Management, Stuttgart 2002, pp. 492 – 520.

Höhmann, K. (1998): Shareholder Value von Banken, Wiesbaden 1998.

Hommel, U. / Scholich, M. / Baecker, P. N. (2003): Reale Optionen: Konzepte, Praxis und Perspektiven strategischer Unternehmensfinanzierung, Berlin 2003.

Hopfenbeck, W. (1989): Allgemeine Betriebswirtschafts- und Managementlehre, Berlin 1989.

Höpflinger, F. (2002): Ausfälle und Verweigerungen bei Befragungen, available from: http://www.mypage.bluewin.ch/hoepf/fhtop/fhmethod1C.html [accessed on September 3rd, 2006].

Hoppenstedt, D. H. (2005): Speech of the president of the DSGV, strategy day of Sparkassen-Finanzgruppe, Berlin, November 07th, 2005, available from: http://www.publicgovernance.de/knowledge_center/13577.asp [accessed on September 3rd, 2006].

Hornbach, F. / Jung, B. (2001): Ermittlung des Adressenrisikos, in: S-Management, No. 41, Stuttgart 2001, pp. 52 – 59.

Hörter, S. (1998): Shareholder Value-orientiertes Bank-Controlling, Berlin 1998.

Hortmann, S. / Seide, A. (2006): Kapitalallokation und Limitsysteme im Kontext der MaRisk, in: *Becker, A. / Gruber, W. / Wohlert, D.* (ed.): Handbuch MaRisk, Frankfurt 2006, pp. 299 – 332, also available from: http://www.ifb-group.com/html/download/ fachartikel/2006/16_Hortmann_Seide_299-332.pdf [accessed on September 3rd, 2006].

IDW (1992): Wirtschaftsprüfer-Handbuch, Volume II, 10th edition, Düsseldorf 1992.

IDW (2002): Wirtschaftsprüfer-Handbuch, Volume II, 12th edition, Düsseldorf 2002.

IDW (2003): Erhebungsbogen zur Unternehmensbewertung, 2nd edition, Düsseldorf 2003.

IDW (2005): Grundsätze zur Durchführung von Unternehmensbewertungen (IDW S 1), October 18th, 2005, in: *Die Wirtschaftsprüfung* 23/2005, Düsseldorf 2005, pp. 1303 – 1321.

ifb AG (2006): Software tool ProVari 4.3.1.

Jacob, H. (1960): Die Methoden zur Ermittlung des Gesamtwertes einer Unternehmung, in: *Zeitschrift für Betriebswirtschaft*, Volume 30, Wiesbaden 1960, pp. 131 – 147, pp. 209 – 222.

Jakob, K. (2002): Aufsichtsrechtliche Anforderungen an eine moderne Zins- und Adressrisiko-Steuerung, in: *Eller, R. / Gruber, W. / Reif, M.* (ed.): Risikomanagement und Risikocontrolling im modernen Treasury-Management, Stuttgart 2002, pp. 329 – 352.

Jakubowicz, V. K. (2000): Wertorientierte Unternehmensführung, Wiesbaden 2000.

Jennen, B. (2006): Der unendliche Sparkassen-Streit, in: *Financial Times Deutschland*, Hamburg, July 3rd, 2006, p. 20.

Jonas, M. / Löffler, A. / Wiese, J. (2004): Das CAPM mit deutscher Einkommensteuer, in: *WPg*, Volume 57, Düsseldorf 2004, pp. 898.

Jung, W. (1983): Praxis des Unternehmenskaufs, Frankfurt 1983.

Kaninke, M. / Wiedemann, A. (n.Y.): Balanced Scorecard als Instrument des Bankcontrollings, available from: http://www.uni-siegen.de/~banken/bsc.pdf [accessed on September 3rd, 2006].

Kaplan, R. S. / Norton, D. P. (1992): The Balanced Scorecard – Measures that drive Performance, in: *Harvard Business Review*, No. 1/1992, Harvard 1992, pp. 71 – 79.

Kaplan, R. S. / Norton, D. P. (1997): Balanced Scorecard – Strategien erfolgreich umsetzen, Stuttgart 1997.

Kaplan, S. N. / Ruback, R. S. (1995): The Valuation of Cash Flow Forecasts: An Empirical Analysis, in: *The Journal of Finance*, Volume 50, no place 1995, pp. 1059 – 1093.

Kengelbach, J. (2000): Unternehmensbewertung bei internationalen Transaktionen, Frankfurt 2000.

Kinast, G. (1991): Abwicklung einer Akquisition; in: *Baetge, J.* (ed), Akquisition und Unternehmensbewertung, Düsseldorf 1991, pp. 31 – 43.

Kirsten, D. W. (2000): Das bankspezifische Shareholder-Value-Konzept – Anwendbarkeit und Konkretisierung für deutsche Kreditinstitute, Wiesbaden 2000.

Koch, T. (2000): Bewertung von Bank Akquisitionen, zeb Schriftreihe, Frankfurt am Main 2000.

Koch, T. (2004): Besonderheiten der Unternehmensbewertung von Banken, in: *Richter, F. / Timmreck, C.* (ed.): Unternehmensbewertung – Moderne Instrumente und Lösungsansätze, Stuttgart 2004, pp. 119 – 135.

Korth, H.-M. (1992): Unternehmensbewertung im Spannungsfeld zwischen betriebswirtschaftlicher Unternehmenswertermittlung, Marktpreisabgeltung und Rechtsprechung – Eine Bestandsaufnahme für die Praxis, in: *Betriebs-Berater*, supplement 19 of Volume 33, Frankfurt 1992.

Kotissek, N. (1987): Zur Berechnung des Konditionsbeitrags bei konstanter effektiver Marge, in: *Bank und Markt*, No. 1, Frankfurt 1987, pp. 34 – 37.

Kotler, P. / Armstrong, G. (2004): Principles of Marketing, 10th edition, 3rd Indian reprint, Delhi 2004.

Krabichler, T. / Krauß, I. (2003): Konsolidierung im europäischen Bankenmarkt – die Länder der EU im Vergleich, study of ibi – "Institut für Bankinformatik und Bankstrategie" of the Regensburg university, February 2003, available from: http://pc50461.uni-regensburg.de/NR/rdonlyres/C91128C0-5E55-49D8-8B04-3C5C79B2E6A3/0/RRKonsolidierung.pdf [accessed on September 3rd, 2006].

Krämer, W. / Schäfer, F. (2005): Der Bondholder Value als Bestimmungsfaktor der Unternehmensbewertung, Frankfurt 2005, available from: http://www.lazardnet.com/lam/de/pdfs/Hintergrund_Juni_2005_Bondholder_Value.pdf [accessed on September 3rd, 2006].

Kruschwitz, L. / Löffler, A. (1997): Ross' APT ist gescheitert – Was nun?, in: *Zeitschrift für betriebswirtschaftliche Forschung*, Volume 49, Düsseldorf 1997, pp. 644 – 651.

Kuhner, C. / Maltry, H. (2006): Unternehmensbewertung, Berlin 2006.

Kümmel, A. T. (1993): Bewertung von Kreditinstituten nach dem Shareholder Value Ansatz in: *Stein, J.H.* (ed.): Studienreihe der Stiftung Kreditwirtschaft an der Universität Hochrhein, Volume 12, 1993.

Kümmel, A. T. (1995): Bewertung von Kreditinstituten nach dem Shareholder Value Ansatz unter besonderer Berücksichtigung des Zinsänderungsrisikos, 2nd edition, Berlin 1995.

Künnemann, M. (1985): Objektivierte Unternehmensbewertung, Frankfurt-Bern-New York 1985.

KWG (2005): Gesetz über das Kreditwesen, available from: http://www.gesetze-im-internet.de/bundesrecht/kredwg/gesamt.pdf [accessed on September 3rd, 2006].

Lach, N. / Neubert, B. / Kirmße, S. (2002): Integrierte Zinsbuchsteuerung, Münster, August 2002, available from: http://www.zeb.de/zeb/download/veroeffentlichungen/Integrierte_Zinsbuchsteuerung.pdf [accessed on September 3rd, 2006].

Laitenberger, J. / Tschöpel, A. (2003): Vollausschüttung und Halbeinkünfteverfahren, in: *Die Wirtschaftsprüfung*, Volume 56, Düsseldorf 2003, pp. 1357 – 1367.

Lakonishok, J. / Shapiro, A. (1986): Systematic Risk, total Risk and Size as Determinants of Stock Market Returns, in: *Journal of Banking and Finance*, Volume 10, no place 1986, pp. 115 – 131.

Lass, T. (2004): Steuerung internationaler Konzerne, Frankfurt 2004.

Lintner, J. (1965): The Valuation of Risk Assets and the Selection of Risky Investment in Stock Portfolios and Capital Budgets, in: *Review of Economics and Statistics*, 47, no place 1965, pp. 13 – 37.

Liu, J. / Nissim, D. / Thomas, J. (2002): Equity Valuation Using Multiples, in: *Journal of Accounting Research*, Volume 40, no place 2002, pp. 135 – 172.

Löhnert, P. G. / Böckmann, U. J. (2002): Multiplikatorverfahren in der Unternehmensbewertung, in: *Peemöller, V.H.* (ed.): Praxishandbuch der Unternehmensbewertung, 2nd edition, Herne-Berlin, pp. 5 – 25.

Lötters, C. (2000): Marktforschung, Cologne 2000.

Lüders, U. / Herrmann, J. / Sternberg, C. (2005): Integration der variablen Produkte in die barwertige Vertriebssteuerung, in: *Wiedemann, A. / Lüders, U.* (ed.): Integrierte Rendite-/Risikosteuerung, Montabaur 2005, pp. 231 – 250.

Luehrman, T. (1997): Using APV – A Better Tool for Valuing Operations, in: *HBR*, Volume 75, no place 1997, pp. 145 – 154.

Mandl, G. / Rabel, K. (1997): Unternehmensbewertung, Wien-Frankfurt 1997.

Mandl, G. / Rabel, K. (2002): Grundlagen der Unternehmensbewertung, part D: Methoden der Unternehmensbewertung (Überblick), in: *Peemöller, V.H.* (ed.): Praxishandbuch der Unternehmensbewertung, 2nd edition, Herne-Berlin 2002, pp. 47 – 85.

Mandl, G. / Rabel, K. (2005): Methoden der Unternehmensbewertung (Überblick), in: *Peemöller, V.H.* (ed.): Praxishandbuch der Unternehmensbewertung, Herne-Berlin 2005, pp. 47 – 88.

Markowitz, H. M. (1952): Portfolio Selection, in: *The Journal of Finance*, Vol VII, No. 1, no place March 1952, pp. 77 – 91, also available from: http://cowles.econ.yale.edu/P/cp/p00b/p0060.pdf [accessed on September 3rd, 2006].

Marusev, A. (1988): Die Marktzinsmethode im Tagesgeschäft der Banken, in: *Bank-Controlling* 1988, Controlling-Workshop Münster, editors: *Schierenbeck, H. / Schimmelmann, W. v. / Rolfes, B.*, Frankfurt 1988, pp. 59 – 68.

Matschke, M. (1979): Funktionale Unternehmensbewertung: Der Arbitriumwert der Unternehmung, Wiesbaden 1979.

Mellerowicz, K. (1952): Der Wert der Unternehmung als Ganzes, Essen 1952.

Menninghaus, W. (2001): Barwertige Zinsbuchsteuerung, in: *Schierenbeck, H. / Rolfes, B. / Schüller, S.* (ed.): Handbuch Bankcontrolling, 2nd edition, Wiesbaden 2001, pp. 1147 – 1160.

Miles, J. A. / Ezzell, J. R. (1980): The Weighted Average Cost of Capital, Perfect Capital Markets, and Project life: A clarification, in: *JFQA*, Volume 15, no place 1980, pp. 719 – 730.

Miller, W. D. (1995): Commercial Bank Valuation, New York 1995.

Modigliani, F. / Miller, M. H. (1958): The Cost of Capital, Corporation Finance and the Theory of Investment, in: *AER*, Volume 48, no place 1958, pp. 261 – 297.

Modigliani, F. / Miller, M. H. (1963): Corporate Income Taxes and Cost of Capital: A Correction, in: *AER*, Volume 53, no place 1963, pp. 433 – 443.

Moser, U. / Auge-Dickhut, S. (2003a): Unternehmensbewertung: Der Informationsgehalt von Marktpreisabschätzungen auf Basis von Vergleichsverfahren, in: *Finanzbetrieb*, Volume 5, Düsseldorf 2003, pp. 10 – 22.

Moser, U. / Auge-Dickhut, S. (2003b): Unternehmensbewertung: Zum Zusammenhang zwischen Vergleichsverfahren und DCF-Verfahren, in: *Finanzbetrieb*, Volume 5, Düsseldorf 2003, pp. 213 – 223.

Mossin, J. (1996): Equilibrium in a Capital Asset Market, in: *Econometrica* 34, no place 1966, pp. 768 – 783.

Moxter, A. (1976): Grundsätze ordnungsgemäßer Unternehmensbewertung, Wiesbaden 1976.

Moxter, A. (1977): Die sieben Todsünden des Unternehmensbewerters, in: *Goetzke, W. / Sieben, G.* (ed.): Moderne Unternehmensbewertung und Grundsätze ihrer ordnungsgemäßen Durchführung, Cologne, pp. 253 – 256.

Moxter, A. (1983): Grundsätze ordnungsgemäßer Unternehmensbewertung, 2nd edition, Wiesbaden 1983.

Münchow, S. / Biehsmann, J. (2006): Ermittlung der barwertigen Risikotragfähigkeit der Sparkasse Bottrop und Einbindung in die operativen Steuerungssysteme, presentation at the ifb SparkassenDIALOG, Cologne, June 29th, 2006.

Nestler, A. / Kraus, P. (2003): Die Bewertung von Unternehmen anhand der Multiplikatormethode, in: *Betriebswirtschaftliche Mandantenbetreuung* No. 09/2003, no place 2003, also available from: http://www.or-ag.de/downloads/Betriebsw.Mandantenbetreuung 11_09_03.pdf [accessed on September 3rd, 2006].

Neumann, J. von / Morgenstern, O. (1944): Theory of Games and Economic Behavior, Princeton 1944.

Nowak, K. (2003): Marktorientierte Unternehmensbewertung, 2nd edition, Wiesbaden 2003.

Olbrich, M. (2000): Zur Bedeutung des Börsenkurses für die Bewertung von Unternehmungen und Unternehmungsanteilen, in: *Matschke, M.J. / Sieben, G. / Schildbach, T.* (ed.): Betriebswirtschaftliche Forschung und Praxis, No. 5/2000, Herne-Berlin 2000, pp. 454 – 465.

OLG Düsseldorf (2003): Resolution of 2003-07-08 – 19 W 6/00, in: *AG*, Volume 48, Düsseldorf 2003, p. 691.

OLG Düsseldorf (2004): Resolution of 2004-02-27 – 19 W 3/00, in: *AG*, Volume 49, Düsseldorf 2004, p. 327.

Örtmann, P. / Zimmermann, H. (1997): Das Zinsänderungsrisiko bestimmt die Kapitalkosten, in: *Schweizer Bank*, Volume 2/97, no place 1997, pp. 39 – 43.

Ossadnik, W. (1984): Rationalisierung der Unternehmensbewertung durch Risikoklassen, Frankfurt 1984.

Parchert, R. / Markus, D. (2002): Treasury-Management im Kontext einer modernen Gesamtbanksteuerung, in: *Eller, R. / Gruber, W. / Reif, M.* (ed.): Risikomanagement und Risikocontrolling im modernen Treasury Management, Stuttgart 2002, pp. 15 – 58.

Peemöller, V. H. (2005): Grundlagen der Unternehmensbewertung, Teil A – Wert und Werttheorien, in: *Peemöller, V.H.* (ed.): Praxishandbuch der Unternehmensbewertung, 3rd edition, Herne-Berlin 2005, pp. 5 – 25.

Perridon, L. / Steiner, M. (1997): Finanzwirtschaft der Unternehmung, 9th edition, Munich 1997.

Perseus (2004): A Complete Guide to a Successful Survey, Braintree May 2004, available from:
http://www.perseus.com/survey/resources/perseus_survey_101.pdf
[accessed on September 3rd, 2006].

Pfeifer, G. (2006): Operationale Risiken als übergreifende Risikoart, in: *Pfeifer, G. / Ullrich, W. / Wimmer, K.* (ed.): MaRisk Umsetzungsleitfaden: Neue Planungs-, Steuerungs- und Reportingpflichten gemäß Mindestanforderungen an das Risikomanagement, Heidelberg 2006, pp. 445 – 454.

Picot, G. / Jansen, S. A. (1999): Mergers & Acquisitions optimal managen – Teil 4: Moderne Bewertungsverfahren von Unternehmen; in: *Handelsblatt*, Düsseldorf, April 16th / 17th, 1999, page K 3.

Piltz, D. (1994): Die Unternehmensbewertung in der Rechtsprechung, 3rd edition, Düsseldorf 1994.

Piltz, D. (2005): Die Rechtsprechung zur Unternehmensbewertung, in: *Peemöller, V.H.* (ed.): Praxishandbuch der Unternehmensbewertung, Herne-Berlin 2005, pp. 779 – 796.

Poddig, T. / Dichtl, H. / Petersmeier, K. (2000): Statistik, Ökonometrie, Optimierung, Bad Soden 2000.

Porter, M. E. (1987): From Competitive Advantage to Corporate Strategy, in: *Harvard Business Review*, Volume 65, Harvard 1987, pp. 43 – 89.

Porter, M. E. (1996): What is Strategy?, in: *Harvard Business Review*, Harvard, November/December 1996, pp. 61 – 78.

Propach, J. / Reuse, S. (2003): Data Warehouses in der Gesamtbanksteuerung: Entwicklung eines idealen Banken Data Warehouses und empirische Untersuchung des Status quo, in: *Controlling*, Volume 15, No. 06/2003, Munich-Frankfurt 2003, pp. 323 – 330.

Propach, J. / Reuse, S. (2005): Integration von Data Warehouse und Balanced Scorecard in ein gesamtbankorientiertes Steuerungskonzept, in: *ControllerMagazin*, Volume 30, No. 05/2005, Offenburg-Wörthsee-Munich, September 2005, pp. 439 – 448.

Rams, A. (1998): Strategisch-dynamische Unternehmensbewertung mittels Realoptionen, in: *Die Bank*, Volume 11-98, Berlin-Cologne 1998, pp. 676 – 680.

Rappaport, A. (1986): Creating Shareholder Value – The New Standard for Business Performance, New York/London 1986.

Rappaport, A. (1995): Shareholder-value – Wertsteigerung als Maßstab für die Unternehmensführung, Stuttgart 1999.

Reuse, S. (2002.12): Marktzinsmethode (Teil 1) – Kalkulation des Zinserfolges, in: *Bankfachklasse*, No. 12.2002, Wiesbaden 2002, pp. 24 – 26.

Reuse, S. (2003.02): Marktzinsmethode (Teil 2) – Ermittlung der GKM-Sätze, in: *Bankfachklasse*, No. 02.2003, Wiesbaden 2003, pp. 28 – 31.

Reuse, S. (2003.03): Messung von Zinsrisiken, in: *Bankfachklasse*, No. 03.2003, Wiesbaden 2003, pp. 26 – 28.

Reuse, S. (2003.10): Risikomessung mit der Kennzahl Value at Risk (VaR), in: *Bankfachklasse*, No. 10.2003, Wiesbaden 2003, pp. 25 – 27.

Reuse, S. (2003.12): Der Spread als Risikomaß für Unternehmensanleihen, in: *Bankfachklasse*, No. 12.2003, Wiesbaden 2003, pp. 16 – 18.

Reuse, S. (2006): Marktpreisrisiken auf Gesamtbankebene, in: *Pfeifer, G. / Ullrich, W. / Wimmer, K.* (ed.): MaRisk Umsetzungsleitfaden: Neue Planungs-, Steuerungs- und Reportingpflichten gemäß Mindestanforderungen an das Risikomanagement, Heidelberg 2006, pp. 377 – 436.

Reuse, S. (2006.07-08): Berechnung des Value-at-Risk mit der Monte-Carlo-Simulation, in: *Bankpraktiker*, No. 07-08/2006, Heidelberg 2006, pp. 366 – 371.

Reuter, M. / Blees, T. (2006): KPMG-Studie: Steuersätze 2006 im internationalen Vergleich / Europäischer Trend: Steuersätze sinken weiter / Deutschland: Steuersatz bleibt hoch, Berlin, April 18th, 2006, available from: http://www.presseportal.de/story.htx?nr=811734 [accessed on September 3rd, 2006].

Reuters (2006): Historical share prices for the DAX and the peer group, no place 2006.

Richard, W. / Mühlmeyer, J. / Bergmann, B. (1996): Betriebslehre der Banken und Sparkassen, Rinteln 1996.

Richter, A. (1942): Die Bewertung von Minderheitsanteilen an Kapitalgesellschaften, in: *Der praktische Betriebswirt*, Volume 22, Berlin 1942, pp. 105 – 110.

Rolfes, B. (1997): Retailbanking: Werttreiber oder Wertvernichter für den Shareholder Value, in: *Baseler Bankenvereinigung* (ed.): Shareholder Value-Konzepte in Banken, Bern-Stuttgart-Wien 1997, pp. 95 – 118.

Rolfes, B. (1999): Gesamtbanksteuerung, Stuttgart 1999.

Rolfes, B. (1999.04): Gesamtbanksteuerung – Risiken ertragsorientiert managen, Institut for economics, university Klagenfurt, Austria, April 1999, available from: http://www-sci.uni-klu.ac.at/wiwi/Forschung/04.pdf [accessed on September 3rd, 2006].

Rolfes, B. / Dartsch, A. (1998): Verrentungskonzeptionen im Spannungsfeld interner und externer Rechnungslegung bei Banken, in: *WISU – Das Wirtschaftsstudium*, No. 1/98, Düsseldorf 1998, pp. 67 – 75.

Schell, G. (1988): Die Ertragsermittlung für Bankbewertungen, in: *Betriebswirtschaftliche Studien Rechnungs- und Finanzwesen, Organisation und Institution*, No. 8, Frankfurt-Bern-New York-Paris 1988.

Schierenbeck, H. (1998): Grundzüge der Betriebswirtschaftslehre, 13th edition, Munich 1998.

Schierenbeck, H. (2001a): Ertragsorientiertes Bankmanagement, Volume 1, 7th edition, Wiesbaden 2001.

Schierenbeck, H. (2001b): Ertragsorientiertes Bankmanagement, Volume 2, 7th edition, Wiesbaden 2001.

Schildbach, T. (1977): Die Berücksichtigung der Geldentwertung bei der Unternehmensbewertung, in: *Goetzke, W. / Sieben, G.* (ed.): Moderne Unternehmensbewertung und Grundsätze ihrer ordnungsgemäßen Durchführung, Cologne 1977, pp. 225 – 240.

Schmidt, J. H. (1995): Die Discounted Cash-flow-Methode – nur eine kleine Abwandlung der Ertragswertmethode? In: *Zeitschrift für betriebswirtschaftliche Forschung*, Volume 47, Düsseldorf 1995, pp. 1087 – 1118.

Schmidt, R. H. / Terberger, E. (1997): Grundzüge der Investitions- und Finanzierungstheorie, 4th edition, Wiesbaden 1997.

Schmidtbauer, R. (2004): Marktbewertung mithilfe von Multiplikatoren im Spiegel des Discounted –Cashflow-Ansatzes, in: *Betriebs-Berater*, Volume 59, Frankfurt 2004, pp. 148 – 153.

Schnell, R. / Hill, P. B. / Esser, E. (1999): Methoden der empirischen Sozialforschung, Wien 1999.

Scholz, C. (2004): Human Capital Management – Wege aus der Unverbindlichkeit, Munich / Unterschleißheim 2004.

Schultze, W. (2003a): Methoden der Unternehmensbewertung, 2nd edition, Düsseldorf 2003.

Schultze, W. (2003b): Kombinationsverfahren und Residualgewinnmethode in der Unternehmensbewertung: konzeptioneller Zusammenhang, in: *KoR*, Volume 3, pp. 458 – 464.

Schulz, C. / Weissenberger, L. (2003): Ein neuer Markenauftritt für die Sparkassen, in: *Sparkasse* SH/2003, available from:
http://www.sparkassenzeitung.de/service/fachzeitschriften/sparkasse/ssh_Schulz.pdf
[accessed on September 3rd, 2006].

Schwetzler, B. (2000): Stochastische Verknüpfung und implizite bzw. maximal zulässige Risikozuschläge bei der Unternehmensbewertung, in: *Matschke, M.J. / Sieben, G. / Schildbach, T.* (ed.): Betriebswirtschaftliche Forschung und Praxis, No. 5/2000, Herne-Berlin 2000, pp. 478 – 492.

Seppelfricke, P. (2003): Handbuch Aktien- und Unternehmensbewertung, Stuttgart 2003.

Sharpe, W. F. (1964): Capital Asset Prices: A Theory of Market Equilibrium under Conditions of Risk, in: *The Journal of Finance*, No. 19, no place September 1964, pp. 425 – 442.

Sharpe, W. F. (1970): Portfolio Theory and Capital Markets, New York 1970.

Sieben, G. (1977): Opening the conference, in: *Goetzke, W. / Sieben, G.* (ed.): Moderne Unternehmensbewertung und Grundsätze ihrer ordnungsgemäßen Durchführung, Cologne 1997, pp. 27 – 31.

Sieben, G. (1992): Wesen, Ermittlung und Bedeutung des Substanzwertes als „vorgeleistete" Ausgaben, in: *Busse von Colbe, W. / Coenenberg, G.A.* (ed.): Unternehmensakquisition und Unternehmensbewertung, Stuttgart 1992.

Sieben, G. (1993): Unternehmensbewertung, in: *Wittmann* (ed.): Handwörterbuch der Betriebswirtschaft, 5th edition, Stuttgart 1993, columns 4315.

Sieben, G. (1995): Unternehmensbewertung: Discounted Cash-flow-Verfahren und Ertragswertverfahren – Zwei völlig unterschiedliche Ansätze? In: *Keufermann, J.* (ed.): Internationale Wirtschaftsprüfung, commemorative publication for H. Havermann, no place 1995, pp. 714 – 737.

Sieben, G. / Maltry, H. (2002): Der Substanzwert der Unternehmung, in: *Peemöller, V.H.* (ed.): Handbuch der Unternehmensbewertung, 2nd edition, Herne-Berlin 2002, pp. 375 – 399.

Sievi, C. R. (1995): Kalkulation und Disposition: Betriebswirtschaftliche Grundlagen, Rechenverfahren, Anwendungen, Bretten 1995.

Sievi, C. R. (1998): Convex3-Mapping – Ein neues Verfahren im Vergleich zu herkömmlichen Mapping-Methoden, in: *Die Bank* No. 05/1998, Berlin-Cologne 1998, pp. 7 – 15, also available from: http://www.gillardon.de/pdfs/presse/fachartikel/convex3-mapping.pdf [accessed on September 3rd, 2006].

Sievi, C. R. (1999): Neugestaltung variabler Passivprodukte, in: *Betriebswirtschaftliche Blätter* No. 01/1999, Berlin 1999, pp. 31 – 39, also available from: http://www.gillardon.de/pdfs/presse/fachartikel/1997-1999/neugestaltung_var_passivprodukte.pdf, [accessed on September 3rd, 2006].

Sievi, C. R. (2000): Projekt „Typische Zinsszenarien und Dispositionskonzept" - Abschlußbericht – DSGV Berlin 2000.

Sievi, C. R. (2001): Studie – Steuerung des Zinsbuches einer Sparkasse - aktives versus passives Management, Abschlußbericht – DSGV Berlin 2001.

Sievi, C. R. (n.Y. a): Wertorientierte Steuerung des Zinsänderungsrisikos Abschlußbericht und Fachkonzeption zum Projektteil 1 der Machbarkeitsstudie: Barwertkonzept und Cash Flow orientiertes Bilanzstrukturmanagement, DSGV Berlin n.Y.

Sievi, C. R. (n.Y. b): Kalkulation und Marktsteuerung im Barwertkonzept Abschlußbericht zum Projektteil 2 der Machbarkeitsstudie: Barwertkonzept und Cash Flow orientiertes Bilanzstrukturmanagement, DSGV Berlin n.Y.

Simmert, D. B. / Benölken, H. (2006): Zur Position der Sparkassen im Gruppenwettbewerb, in: *Betriebswirtschaftliche Blätter*, No. 04/2006, Berlin 2006, pp. 238 – 347.

S-Investor (2006aa): Fundamental data of Aareal Bank, available from:
http://sinvnet.teledata.de/sis/unternehmen/portrait.html?INST_ID=0000362&company_id=3389
[accessed on Mai 29th, 2006].

S-Investor (2006ab): Market data of Aareal Bank, available from:
http://sinvnet.teledata.de/sis/detail/index.html?INST_ID=0000362&sym=ARL.ETR
[accessed on Mai 29th, 2006].

S-Investor (2006ba): Fundamental data of Comdirect, available from:
http://sinvnet.teledata.de/sis/unternehmen/portrait.html?INST_ID=0000362&company_id=1626
[accessed on Mai 29th, 2006].

S-Investor (2006bb): Market data of Comdirect, available from:
http://sinvnet.teledata.de/sis/detail/index.html?INST_ID=0000362&sym=COM.ETR
[accessed on Mai 29th, 2006].

S-Investor (2006ca): Fundamental data of Deutsche Postbank, available from:
http://sinvnet.teledata.de/sis/unternehmen/portrait.html?INST_ID=0000362&company_id=2566
[accessed on Mai 29th, 2006].

S-Investor (2006cb): Market data of Deutsche Postbank, available from:
http://sinvnet.teledata.de/sis/detail/index.html?INST_ID=0000362&sym=DPB.ETR
[accessed on Mai 29th, 2006].

S-Investor (2006da): Fundamental data of Hypo Real Estate, available from:
http://sinvnet.teledata.de/sis/unternehmen/portrait.html?INST_ID=0000362&compan
y_id=3440
[accessed on Mai 29th, 2006].

S-Investor (2006db): Market data of Hypo Real Estate, available from:
http://sinvnet.teledata.de/sis/detail/index.html?INST_ID=0000362&sym=HRX.ETR
[accessed on Mai 29th, 2006].

S-Investor (2006ea): Fundamental data of IKB Deutsche Industriebank, available from:
http://sinvnet.teledata.de/sis/unternehmen/portrait.html?INST_ID=0000362&compan
y_id=523
[accessed on Mai 29th, 2006].

S-Investor (2006eb): Market data of IKB Deutsche Industriebank, available from:
http://sinvnet.teledata.de/sis/detail/index.html?INST_ID=0000362&sym=IKB.ETR
[accessed on Mai 29th, 2006].

S-Investor (2006fa): Fundamental data of Deutsche Bank, available from:
http://sinvnet.teledata.de/sis/unternehmen/portrait.html?INST_ID=0000362&compan
y_id=515
[accessed on Mai 29th, 2006].

S-Investor (2006fb): Market data of Deutsche Bank, available from:
http://sinvnet.teledata.de/sis/detail/index.html?INST_ID=0000362&sym=DBK.ETR
[accessed on Mai 29th, 2006].

S-Investor (2006ga): Fundamental data of Hypovereinsbank, available from:
http://sinvnet.teledata.de/sis/unternehmen/portrait.html?INST_ID=0000362&compan
y_id=509
[accessed on Mai 29th, 2006].

S-Investor (2006gb): Market data of Hypovereinsbank, available from:
http://sinvnet.teledata.de/sis/detail/index.html?INST_ID=0000362&sym=HVM.ETR
[accessed on Mai 29th, 2006].

S-Investor (2006ha): Fundamental data of Commerzbank, available from:
http://sinvnet.teledata.de/sis/unternehmen/portrait.html?INST_ID=0000362&compan
y_id=513
[accessed on Mai 29th, 2006].

S-Investor (2006hb): Market data of Commerzbank, available from:
http://sinvnet.teledata.de/sis/detail/index.html?INST_ID=0000362&sym=CBK.ETR
[accessed on Mai 29th, 2006].

Soffer, L. C. / Soffer R. J. (2003): Financial Statement Analysis: A Valuation Approach, Upper
Saddle River 2003.

Sonntag, A. (2001): Bewertung von Banken: Ein Discounted Cash Flow-Ansatz für Commercial Banks unter Berücksichtigung der Marktzinsmethode, Schriftreihen der Handelshochschule Leipzig, Wiesbaden 2001.

SPSS (2003): How to Get More Value from Your Survey Data, Chicago 2003, available from: http://www.spss.com/dk/dimension/morevalue.pdf
[accessed on September 3rd, 2006].

Standard and Poor's (2006): Ratings Definitions, no place 2006, available from: http://www2.standardandpoors.com/servlet/Satellite?pagename=sp/Page/FixedIncom eRatingsCriteriaPg&r=1&l=EN&b=2
[accessed on September 3rd, 2006, registration required].

Steiner, M. / Bruns, C. (2000): Wertpapiermanagement, 7th edition, Stuttgart 2000.

Steinöcker, R. (1993): Akquisitionscontrolling – Strategische Planung von Firmenübernahmen, Berlin-Bonn-Regensburg 1993.

Stewart, G. B. (1991): The Quest for Value – The EVA[TM] Management Guide, New York 1991.

Strutz, E. (1993): Wertmanagement von Banken, Bern 1993.

Stulz, R. M. (1996): Rethinking Risk Management, in *JoACF*, Volume 9, no place 1996, pp. 8 – 24.

Stützer, W. (1976): Wert und Preis, in: *HWB*, No. 4, 4th no place 1976, columns 4404 – 4425.

Süchting, J. / Paul, S. (1998): Bankmanagement, 4th edition, Stuttgart 1998.

Sudman, S. (1998): Marketing research: A Problem-Solving Approach, Boston 1998.

Täubert, A. (2005): European Banking Study 2004: Europas Bankenmarkt wird homogener – Rentabilität europäischer Kreditinstitute gleicht sich an / Deutsche Banken bilden trotz gestiegener Erträge nach wie vor das Schlusslicht in Europa / Top-Regionalbanken übernehmen in Deutschland Führung vor Groß- und Privatbanken, no place, March 10th, 2005, available from: http://www.zeb.de/zeb/de/presse/pressemitteilungen/newsdetails.html?newsId=747& cmsframe=haupt
[accessed on September 3rd, 2006].

Thaller, A. (2005): Barwertige Risikotragfähigkeit und Limitierung von Marktpreisrisiken, in: *Wiedemann, A. / Lüders, U.* (ed.): Integrierte Rendite-/ Risikosteuerung, Montabaur 2005, pp. 141 – 156.

Thompson, A. / Strickland A. (2003): Strategic Management: Concepts and Cases, 13th edition, New Delhi 2003.

Tichy, G. E. (1992): Die Bedeutung einer Unternehmensbewertung für die Kaufpreisfindung; in: *Seicht, G.* (ed.), Jahrbuch für Controlling und Rechnungswesen '92, Wien 1992, pp. 329 – 346.

Trigeorgis, L. (2000) Real Options: Managerial Flexibility and Strategy in Resource Allocation, The MIT Press, 5th print, Cambridge MA 2000.

Vettiger, T. (1996): Wertorientiertes Bankcontrolling, Bern 1996.

Viel, J. / Bredt, O. / Renard, M. (1970): Die Bewertung von Unternehmen und Unternehmensanteilen, 3rd edition, Stuttgart 1970.

Vitt, M. (2002): Das Nullbank-Konzept im Rahmen der Steuerung des Zinsbuches, in: *Eller, R. / Gruber, W. / Reif, M.* (ed.): Risikomanagement und Risikocontrolling im modernen Treasury-Management, Stuttgart 2002, pp. 547 – 567.

Vogler, S. (n.Y.): Regeln für das Branding von Banken, pp. 459 – 472, available from: http://www.markenexperte.ch/pdf/regeln_fuer_das_branding_von_banken_459-472.pdf
[accessed on September 3rd, 2006].

Voigtländer, D. (2004): Drei Säulen des Deutschen Bankenmarktes, DZ Bank, presentation for the conference "Zahlungsverkehrssymposium", Frankfurt, June 21st, 2004, available from:
http://www.bundesbank.de/download/zahlungsverkehr/zv_symposium_2004/vortrag_voigtlaender_040621.pdf
[accessed on September 3rd, 2006].

Volkart, R. (n.Y.): Wertkommunikation, Aktienkursbildung und Managementverhalten als kritische Eckpunkte im Shareholder value-Konzept, available from: http://www.isb.unizh.ch/publikationen/pdf/workingpapernr04.pdf#search=%22shareholder%20value%20shareholder%20wealth%22
[accessed on September 3rd, 2006].

Weber, J. (2004): Einführung in das Controlling, 10th edition, Stuttgart 2004.

Weinzirl, V. (2002): Implementierung einer barwertigen Zinsbuchsteuerung, in: *Eller, R. / Gruber, W. / Reif, M.* (2002): Risikomanagement und Risikocontrolling im modernen Treasury-Management, Stuttgart 2002, pp. 84 – 101.

Weston, J. F. / Chung, K. S. / Siu, J. A. (1998): Takeovers, Restructuring, and Corporate Governance,
2nd edition, no place 1998.

Widmann, B. / Schieszl, S. / Jeromin, A. (2003): Der Kapitalisierungszinssatz in der praktischen Unternehmensbewertung, in: *Finanzbetrieb*, Volume 5, Düsseldorf 2003, pp. 800 – 810.

Wiedemann, A. (2002): Die Messung von Zinsrisiken anhand des Value at Risk-Konzepts (I), in: *WISU – Das Wirtschaftsstudium*, No. 11/02, Düsseldorf 2002, pp. 1416 – 1423.

Wiedemann, A. / Hager, P. (2002): Performancemessung und Erfolgsspaltung bei Anleihen mit Bonitätsrisiko, Dietzhölztal 2002, available from: http://www.riskbooks.de/zinsrisiko/downloads/Creditspreads.pdf [accessed on September 3rd, 2006].

Wimmer, K. (2006): Ableitung der Gesamtbankstrategie und der Teilstrategien, in: *Pfeifer, G. / Ullrich, W. / Wimmer, K.* (ed.): MaRisk Umsetzungsleitfaden Umsetzungsleitfaden: Neue Planungs-, Steuerungs- und Reportingpflichten gemäß Mindestanforderungen an das Risikomanagement, Heidelberg 2006, pp. 296 – 341.

Winckelmann, H. (1953): Zum Einfluß der Gewinnsteuern auf den Unternehmenswert, in: *Die Wirtschaftsprüfung*, Düsseldorf 1953, pp. 181 – 183.

Witt, P. (2003): Die Bedeutung des Realoptionsansatzes für Gründungsunternehmen, in: *Hommel, U. / Scholich, M. / Baecker, P. N.* (ed.): Reale Optionen: Konzepte, Praxis und Perspektiven strategischer Unternehmensfinanzierung, Berlin 2003, pp. 121 – 141.

Wiwo (2006): Privatbanken fordern mehr Chancengleichheit, Düsseldorf, April 26th, 2006, available from: http://www.wiwo.de/pswiwo/fn/ww2/sfn/buildww/id/97/id/173570/SH/0/depot/0/index.html [accessed on September 3rd, 2006].

Wöhe, G. (1996): Einführung in die Allgemeine Betriebswirtschaftslehre, 19th edition, Munich 1996.

Yegge, W. M. (1996): A Basic Guide for Valuing a Company, New York-Chichester-Brisbane-Singapore-Weinheim 1996.

Zessin, A. (1982): Unternehmensbewertung von Kreditinstituten, Göttingen 1982.

Zimmermann, H. (1995): Bestimmungsgrößen der Kapitalkosten bei Banken, lecture at the institute for Swiss banking of Zürich university, according to the topic: "Shareholder-value-Management – Wertorientierte Unternehmensführung im Spannungsfeldsfeld von Kunde, Arbeitnehmern und Aktionären", Zürich 1995.